Women's Activism, Feminism, and Social Justice

Studies in Feminist Philosophy is designed to showcase cutting-edge monographs and collections that display the full range of feminist approaches to philosophy, that push feminist thought in important new directions, and that display the outstanding quality of feminist philosophical thought.

STUDIES IN FEMINIST PHILOSOPHY

Published in the Series:

Women's Activism, Feminism, and Social Justice

MARGARET A. MCLAREN

OXFORD
UNIVERSITY PRESS

Oxford University Press is a department of the University of Oxford. It furthers
the University's objective of excellence in research, scholarship, and education
by publishing worldwide. Oxford is a registered trade mark of Oxford University
Press in the UK and certain other countries.

Published in the United States of America by Oxford University Press
198 Madison Avenue, New York, NY 10016, United States of America.

CIP data is on file at the Library of Congress
ISBN 978–0–19–094769–9 (pbk.)
ISBN 978–0–19–094770–5 (hbk.)

For my partner in life and love, Chuck Weise,
and for my parents, Jean Lawrence and John McLaren

CONTENTS

ACKNOWLEDGMENTS

Over the years that I have been working on this book, I have benefited from numerous conversations with colleagues and friends. I have had the opportunity to give papers on the ideas and topics in the book at a number of conferences, including the Feminist Ethics and Social Theory conference, the Radical Philosophy Association, an International Women and Globalization conference, the National Women's Studies Association, the Socialist Feminist Philosophers Association, and an International Colloquium on Iris Young. I am grateful for the questions and responses of conference participants, which helped me to push and clarify my ideas. Audiences at papers I presented at Bhawanipur Education Society College (Calcutta), Visva-Bharati University (Shantiniketan), and the National Conference for the Association of American Physicians of Indian Origin (United States) also provided valuable perspectives and feedback.

Special thanks are due to those who read drafts of the chapters along the way. Shelley Park read drafts of most of the chapters in their earliest version and provided both encouragement to continue and critical feedback. As the book progressed, many people generously provided feedback on chapters, and I acknowledge with gratitude the time and energy they invested in helping to improve my work; thanks are due to Hoyt Edge, Serene Khader, Cory Aragon, Celia Bardwell-Jones, Mecke Nagel, Julia Maskivker, Grant Cornwell, Dan Chong, and Eric Smaw. Thanks also to the two anonymous reviewers for Oxford University Press and to my editor at Oxford University Press, Lucy Randall. And much gratitude to Cheshire Calhoun, series editor for Studies in Feminist Philosophy, for her very helpful feedback on the book and for believing in the project.

I was fortunate to have proofreaders and formatters whose hard work and attention to detail is much appreciated; many thanks to Ryan Hudnall, Cyndi Fridlich, and Veronica Leary. Veronica Leary also prepared the index.

Over the years that I have worked on this project, I have been sustained and supported by my colleagues, my friends, and my family, and I appreciate each and every one of them. My spouse, Chuck Weise, deserves special recognition for his patience, love, and unfailing support through the long process of writing this book.

My deep gratitude also goes to the women of the Self-Employed Women's Association and MarketPlace India from whom I learned so much.

While some of the ideas in this book originated in previously published work, over the years the project has developed these initial ideas have been extended and refined. A shorter and modified version of Chapter 5 is forthcoming with the journal *Critical Horizons*.

Introduction
Situating the Project

Clearly, we need to build a new language in which to frame our
vision and strategies for social transformation at the local, national,
or global level. I for one intend to do so not by re-reading Foucault or
Gramsci or other great political philosophers, but *by listening to poor
women and their movements, listening to their values, principles,
articulations, and actions, and by trying to hear how they frame
their search for justice.* From this, I suspect, will emerge not only a
new discourse, but also new concepts and strategies that have not yet
entered our political or philosophical imaginations.

—SRILATHA BATLIWALA (2007, 564)

Beginning from the social location of poor women of color from the
Two-Thirds World is an important, even crucial, place for feminist
analysis; it is precisely the potential epistemic privilege of these
communities of women that opens up the space for demystifying
capitalism and for envisioning transborder social and economic
justice.

—CHANDRA TALPADE MOHANTY (2003, 250)

If you have come to help me, I don't need your help, but if you have
come because your liberation is tied to mine, come, let us work
together.

—LILA WATSON (2005, 401)

FEMINISTS, LIKE OTHERS WHO work for social justice, freedom, and
equality, often walk a fine line between working with and for others,
and for themselves. Like other marginalized groups, women often seek

justice for themselves and those similarly affected by oppressive social conditions, focusing on issues like sexual harassment or violence against women. Within feminism there has been much discussion about the ways that constructing women as a group falsely assumes commonalities among women and overlooks significant differences, including race, ethnicity, economic status, nationality, religion, sexual orientation, gender identity, and ability. Overlooking differences of social location among women, an already oppressed group, further oppresses and disenfranchises women who do not hold privileged locations within the social structure. That is, when feminists organize around the category of "women," it has often been assumed that women share a social location, and that challenging sexism is the primary goal for feminism. In the history of Anglo and US feminism, the shared location often defaults into the dominant group—white, middle class, heterosexual, and able bodied. And yet sexism is never isolated from other forms of oppression such as racism, class exploitation, religious bias, heterosexism, ableism, and ethnic discrimination. This presents an apparent dilemma: how can feminists organize a liberatory politics around ending women's oppression without invoking the category "women," which itself plays a normalizing role by its presumption of commonality? For many of us, this is an old and familiar story.

But this was not the story I heard when I spent time with women's activist groups in India, nor at the United Nations Conferences for Women in Nairobi, Kenya, in 1985 and in Beijing, China, in 1995. And it was not the story I heard when I went to demonstrations with the Florida Farmworkers Association and the Coalition of Immokalee Workers. It was not the main issue when testifying in support of nondiscrimination laws for lesbians and gays, and later for transgendered women and men, in the city of Orlando and in Orange County, Florida. Although each of these groups and their struggles may seem unrelated—poor women in India seeking ways to survive; nongovernmental organizations (NGOs) and politicians at UN conferences in Kenya and China discussing policies and recommendations for improving the status of women and girls globally; migrant farmworkers in Florida demonstrating for fair wages and safer working conditions; and lesbian, gay, and transgender people in Florida demanding fair treatment and nondiscrimination in jobs and housing—they weave together to create a larger picture of social justice.

Social justice must attend to peoples' basic survival needs and the need for decent work with decent pay and safe working conditions, as well as the need for marginalized groups to be both recognized as members of a specific group and treated fairly. The scope of social justice is both larger and smaller than classic theories of justice that focus on the state: smaller because social justice acknowledges the importance of redressing social injustice and the social and cultural marginalization of groups within specific nation-states. And larger in the sense that those concerned with social justice must acknowledge the interconnections among the local and the global, not only by recommending global guidelines and goals but also by looking at the effects of global economic policy on local communities. Moreover, as I discuss, classic theories of justice emphasize legal and political remedies to redress injustices, and often focus on redistribution, rather than the radical restructuring of institutional arrangements.

The Project

In this book, I show the limitations of specific philosophical approaches to global justice for women by beginning with women's real-life struggles for social justice. Taking a feminist approach to social justice issues, I develop a normative framework drawing upon a number of different strands of feminist and social justice theories that I call the feminist social justice framework. I argue that social justice feminism provides a framework for transnational feminist analysis that is more comprehensive than the frameworks offered by human rights, liberalism (including neoliberal economic projects), and cosmopolitanism. I explore each of these frameworks for transnational justice in turn, paying particular attention to their applicability to issues of global gender justice. For instance, in chapter 2, I address the ways that feminists have advocated for a universal conception of human rights to secure gender equality transnationally. In chapter 3, I explore the issue of economic justice with a focus on the intersections between economic and gender justice. And in chapter 4, I show how dominant models of cosmopolitanism that rely on the liberal individualist framework do not fully capture our relationality or our rich differences. I develop a model of relational cosmopolitanism that acknowledges our interdependence and values cultural difference.

Chapter 5 looks at Iris Marion Young's concept of political responsibility as a framework for global justice. Political responsibility moves away from the individualism and abstraction prevalent in the three frameworks that I criticize: rights, neoliberal economic empowerment, and cosmopolitanism. I extend the model of political responsibility to show how remedying structural injustice and small-scale interventions are connected. In fact, I argue that large-scale structural changes require the creation of new institutions on a smaller scale; macro-level (structural) changes cannot be sustained without correlative changes at the meso-level (institutional). The positive transformation toward structural and institutional justice, in turn, relates to increased empowerment at the individual and interpersonal level. I provide more detailed summaries of each chapter later in this introduction.

I conclude with a call for a shift in our thinking and practice toward reimagining the possibilities for justice from a relational framework.

The frameworks of liberalism, human rights, and cosmopolitanism abstract from real-world situations and the complexities of human existence and interdependence; they propose single-issue approaches to complex problems. I call these single-issue approaches "rights-justice approaches" as a shorthand way of distinguishing them from the feminist social justice approach. By contrast with philosophical theories that advocate a rights-justice approach, I demonstrate how actual struggles for social justice, such as the struggles of the women of the Self-Employed Women's Association (hereafter also referred to as SEWA) and MarketPlace India (hereafter also referred to as MarketPlace), enact an approach to social justice that is multifaceted and complex. They enact social justice feminism.

Women's Activism and Social Justice

Development theorists, practitioners, and ethicists suggest that qualitative studies may illuminate aspects of empowerment from the point of view of the women involved (Kabeer 1998, 2001; Koggel 2010; Krenz et al. 2014). Following this trend, I illustrate my theoretical arguments for the feminist social justice framework with specific examples from my research conducted with MarketPlace and with SEWA.

In order to learn from these grassroots organizations, I engaged in participatory action research. Participatory action research "consists of systematic, empirical research in collaboration with representatives of the population under investigation, with the goal of action or intervention in the issues or problems being studied" (Hill-Collins and Bilge 2016, 60). Over a two-year period, I conducted qualitative interviews with members of these groups, and I visited their projects in and around Mumbai, India, as well as in Ahmedabad and in rural Gujarat. In addition to this primary research, my knowledge about these organizations relies on analyses and research reports produced by SEWA members and staff, and three book-length studies of the organizations.[1]

The stories and examples of SEWA and MarketPlace members, poor women who face social oppression as well as economic exploitation, show the limitations of single-issue approaches and point to the necessity of a multifaceted, comprehensive feminist social justice approach. Listening to the stories of women in MarketPlace and SEWA revealed the inadequacies of universal rights–based approaches to global justice, including with respect to gender equality. The issues they routinely confronted—lack of shelter, no health care, children suffering from malnutrition, domestic violence, riots in their neighborhoods because of religious differences, social pressure to support gender norms such as dowries for daughters, false land claims—highlighted that changes in laws alone would not be sufficient to remedy these problems.

Addressing poverty, oppressive social norms, and violence in interpersonal relationships requires a broad based approach to social change. While the law and politics can provide some protections for individuals and promote equality, changes need to be made at multiple levels and areas of life—economic, social, and cultural, in addition to political and legal. Most important, in order to combat the poverty these women face, we must explicitly challenge structural injustice. Challenging structural injustice means questioning the ways in which institutions and systems reproduce economic and social inequality through practices that systematically disadvantage one group of people, often on the basis of their membership in social groups such as gender, race, caste, ethnicity, and so on.

Some aspects of the feminist movement focus on attaining political and legal equality for women; but this focus on formal structures leaves aside issues of class and economic exploitation. Many feminists recognize the ways that gender and the category "women" never exist in isolation from other identities. Understanding identity as intersectional underscores the necessity of working against multiple systems of oppression. Social group identities are often created and maintained through the very systems and structures of injustice that social justice aims to dismantle (e.g., sexism, racism, classism, heterosexism, ableism, etc.); thus, social change requires an intersectional, multipronged approach to challenging systemic injustice, not merely remedying gender inequality.

Because there is a range of feminist positions and approaches, I call my multifaceted approach a *feminist social justice approach.*[2] The feminist social justice approach draws on the insights of intersectionality in terms of recognizing both the complexity of identity and the sociopolitical context of structural oppression. Additionally, the feminist social justice approach acknowledges the different domains in which oppression, domination, and exploitation occur. I offer this approach as one method that can contribute to ongoing feminist transnational solidarity projects, keeping in mind that like all methods it is fallible, revisable, and limited. In what follows I articulate both the elements of the social justice approach and the normative commitments of the feminist social justice framework.

The Feminist Social Justice Approach: Methodology and Grounding

First, a feminist social justice approach is grounded in the real struggles and issues of women, and *recognizes the link between theories and practices*. Recognizing the link between theory, analysis, and real-life struggles allows for an analysis that is informed by, and may inform, struggles for social justice on the ground. This approach departs from mainstream philosophical theory, which often begins from hypothetical situations, or ideal principles. Feminists, such as Alison Jaggar, have criticized prominent approaches to justice such as that of John Rawls as "ideal theory" that assumes conditions of injustice can be resolved simply by selecting fair principles and procedures (Jaggar 2009). Jaggar and others argue that "nonideal" theories of justice are better suited to effectively counter injustice by beginning from actual social and political conditions. Nonideal theorists recognize that actual social, political, and economic contexts provide the starting point for approaching questions of justice.

Second, a feminist social justice approach must address *systemic and structural injustices* both within and across borders. Systemic or structural injustice can be characterized by the patterns and structures that inhibit equal access and opportunity to fair treatment and equality. The barriers to fair treatment and equality can be economic, political, legal, cultural, or social; they are expressed through policies, laws, gendered and raced patterns of economic discrimination and exploitation, cultural traditions and practices, and social norms.

In her classic article "Oppression," Marilyn Frye uses the analogy of a birdcage to describe oppression as systemic injustice: if we focus on just one wire of the birdcage, it seems that there is no barrier to being free; the bird can just fly around the wire. But when we see that the single wire is part of a larger structure with multiple wires close together, we recognize that the bird is closed in, and cannot simply fly around the single wire. This analogy illustrates the ways in which oppression of all types has a variety of different institutions and social practices reinforcing it. In order to overcome the oppression, work must be done on multiple fronts. A key factor in this analogy is seeing the *relationship* of the various wires/barriers.

Relationships are significant for the feminist social justice approach in two ways. First, acknowledging *relationality* and *interdependence* is important for a feminist social justice approach; feminists have criticized the model of exaggerated independence prevalent in mainstream political and ethical theory (Benhabib 1987; Ruddick 1989; Held 2006). Second, addressing systemic structural injustice means recognizing that our social, political, and economic interdependence takes place within an uneven social and political landscape. Because we are deeply implicated in others' lives in an unequal social and political landscape, we stand in complicated *relationships of power* to one another. Examining issues of justice from a feminist social justice approach means exposing structural injustice both in local contexts, and across national borders, and also attending to historical, political, and material contexts. Because of this interdependence that crosses borders, I situate my analysis with respect to the effects of globalization.

Relationships of power exist both interpersonally, in terms of social groups, and historically. Interpersonally, relationships of power (and privilege) have been discussed in feminist literature as differences of social location (Rich 1984), positionality (Alcoff 1988), standpoint (Hartsock 1998), and privilege (McIntosh 1988). Each of us occupies a particular place in social systems based upon our social group identity; those in dominant social groups have unearned advantages because of the social system that privileges them. Conversely, the social system oppresses those from nondominant groups. Recognizing these relationships of power interpersonally, and within and among groups, is an important step to dismantling systems of oppression.

Historically, colonization was an overt exercise of power of European countries over Asia, Africa, and Latin America. Neocolonialism and imperialism still persist in practice and theory. One of the aims of my feminist social justice approach with respect to *relationships of power* is to unmask them, for instance, to reveal the specific historical and social locations of certain philosophical assumptions as originating from post-Enlightenment, Western thought. Revealing the origins of these assumptions allows us to critically examine them and to assess their relevance to the wide range of issues and problems they purport to solve. One of the primary assumptions of much post-Enlightenment moral and political philosophy is an exaggerated view of human independence, and the idea that similarity among humans is the key to justifying global moral obligations.

Many feminists have criticized the exaggerated independence foundational to these post-Enlightenment philosophical approaches; instead, they argue for *relationality* and *interdependence.*[3] *Relationality* and *interdependence* not only better describe the human condition (from the interdependence of children and parents, to the interdependence of global chains of production and consumption), but they can also serve as worthy ideals. Recognizing that we are interdependent and exist in a web of relationships fosters cooperative, rather than competitive relationships.

Western philosophical theory in the tradition of political liberalism often assumes an ideal of human similarity achieved by abstracting people from their social and historical context, by neglecting the ways that they are positioned differently in social networks of power, and by overemphasizing rationality as the most prized human trait.

By contrast, the feminist social justice approach acknowledges the rich *differences* among people: differences of power, differences of social group membership and identity, and cultural differences. Differences need not be essentialized, nor seen as an impediment to connection. Rather than being seen as discrete, or static, or essentialized, these differences are intersectional. Following Audre Lorde, a feminist social justice approach sees difference as a resource for creativity and connection (Lorde 1984).

Intersectionality has been a key feminist methodology for several decades (King 1988; Crenshaw 1991; May 2015; Hill-Collins and Bilge, 2016). My feminist social justice approach takes *intersectionality* as central in two ways: first, intersectionality means that you cannot separate out the aspects of issues; you must approach them as *interconnected.* Second, intersectionality as a framework *connects the personal to the political* because it shows the ways that individual identities are shaped and formed by structural forces. Specifically, intersectionality as a feminist concept emerged out of social movements that argued that identities are formed in relation to social structures; in order for those who are oppressed to be liberated, structural oppression must be eradicated.[4] Intersectionality is not about identity alone, but about the relationship between identities and social structures. This connection between individuals and social structures reveals a connection between the personal and the political.

One way that the feminist social justice approach ascribes to this connection between the personal and the political is by recognizing that in order for oppression to be overcome, internalized oppression must also be overcome. If oppression correlates to external structural barriers, internalized oppression correlates to internal psychological barriers. For instance, when women are not seen as leaders, not valued for their knowledge and expertise, and are seen as lacking authority, this cultural and social devaluation often undermines their self-confidence. This diminished sense of self, in turn, constricts their ability to speak up and take action. For those impacted by internalized oppression, an expanded range of power and agency by overcoming internalized oppression results in *empowerment*.

My feminist social justice approach recognize*s empowerment* as a significant aspect of the work for social justice. *Empowerment*, as I will argue, exemplifies the relationship between individual change and structural change. I show the connections between individual empowerment and the collective ability to create positive social and political change.

The Feminist Social Justice Approach: Normative Framework

The normative framework for the feminist social justice approach includes the ideals of equality and justice promoted under legal and political models of justice. But it goes beyond standard models by recognizing that in the face of structural injustice the ideals of equality and justice are undermined unless the structural forces producing injustice are changed. These structural forces include economic systems, as well as cultural and social systems. Moreover, the feminist social justice approach questions how standard approaches to justice may actually result in injustice; for instance, by demonstrating the ways that the law and justice system work to disadvantage those who are poor, or black, or both.[5]

Although the feminist social justice approach is critical of how legal and political systems may reinforce existing inequalities, political and legal justice still plays a role in its normative framework. One can be critical of state power and still believe that everyone deserves equal protection under the law. Many social movements primarily address political and legal injustices. They work for political rights, such as the right to vote, and legal rights, such as the right to a fair trial, the right to marry, the right to property, and nondiscrimination in employment and housing. Political and legal injustices can often be effectively remedied through changes in laws, including laws about political representation and voting. Yet even when laws promote, for example, racial equality, if systemic racism persists, the outcome of judicial and legal systems will not serve its purported aim of equal treatment. In this case, nondiscrimination laws must be accompanied by changes in social and cultural norms and attitudes, as well as changes in a host of institutions that support and perpetuate racism, such as redlining in housing and real estate, lack of support for inner-city schools, racial profiling by police, and media stereotyping.

As mentioned, the feminist social justice approach has a systemic view of structural injustice; this means that interrelationships and interconnections of large structural forces must be accounted for in our analyses. When we individuate specific institutions and systems, such as the legal system, we obscure the ways that other institutions and systems, such as the economic system, may still hold inequalities in place. For example, in the United States, women are equal under the law, and yet women still make less than men, still face sexual harassment in the workplace, more women live in poverty than men, and women are more likely to be subject to sexual violence than men. And singling out one aspect of identity, such as gender, obscures the differences within that group, as previously noted. According to the US National Commission on pay equity, although across the board all women are paid less than white men, there are differences in the disparity of wages among women: white women are paid on average 81.0 percent; black women, 65.3 percent; Hispanic women, 57.6 percent; and Asian women, 89.8 percent of the wages of white men.[6] In this case, legal equality does not guarantee economic equality, and inequalities within groups are not addressed. And it is easy to see how structural injustice (racism) positions women differently depending on their race and ethnicity. The interconnections among gender, race, and poverty mean that in order for structural oppression based on social group membership to be eradicated, so must the systems of economic inequality that both support and perpetuate aspects of social inequality.

Economic justice is central to the feminist social justice framework. Economic justice involves not only the redistribution of material benefits but also changing the systems that perpetuate economic inequality. Economic injustice can be characterized as a form of exploitation. *Economic exploitation* occurs when the labor and powers of one group are transferred to another—workers to capitalists, women to men, people of color to whites—in an ongoing and systematic manner (Young 1990). Recognizing economic exploitation requires systemic and structural analyses. The feminist social justice framework includes *anti-exploitation* as one of its primary normative commitments

As noted, the rights-justice framework operates within the legal and political system, but it leaves aside issues in the sphere of social and economic equality. Addressing legal and political inequality and discrimination achieves formal, but not substantive equality. Unless social and economic inequalities are addressed, those who are poor, uneducated, or illiterate will not be able to actualize some of their formal rights. Moreover, economic resources and material circumstances are significant issues for any theory of justice.

When the rights-justice theory does include considerations of economic justice, this approach remains within the paradigm of reform and redistribution. Redistribution allocates resources differently within the existing economic system, and reform might mean incremental adjustments or improvements to the existing laws and institutions. Thus, the rights-justice framework is not well suited to address issues of structural systemic inequality because it generally seeks to redress existing inequalities rather than change the structural conditions that create the inequalities.

A feminist social justice approach sees economic justice as fundamental to its goal. Economic justice involves not merely redistribution, but a radical rethinking of the ways that our economic systems are structured. Nonexploitative economic relationships are central to economic justice; adopting a nonexploitative perspective will involve a major rethinking of the role of economics.

This legacy of including economic, material issues as central to accounts of justice runs through many contemporary critical traditions and has its roots in Marxism. Countering exploited labor and alienated labor reorients the relationship between economics and society; human needs and social aims should determine economic institutions and arrangements. Such a perspective guides current movements for solidarity economics. Solidarity economics approaches are committed to egalitarian social relationships, environmental sustainability, and putting people before profit.

In addition to a commitment to anti-exploitation, the feminist social justice approach includes a normative commitment to *anti-oppression*. Oppression is the systematic constriction of agency, movement, and opportunities (Frye 1983). Overcoming sexist oppression is a fundamental aspect of feminism, and intersectional feminists recognize that sexist oppression is entwined with other forms of oppression, such as racism, classism, heterosexism, and ableism. Anti-oppression work must be systemic because the social structures and forces that cause oppression are interrelated barriers.

As noted, legal and political barriers can be partially addressed through legal and political reforms. But anti-oppression work must also be *sociocultural* because it includes social and cultural norms and practices, and power relationships based on social and cultural arrangements. Oppression occurs through the imposition of dominant norms on minority groups. Imposition of dominant norms occurs through everyday social and cultural practices as well as institutions such as schools, the workplace, political institutions, legal institutions, and religious institutions. Dominant groups' values hold sway over others; for example, Sunday store closures in the United States reflect the dominant Christian religious culture, as do public school holiday closures.

The injustices of oppression may link to economic injustice, for instance, when a job candidate is discriminated against because of race or ethnicity. This type of outright discrimination can be addressed through changes in laws and their enforcement. However, other types of social marginalization cannot be remedied through legal means; for example, the devaluation and social marginalization of a particular caste, race, or ethnic group, or slights experienced during interpersonal interactions.

This social marginalization and devaluation can result in a lack of self-respect and self-esteem; as theorists of oppression have noted, oppression is often internalized (Fanon 1967; Bartky 1990; Taylor 1994). While oppression deprives a person of the social good of respect, internalized oppression deprives a person of the social good of self-respect. As Iris Marion Young points out in her discussion of the five faces of oppression, those who are powerless do not command respect; they lack "authority, status, and sense of self." In contrast to the powerless, those with power have "authority, expertise, or influence" (Young 1990, 57).[7]

Authority, expertise, influence, and status derive from one's social position and the perception of one's peers and interpersonal interactions. Although sociocultural elements and laws may be related—for instance, laws supporting racial segregation and discrimination support racist behavior and attitudes—social norms are not reducible to laws and cannot be changed through legal means alone. Respect as a social good belongs to the sociocultural arena of interpersonal interactions and may be achieved through changes in social status or perception of one's social status. Respect has to do with social standing; through examples drawn from SEWA and MarketPlace, I show the connection between women working against economic exploitation and sexist oppression and their newfound sense of self-respect and self-confidence.

Like respect, the social good of recognition is realized through interpersonal and social relationships. While respect can be, indeed should be, conferred regardless of one's identity, recognition involves acknowledgment of one's particular identity. Often recognition of particularity is especially important for members of nondominant social groups. The concept of recognition as a political demand is well articulated by Charles Taylor: "our identity is partly shaped by recognition and its absence, often by the *mis*recognition of others, and so a person or group of people can suffer real damage, real distortion, if the people or society around them mirror back a contemptible picture of themselves. Nonrecognition or misrecognition can inflict harm, can be a form of oppression, imprisoning someone in a false, distorted and reduced mode of being" (Taylor 1994, 25). This view holds that, at least in part, individuals derive their identities from their social group identity, and that nonrecognition of their particular identity is a form of oppression. Thus, recognition of particular identities is an aspect of the normative commitment to anti-oppression.

This commitment to overcoming internalized oppression connects the structural barriers people face with the psychological effects. As I will argue, empowerment involves an overcoming of internalized oppression in part as a result of acting collectively against structural barriers. A feminist social justice approach recognizes that people exist in social, historical, and political contexts and have identities, histories, and group affiliations that shape their experiences, and that hold significance for them and that social justice includes transformations at individual, institutional, and structural levels. The feminist social justice framework begins from these insights and holds normative commitments to anti-exploitation and anti-oppression.

In sum, a feminist social justice framework includes normative commitments to economic justice (anti-exploitation) and sociocultural justice (anti-oppression, including social recognition and respect), in addition to legal and political justice. Additionally, social justice feminism recognizes that we are all implicated in systems of unequal power, and because of this, we all have a responsibility to work to make these institutions and systems fairer and more just.

Chapter Summaries

In chapter 1, I discuss the background and work of SEWA and MarketPlace. I situate my analysis with respect to other feminist projects that advocate beginning from the situation of struggles of Third World women workers to illuminate the ways that they negotiate the complex intersections of class, gender, religious, ethnic, and caste differences and neocolonialism and imperialism (Mohanty 2003).[8] Beginning with real-life situations of injustice, and struggles for justice, is consistent with the feminist social justice approach, which recognizes the links between theory and practice.

I identify four major themes in the work of these two organizations: Collaboration and Participation; Women's Leadership; Women's Empowerment; and Respect for Diversity and Global Connections. These four themes resonate with elements of the feminist social justice approach. Collaboration and participation involve an awareness of *power relations.* As much as possible within these groups, power is shared among members. This power sharing is an intentional strategy to disrupt the unequal power relationships present in the society at large among women of different religions, castes, and socioeconomic status. One element of this intentional disruption of power relations is to accord *respect* to each member's abilities and knowledge. Respecting the abilities and knowledge of each woman and countering pervasive social inequalities in the larger society includes having women in positions of leadership within the organizations.

As a women-only organization, SEWA offers women leadership positions that allow them to increase their skill base and their confidence. MarketPlace has mainly women as members, and they also remark on the ways that being placed in significant leadership roles changed their view of themselves. This increased range of capacities and increased self-confidence is one aspect of *empowerment.*

Empowerment, I will argue, involves both *anti-exploitation* work and *anti-oppression* work. Disempowerment comes from both external forces that perpetuate social inequality, as well as the internalization of oppression that results in a devaluation of self. Both must be affectively countered. Because the systemic forces that produce structural inequality require collective political action to eradicate them, empowerment also involves political and social activism.

These organizations show respect for *diversity* in a variety of ways: in rural settings many of the women involved in the group are from different indigenous groups; in urban settings one of the most significant differences is in terms of religion. In both settings, all members work with women of different castes, ethnicities, and religions than themselves. Rather than acting as though they are the same, the women bring their religious, caste, and ethnic differences into their work and learn from one another's differences. The members of these organizations model a solidarity that comes not from ignoring differences among them, but from embracing them.

Each organization makes *global connections* in its own way. SEWA began with local struggles around home-based work and harassment of street vendors. After success at the local level, they participated in international meetings, such as the International Labor Organization, to help pass international policies and guidelines for home-based work. They also connected with several international coalitions that organize workers in the informal economy. MarketPlace engages its members in discussions about global issues. They also make global connections between the co-operative members who produce the clothing in India and the women who buy it in the United States.

In chapter 2, I argue that transnational feminism must go beyond the universal human rights approach. For the last half of the twentieth century, human rights scholars and activists have been the dominant voice in making global claims for justice. Feminists took up this project advocating for "women's rights as human rights" (Cook 1994; Peters and Wolper 1995). I explain both the important contribution the women's rights as human rights movement made, and I also explore some of the limitations of using the discourse of human rights. Even established human rights organizations such as Amnesty International now see human rights as "instruments for attaining other goals such as dignity, equality, or social justice" (Lettinga and Troost 2015, 7).

Employing a human rights strategy for global gender justice, I argue, overemphasizes legal and political remedies while downplaying social and economic inequalities. Even when feminists include social and economic rights (Bunch 1995) and argue for the indivisibility of rights (Petchetsky 2002), without an account of structural inequality and an analysis of power relations, gender inequality cannot be fully addressed. As I have discussed, economic inequality is a form of structural inequality that must be addressed through substantive systemic social and institutional change that goes far beyond formal legal and political changes, which are the primary types of changes called for by the human rights framework. Using a feminist social justice approach highlights issues of economic inequality and exploitation that the rights framework does not account for because it lacks an analysis of *power relations*.

Beyond its focus on legal and political remedies for inequality, using a human rights framework often overlooks significant social group and cultural differences among people. For feminists, acknowledging the significance of cultural traditions and practices has proven to be tricky territory. Some feminists claim that gender equality requires ignoring, or even abolishing, culture (Bunch 1993; Okin 1999). Other feminists speak up about the importance of culture (Abu Lughod 2002; Mahmood 2005). Several issues arise from this conflict of views about the role of culture in global gender justice. In terms of a feminist social justice approach, separating gender from culture neglects the role of intersectionality; we know that gender cannot be isolated from other social group identities, including culture.

This neglect of culture has resulted in charges of cultural imperialism because calling for the abolition or change of cultures only in non-Western countries reinforces the stereotypical view of non-Western cultures as primitive, barbaric, and backward. As Uma Narayan and others have pointed out, challenging the imperialism of these views does not mean one cannot criticize cultural practices in non-Western countries. Drawing on Narayan's work on the colonialist stance, and her work on complicating our ideas about culture, I show that an appreciation of one's culture can be consistent with criticizing specific practices. And that this more complicated relationship to cultural practices serves feminists well and avoids pitting gender equality and respect for culture against one another.

Often calls for gender equality have relied on the framework of human rights. In addition to the issues raised earlier, the human rights framework is individualist. Feminists' work on conceptions of the self emphasizes the interdependence and relationality of selves (Held 2006; Koggel 2013). Recognizing our interdependence, rather than assuming our individualism, can shift our prescriptive ideals as well toward valuing cooperation more than competition.

In chapter 3, I address what Serene Khader calls the "global justice dilemma" (Khader 2011, 24). Khader aptly characterizes this dilemma as asking "feminist philosophers to choose between addressing systemic injustice and promoting small-scale interventions to improve women's lives" (Khader 2011, 36). Arguing that this is a false dilemma, I demonstrate the connections between small-scale interventions and addressing systemic injustice.

First, I show the ways that economic inequality and gender inequality are interrelated. The feminization of poverty is a global phenomenon, and it has been exacerbated through neoliberal economic policies of privatization of public services, liberalization of trade, and the outsourcing of labor.

One of the most prevalent small-scale interventions to improve women's lives has been the introduction of income-generating enterprises often funded through microfinance institutions (MFIs). Supporters of this strategy often claim that women become empowered by their access to the money and opportunities created by MFIs. Yet critics raise issues about whether or not MFIs actually result in women's empowerment. At issue here is the definition of empowerment as well as the practical outcome of MFIs. I argue for a definition of *empowerment* that includes structural change, as well individual changes in self-confidence, through small-scale interventions. Linking these aspects shows that the either/or dilemma of structural change or small-scale solutions can be countered with a both/and solution; large-scale structural change is related to other types of smaller institutional changes, and vice versa.

Specifically, I show how the small-scale intervention of creating women's cooperatives has led to women's leadership and social and political activism in their communities. Cooperatives, I argue, have a significantly different impact than MFIs because of their structure: they are committed to social equality, not only economic advancement. Because of this twin goal of social and economic equality, cooperatives foster gender equality and economic equality simultaneously. In chapter 5, I link up women's cooperatives with the worldwide Fair Trade movement and the global solidarity economy movement.

The types of collective organizing that SEWA and Marketplace engage in for gender equality and fair labor practices have crossed national boundaries as both organizations focus on structural barriers to women's equality, and the greatest structural barrier is economic inequality. SEWA has fought and won cases in India's Supreme Court, and it has changed international policies through its advocacy work at the International Labor Organization. MarketPlace has held demonstrations in the streets to improve the process of government rationing, and members promote campaigns for local changes in the communities where they live.

In chapter 4, I introduce a new concept of cosmopolitanism that I call "relational cosmopolitanism." Relational cosmopolitanism accounts for power differences, the history of colonialism and its neoimperialist legacy, the interdependence of persons, and the significance of cultural and social differences. My concept of relational cosmopolitanism draws on Rabindranath Tagore and contemporary feminist work (Lorde 1984; Lugones 1987).

Feminist projects aiming at global justice must also consider cosmopolitan approaches to global justice. I consider two prominent approaches to cosmopolitanism before developing my concept of relational cosmopolitanism, Martha Nussbaum's individualist ethical cosmopolitanism, and Thomas Pogge's institutional cosmopolitanism. I argue that Nussbaum's account of cosmopolitanism relies on an exaggerated notion of the individualism and rationality of the self. Because of the strongly individualist bias in her account, her cosmopolitanism lacks an analysis of power relations, specifically an analysis of structural inequality. Accounts of global justice cannot ignore structural inequality, including the history of colonialism that caused much of the current unjust economic global order.

I then examine Thomas Pogge's institutional cosmopolitanism. While institutional cosmopolitanism provides an analysis of structural injustice, specifically structural economic injustice, it leaves aside issues of cultural difference and lacks a gender analysis. As I argue in chapter 3, global gender justice and global economic justice are intimately linked because gender inequality is connected to economic inequality. In addition to a lack of gender analysis, both Nussbaum's and Pogge's versions of cosmopolitanism dismiss cultural difference as morally irrelevant. Both assume it must be overcome or ignored to justify global moral obligations; we are obligated to others because they are similar to us, on Nussbaum's account. On Pogge's account, we are obligated to others because we stand in a structural relationship in which we benefit from an unjust global economic order.

I draw on Tagore's cosmopolitanism to construct a relational cosmopolitanism that values cultural differences without reifying them. Tagore maintains a fine balance between valuing cultures and still criticizing specific cultural practices. He also provides a trenchant critique of nationalism. Nationalism, according to him, is based on greed, efficiency, and militarism; and it drives colonialism. Tagore's model of cosmopolitanism exemplifies feminist social justice concepts of *relationality, power relations*, and *interdependence*. His criticism of nationalism clearly includes economic anti-exploitation as well as anti-oppression on the basis of culture and society. Tagore's relational cosmopolitanism, with its rich understanding of power relations and cultural differences, provides a better starting point for feminist accounts of cosmopolitanism, although it does not include a gender analysis.

Using Audre Lorde's insight that it is our differences that enable us to learn and transform, and Maria Lugones's concept of "world traveling," I extend Tagore's ideas about cosmopolitanism to embrace these feminist ideas of difference as a resource for creativity and as the basis for solidarity and connection.

Finally, I provide examples of this type of relational cosmopolitanism from the work and practices of SEWA and MarketPlace.

In chapter 5, I explore the framework of political responsibility advocated by Iris Marion Young. Young's concept of political responsibility identifies our material social and economic connections as the source of our moral obligations to one another.[9] She develops her model of political responsibility as an alternative to the liability model of responsibility. Her criticism of the liability model of responsibility shares some of the same concerns that I raise with the rights framework; both are legalistic, individualist, and ignore structural inequality as the root of injustice. Young's responsibility model recognizes that structural inequality, especially economic inequality, but also other types of social inequalities, must be changed in order to achieve social justice. Her account, like my feminist social justice framework, includes norms of economic anti-exploitation and anti-oppression.

In spite of this congruence of norms between her model of political responsibility and my feminist social justice framework, the model of political responsibility that Young develops is not explicitly feminist. I bring her account of political responsibility together with feminist notions such as intersectionality, power relations, and privilege to argue that her model of political responsibility as a transnational conception of justice is well suited for feminist analyses.

I defend Young's model of political responsibility from critics who argue for a predominately rights-based model of transnational justice, and I extend her model to accommodate criticisms that political responsibility is silent on cultural abuses of women (Gould 2009; Ferguson 2009d). This latter criticism is, of course, partially deflected by defusing the antagonism between gender equality and culture, which I do in chapter 2.

The "global justice" dilemma between large-scale structural solutions and small-scale interventions arises again in the opposition between advocates for political activism against sweatshop labor, and Fair Trade advocates. Once again, I argue that small-scale interventions do not preclude large-scale structural solutions. I point out that systemic structural change actually requires the development of new small-scale institutions that do not reproduce the systemic inequalities. For instance, in the case against sweatshops, fair wages and better working conditions within the same institutional framework of transnational corporations is an incremental improvement. Moving toward worker-owned and worker-managed cooperatives is a radical shift in the relations of social and economic power. This shift in social relations happens at several levels—at the interpersonal level within the cooperatives by virtue of their egalitarian and participatory democratic structure; at the institutional level by creating alternative organizations and enterprises; and at the structural level as these institutions form cross-border relationships in the interest of economic solidarity, a global economic movement committed to worker justice, and to social justice.

In my conclusion, I urge a shift in thinking: from individualism to interdependence, from identity to intersectionality, and from interest to imagination. I believe that the feminist social justice approach requires this shift and opens up new imaginative possibilities for feminist social justice projects.

The Relationship Between Theory and Practice

Watson's view of collaboration—"If you have come to help me, I don't need your help, but if you have come because your liberation is tied to mine, come, let us work together"—both captures our interdependence and recognizes power differences; because we are all connected through unequal social relationships, our liberation is bound up with one another.[10] I share her view that justice and liberation cannot be realized for and by a single group or a single person; they involve transforming sociocultural, political, and economic systems so that they are not exploitative, oppressive, or exclusionary. This transformation to a just society will need to be a shared, collective project. As a philosopher versed in social, political, moral, and feminist theory and an activist, I approach the relationship between theory and practice with some ambivalence. On the one hand, I am keenly aware of the gaps between theory and practice. On the other hand, I remain convinced that theory and practice are inseparable, and mutually inform one another.

And as a feminist philosopher and activist committed to working for social justice, I find myself confronted with the limitations of theory and language, as well as the gap between theory and practice. Philosophy, at least ideal theory, pushes us toward an "either/or" mentality, whereas real-life situations often call for the possibility of a "both/and" approach. This gap between "either/or" and "both/and" approaches is well illustrated in a story that is used in community organizing: "Babies in the River."[11] Here is an abbreviated version of the story:

> There was a small village downstream on the edge of a river. The villagers enjoyed satisfying lives and treated one another well. They considered themselves good people and were always ready to help others. One day, a villager saw a baby floating by in the river, and rushed in to save her. The villager rescued the baby. But the next day, two babies went floating

by. The villager called for help, and both babies were pulled from the river and saved. But the next day, four babies were seen floating down the river. Soon everyone in the village was occupied with saving this endless stream of babies from drowning. It became obvious that the babies were not getting in the river on their own, but were being thrown into the river. The villagers were faced with a dilemma: if any of them left to investigate who was throwing the babies into the river upstream, there would not be enough of them to save the constant stream of babies now floating by. Should the villagers send someone upstream to investigate knowing that some of the babies would die? Or should they continue to pull the babies out of the river in order to save them?[12]

As is often the case with hypothetical dilemmas, neither of these choices seems palatable. On the one hand, if someone goes upstream to investigate, and, hopefully, stops more babies from being thrown into the river, some babies will die. On the other hand, if no one goes upstream to stop the babies from being thrown in, the situation will continue indefinitely and may even get worse. In the first case, going upriver will get to the root of the problem and stop the need for the ongoing rescue mission by the villagers. In the second case, rescuers face an endless stream of babies to rescue. Obviously, both need to be done.

The difference in these two approaches can be viewed as the difference between a structural approach to a social problem that aims to change the systems that cause the problem in the first place, and a services approach that focuses on immediate needs in order to keep people from dying. In cases of economic hardship and material deprivation, people often need services provided, such as access to food and shelter, to meet their basic needs. At the same time we should question a system that systematically disadvantages some people while benefiting others. And, finally, because we are all implicated in complex systems of power and privilege, each of us can play a role in resisting and transforming unjust social and economic systems: "It is important to note a crucial limitation of this particular story. The way it is framed, the people in the river are basically hopeless victims. In the real world, this is almost never the case. No matter how oppressed, people almost always have the capacity to organize and resist in one way or another. Organizing for social justice should never be about "rescuing" people. Instead, it is about helping people who are oppressed learn skills that can help them resist."[13] Resisting oppression and addressing systemic injustice involve collective struggles for social change.

SEWA and MarketPlace employ a "both/and" strategy, not an "either/or" strategy. This both/and approach means that the women are involved in the organizations as workers seeking both to earn a living in order to meet basic needs and to combat the social and political forces that marginalize them as poor women, and often also as lower caste women. Both organizations use the language of empowerment to capture this dual sense of increasing poor women's material and status, and fostering capacities for social and political change.

Poverty and Gender Inequality in India

The women's cooperatives that I researched in India combine economic empowerment with social and political empowerment. Their innovative and comprehensive strategies exemplify a multifaceted social justice approach. Exploring their strategies for women's social and economic empowerment requires at least a brief discussion of the background conditions in which their struggles take place.

In the past decade, India's rapidly growing emerging economy holds out the possibility for an improved quality of life for all of its citizens. However, for the majority of Indians an improved quality of life is still an unfulfilled promise. India is the second most populated country in the world, and the largest democracy, but is still a country in which there is widespread poverty. According to recent statistics gathered by the United Nations Development Programme, 21 percent of the population live on less than $1.90 a day, while 53 percent are considered working poor earning less than $3.10 per day.[14] As a result of this widespread poverty, many people in India lack access to basic necessities. According to statistics gathered by UNICEF through 2013, 43 percent of children in India under five years old are underweight and undernourished. Moreover, nearly 10 percent of the population lack access to safe water, and 65 percent do not have access to proper sanitation (UNICEF-India-Statistics 2015). The immediacy of meeting basic needs often eclipses the importance of education; according to 2015 statistics, an estimated 37 percent of adults in India are illiterate.

As in many countries, the widespread poverty in India has a greater impact on women. The 2014 Global Gender Gap Report (published by the World Economic Forum to assess how countries are doing on gender parity) ranks 142 countries on a variety of indices for gender parity. India ranks 134 for Economic Participation and Opportunity, 126 for Educational Attainment, 141 for Health and Survival, and 15 for Political

Empowerment. The indices for the greatest gender disparity in health, education, and economic opportunity are clustered near the bottom of these rankings.

In terms of health and survival for women and girls, India ranks very low, second to the bottom. Amartya Sen's well-known observation that "more than 100 million women are missing" (1990) refers to the disparity in the ratio of men to women—a disparity that is incongruous since women typically live longer than men. This disparity can be attributed to sex-selective abortion, infant mortality from malnutrition, and inadequate medical care for female children. Maternal mortality is high in most impoverished countries, but it is rarely noted as a possible reason for the discrepancy in the number of women and men. Maternal mortality often results from the kinds of deprivations related to poverty: poor nutrition and lack of access to health care. And in many countries, women are particularly vulnerable to the effects of poverty and social discrimination, both of which can be addressed through a comprehensive feminist social justice approach.

In contrast to the low ranking for health and survival for women, India ranks fifteenth in political empowerment for women. I do not have the space here to address why women's political participation stands out as an anomaly, although it may be partly attributed to India's status as a constitutional democracy as well as gender quotas for certain elected offices. During the past ten years most indicators of quality of life, such as adult literacy, infant mortality, and access to safe drinking water, have slightly improved in India. However, in some parts of South Asia, women's participation in the labor market is dropping rather than increasing. According to the ILO's Global Employment Trends 2013 report, India's labor force participation rate for women fell from 37 percent in 2004 to 29 percent in 2010. Out of 131 countries with available data, India ranks 120 out of 131 (eleventh from the bottom) in female labor force participation (ILO 2013).

In the next chapter, I examine the responses of two women's organizations in India to these conditions of poverty and gender inequality, SEWA and MarketPlace. The approaches of these grassroots women's organizations demonstrate the power of collective action; the connections between economic justice and gender justice; links between structural change, institutional change, and personal transformation; and a critical appreciation of cultural and religious diversity.

Having observed the work of these organizations first-hand, I think they offer a novel approach to feminist struggles for social justice. I am not alone in this impression. For instance, Gayatri Chakravorty Spivak says

SEWA is "one of the most spectacular social experiments in the Third World" (Spivak 2003, 319). And Chandra Talpade Mohanty credits SEWA with doing "some of the most creative and transformative collective organizing" against Third World women's exploitation (Mohanty 2004, 164).[15] The work of MarketPlace and SEWA exemplifies a complex and multifaceted approach to social justice and the possibilities for systemic change when women work collectively for social justice.

CHAPTER 1 | Women's Activism as a Model
for Feminist Theorizing

MarketPlace India and the Self-Employed Women's Association

Change, to be real, has to come from the people; it cannot be trickled down, imported, or imposed.

—ELA BHATT (2006, 215)

MUMBAI, 2004—WE WALK THROUGH the narrow lanes of a poor community, corrugated tin shacks open to the elements, cook fires burning inside, clothes drying on the open walls. Roosters run underfoot, dogs and children play in the lanes, raw sewage rushes by our feet. We arrive at our destination, the MarketPlace India clothing cooperative, Udan Mandel. Udan Mandel employs women, especially widows, to sew and embroider clothing and provides a fair wage and safe working conditions. The space is no more than 10 by 12 feet, full of women talking, laughing, and sewing. They interrupt their work to talk with us and drink tea. Asmita, widowed ten years earlier, begins to speak: "When my husband died, I didn't know what to do. I had two small children and a blind mother to support. My in-laws were cruel to me and wanted nothing more to do with me after my husband's death." Tears welling up in her eyes, she says softly, "I thought of killing myself."

Like many other widows in India, Asmita felt she had few choices for survival. Because women are often barred from working outside the home, this leaves them dependent on their husbands, male relatives, or in-laws for economic support. In Asmita's case, the death of her husband, the lack of support from her in-laws, and the lack of resources in her own family made her economic situation desperate. Without employment opportunities and lacking the social safety net often taken for granted in wealthy, postindustrialized countries, or among those of the middle and upper class in some countries in the global South, widows without family support have few options for survival, and sometimes commit suicide rather than face starvation. But Asmita did not commit suicide; instead, she found employment at MarketPlace India, earning enough to support herself, her two children, and her mother. MarketPlace India is one of a number of nonprofit organizations that aims to empower women by providing economic and social opportunity, specifically employment, skills training, and social programs.

In this chapter, I discuss the work of two nonprofit membership organizations in India: MarketPlace: Handwork of India and the Self-Employed Women's Association (SEWA), which are both exemplary in addressing women's economic and social inequality.[1] Both organizations aim to ameliorate the situation of poor women; they focus on empowering women as workers. SEWA's main goal is to organize women workers in the informal sector for full employment and self-reliance. SEWA defines full employment as security with regard to work and income, as well as security to cover basic needs such as food, shelter, and health care. SEWA and MarketPlace India both seek to address a range of inequalities and social injustices, including economic, social, gender, ethnic, caste, religious, and educational inequalities. Each organization has women at the forefront of its mission. MarketPlace: Handwork of India defines its mission as "a pioneering nonprofit that empowers women in India to break the cycle of poverty, as they become leaders in their work, their homes, and their neighborhoods, and effect lasting change in their communities. In MarketPlace's comprehensive and creative organization, economic development is only the first step for these brave and resourceful women."[2]

As I discuss in chapter 3, the forces of neoliberal globalization impact women more negatively; free trade policies and export-processing zones contribute to the exploitation of women's labor in the global South. Outsourcing jobs from the postindustrial global North to the global South allows global capitalism to impose new forms of labor exploitation that draw upon hierarchies of race, gender, caste, class, and ethnicity. The situation of women workers, specifically Third World women, including immigrants of color in the United States, and women in the global South, illuminates the ways that neoliberal capitalism exploits these hierarchies as well as the history and legacy of colonialism.[3]

I agree with Chandra Talpade Mohanty's insight that "From these struggles [the dignity of Third World women workers' struggles] we can learn a great deal about the processes of exploitation and domination as well as about autonomy and liberation" (2004, 139–140). Mohanty examines the situations of lacemakers in Narsapur, India, electronics workers in the Silicon Valley, and migrant women workers in Britain to illustrate the processes of exploitation and domination of contemporary global capitalism. To illustrate the processes of autonomy and liberation, she discusses the Working Women's Forum (WWF) and SEWA. Organizing women as workers, according to Mohanty, serves to challenge some of the gendered scripts of labor exploitation that see women primarily as housewives, sisters, daughters, and mothers whose labor is supplemental to a family income and therefore can be underpaid, temporary, and undervalued.

The specific struggles of Third World women workers can be instructive in organizing against global capitalism, and finding grounds for feminist solidarity transnationally. This feminist solidarity would require women coming together not only on the basis of their common situation as women workers, but also on the basis of shared or common interests. As Mohanty puts it: "How do we conceptualize the question of 'common interests' based in a 'common context of struggle' such that women are agents who make choices and decisions that lead to the transformation of consciousness and of their daily lives as workers?" She suggests that feminists look to "the predicament of poor working women and their experiences of survival and resistance in the creation of new organizational forms to earn a living and improve their daily lives" to find "new possibilities for struggle and action" (Mohanty 2003, 161).

Taking this to heart, I have spent over a decade engaging with these two exemplary grassroots organizations of women workers in India. Like Mohanty, I believe that the creative organizing and resistance of these women provide a model for transnational feminist solidarity among Third World women workers. Furthermore, I argue that this model also holds potential for transnational solidarity between producers and consumers, if both groups share a vision of a just world and participate in relationships that support transnational economic solidarity, while also engaging in political work that challenges oppressive, exploitative, and unjust institutions, laws, policies, and relationships.

As I discussed in the Introduction, a feminist social justice approach is multipronged and comprehensive; by this, I mean that concerns about gender should be considered alongside concerns about economic exploitation, racism, caste and class discrimination, and religious intolerance. Moreover, because of its focus on power relationships, feminist social justice analyses must be cognizant of the histories and legacies of colonialism and imperialism, and how these play into contemporary power differences. I follow Mohanty's suggestion that feminists can learn from the successful struggles of Third World women workers how to develop new modes of feminist solidarity and social change. Both SEWA and MarketPlace India have developed a creative and comprehensive model for social change that empowers poor women as agents of change.

Both SEWA and MarketPlace India exemplify a comprehensive approach to gender justice that can serve as a model for transnational feminist solidarity. Although the two organizations are different sizes and have different histories, they both focus on organizing women workers. MarketPlace India was founded in 1980 in Mumbai and currently employs just over 500 members. SEWA began in 1972 in Ahmedabad, and by 2004 had become the largest primary union in India with over 700,000 members; this also made it the largest all-female union in the world (Bhatt 2006, 16). Despite these differences, both organizations share a vision that includes work with dignity and increased access to the basic necessities for poor women and their families. They cultivate values of solidarity and sisterhood among members of their organizations while providing important economic opportunities. In *NGOs in India: The Challenges of Women's Empowerment and Accountability*, Patrick Kilby identifies two main types of nongovernmental organizations (NGOs) in India, those that are action oriented and those that are welfare oriented. Welfare-oriented NGOs see themselves as apolitical and provide services to the poor, whereas action-oriented NGOs seek to empower their constituencies to challenge the very structures that disenfranchise them (Kilby 2011, 17–18). Both MarketPlace India and SEWA are action-oriented NGOs; moreover, they do not fit neatly into the NGO category because they are membership-based, democratic organizations.

In this chapter, I discuss the history, as well as the collaborative structure and participatory organizational models, of MarketPlace India and SEWA and suggest that they provide an interesting model for transnational feminism. Specifically, both organizations began locally but now have an international reach and presence; both focus on women and employment; both employ an inclusive and power-sharing model where the members themselves make organizational decisions; both have a comprehensive program of training, skills building, and support designed to build capacity and empower their members; both recognize the interconnections among various aspects of inequality and social injustice, and seek to transform these injustices individually, collectively, and systemically.

In the final chapter of *Feminism Without Borders*, Chandra Mohanty suggests that transnational feminism would do well to ally itself with anti-globalization movements, especially because gender and labor figure prominently in anti-globalization struggles (2003). Both SEWA and MarketPlace India begin their social justice work at the intersection of gender and labor by specifically focusing on women and work, but both organizations also employ a multilevel systemic approach to social justice that includes attention to diversity, social and cultural context, social and economic inequalities, and the connections among these issues. Looking at how these organizations balance these various issues may be instructive for feminist theorists to help avoid promoting a single framework or analyzing situations of injustice and social inequality along single parameters (e.g., economic, social, political, cultural, gender, class, etc.). As a feminist, a philosopher, and an activist, I have seen too often how a framework for analysis can single out one aspect of injustice while ignoring other types of injustice, thereby minimizing the legitimate concerns relating to other types and aspects of injustice.[4] When activism and praxis inform theory, it becomes clear that working for social justice requires a comprehensive model attentive to the realities of peoples' particular, complex, and situated daily lives.

Both MarketPlace India and SEWA have a dual focus on women's economic and social vulnerabilities, and both work to strengthen women's position by either creating employment, in the case of MarketPlace, or organizing labor, in the case of SEWA, while also providing resources and support for women to become leaders and promoting social and political transformation. The comprehensive approach of these organizations ensures not only that poor women who previously had little or no employment opportunities now earn a living wage, but also that the women develop their own voices, make their own decisions, and become politically empowered to change the social conditions that marginalized and oppressed them in the first place. Political empowerment includes an expansion of women's capacity to speak up, to make decisions and choices; an increase in the range of activity, for instance, related to entering the public domain; and an encouragement of women to become agents of social and political change.[5]

One of the signature characteristics of both MarketPlace India and SEWA is that they are membership-based, power-sharing organizations. This has a number of different aspects. It means that leadership is developed from within the organization, that decisions are made collectively and collaboratively, and that the economic institutions they support (unions and cooperatives) are also based on these principles of participation and inclusivity. This dual focus on economic and social empowerment for women, and the participatory, democratic structure in both of these areas, distinguishes the approach of MarketPlace India and SEWA from the approach of many other poverty alleviation programs that target women.[6] Furthermore, both organizations employ a holistic approach wherein labor, gender, culture, religion, caste, ethnicity, and environment are all considered in various projects and campaigns that they undertake. Organizations such as SEWA and MarketPlace India offer a promising model for transnational feminism as they are grounded in local contexts and needs, yet have a global reach through the transnational relationships they have established. Their comprehensive approach to remedying inequality and social injustice discussed earlier makes a valuable contribution to our understanding of the systemic nature of oppression and social inequality, and it provides solutions that are simultaneously individual and collective, as well as both local and global.

MarketPlace India: Background

MarketPlace India is the smaller and newer of the two organizations; it consists of production cooperatives, and its membership is almost exclusively women. I first learned about MarketPlace India when discussing my research interests with friends. I was puzzled by what seemed to me to be a false dichotomy in some feminist work between equal rights for women and cultural traditions.[7] As I discuss in chapter 2, some feminist positions advocate a strong defense of universal human rights at the expense of cultural tradition. My experiences at international women's conferences and during my travels provided evidence that some traditions, specifically craft and textile traditions, could be a source for women's empowerment through economic opportunities.[8] MarketPlace India exemplifies a successful model of drawing upon traditional textile skills, such as block printing, batik, and embroidery, to empower women through dignified and sustainable employment and ongoing educational and enrichment opportunities. The motto printed on every clothing label, "Dignity, not charity," sums up the mission of MarketPlace. The organization promotes principles of equality and power sharing among the women, and simultaneously equips them to challenge their devaluation in society. As an organization composed of cooperatives, it exemplifies the principles that cooperatives are based upon: self-help, self-responsibility, democracy, equality, equity, and solidarity.[9]

MarketPlace India is an umbrella organization for a group of thirteen cooperatives providing job training, educational programs, and a centralized structure for marketing goods. During my first visit to MarketPlace, I conducted interviews with the women in the cooperatives in Mumbai, India, in February and March of 2004. In a two-week period, I conducted eleven individual interviews and three group interviews (with approximately twenty people in each group). Each individual interview lasted an hour, and the group interviews lasted between one and two hours. The interviews were arranged by MarketPlace, and I also spent a good deal of time talking with the staff and learning about the organization. At the time of my visit, the staff consisted of an executive director, two social workers, and an office manager. The staff of MarketPlace served as coordinators, support staff, and facilitators for the cooperatives. Staff helped cooperatives during the initial organization phase, and also to connect with outside groups and organizations when needed. MarketPlace staff also served as the central unit for marketing and exporting the clothing, as well as coordinating among the cooperatives for social programs. At the time of my initial interviews, the four full-time staff members were educated, middle-class Indian women from Mumbai. Their education, training, and interest were in nonprofit organizations, women's empowerment, and social work. In addition to this small paid staff, each cooperative had leaders that took an active role in developing social programs and trainings for the cooperative members. Most of the four full-time staff spoke fluent English as well as Hindi and Marathi. The two social workers, Suchira and Devi, worked closely with the cooperatives, and during the interviews either Suchira or Devi or both accompanied me and translated for me. The group interviews took place in the workspaces of the cooperatives—tiny spaces filled with sewing machines. Individual interviews took place in a new space acquired by MarketPlace for group meetings, an empty room off a busy street in the urban slums. In both the individual interviews and the group interviews, participants were remarkably open, not only about their relationship to MarketPlace but also about the circumstances of their lives. My initial research in 2004 led to opportunities to visit MarketPlace India again in 2006, and most recently in 2017.

Originally founded in Mumbai, India, in 1980 as SHARE by two sisters, Pushpika Freitas and Lalita Monteiro, MarketPlace began as a nonprofit

organization intended to provide employment for socially and economically marginalized members of society, primarily men with disabilities
and leprosy. Pushpika and her sister had grown up in a progressive middle-
class family in Mumbai. Their mother was involved in social work, and
their father believed in education for girls and women, so he promoted education for his six daughters. Pushpika pursued a bachelor's degree in social work at the University of Mumbai and then went to the United States,
where she earned a master's degree in sociology. When Pushpika returned
to Mumbai, she started an organization to combat the social and economic marginalization of lepers by providing social services and employment through microenterprise. During her work in the poor communities,
Pushpika began to realize that women were especially marginalized and
vulnerable. She recounts a pivotal experience that led her to focus on the
barriers poor women face:

> Late one evening a woman came to my house and asked, "Pushpika, can
> I leave this stove with you because my husband is drunk and he's going to
> sell it and it will take months to save enough money to buy a new one, so
> can you keep it for me for a couple of days?" That was when it hit me that
> women had so little control over their lives. A woman is defined by her re-
> lationship to a man. And although she may be the sole breadwinner in the
> family, she still has no decision-making power to say that their daughter
> should go to school or how many children they should have, nothing. It just
> didn't seem fair. (Littrell and Dickson 2010, 55)

This encounter changed the focus of her work; instead of working with
male lepers, she began to work with poor women to improve their economic and social situation. At first, she worked with just a few women
to make handmade patchwork quilts. They chose to make quilts because
the women knew how to sew by hand, but not by machine. Additionally,
they could neither afford sewing machines, nor did they have the space
in their homes for one. It was also important that they be able to work at
home because they all had small children and could not afford childcare.
During this first year, only three women were involved in the group, in
addition to the founders. Producing the quilts was labor intensive, and the
sales at venues in Mumbai were disappointing. So the women already involved in the production of the quilts shifted their product line to clothing,
reasoning that everybody needs clothing to wear. Their sales were not
strong in India, but on a trip to the United States, Pushpika held a very
successful trunk sale of MarketPlace clothing. So, in 1986, she founded

MarketPlace: Handwork of India to market the artisans' products in the United States.

Collaboration and Participation

Since its founding, the organization has grown to include thirteen cooperatives that employ over five hundred members.[10] They have also expanded their product line to include clothing and household items, and continue to broaden their markets. Five of the thirteen cooperatives produce hand-printed fabric, while the other eight cooperatives sew and hand-embroider the products. Four of the five fabric-producing cooperatives are located at quite a distance from Mumbai, between twelve to twenty-four hours away by train. The eight cooperatives that do the sewing and embroidery are all located either in Mumbai or within a two-hour train ride. Every two weeks, representatives from the sewing cooperatives meet to share information and ideas and to discuss any problems with the production work. This collaboration enables the groups to share their experience and wisdom and to collectively problem-solve. This spirit of collaboration permeates every aspect of MarketPlace India. And, although there are educational and class differences between MarketPlace staff and cooperative members, the commitment to a democratic, participatory structure runs throughout the organization. From the beginning the founders listened to the women and created the organization to respond to the needs that they raised and prioritized: "This democratic approach would become a bedrock for social action projects that would build greater self-confidence among the women and expand the impact of the work to their communities" (Littrell and Dickson 2010, 57–58). The organization combines gainful employment for marginalized women with social programs that educate and empower them; this dual focus on economic opportunity and social and gender equality is crucial to the success of MarketPlace India.

While the organization provides some access to outside programs, most are developed, modified, and managed by the women themselves. This involvement at every level serves to empower the women at MarketPlace India. According to Sharda, *"The best part of my training is the education and information I am getting: even if I'm not the smartest person in the room, just the feeling of sitting in that chair and learning makes me feel equal and worthy."* The organization does not seek to control the production and programs of the various cooperatives; rather, they facilitate the interaction among the various groups and coordinate the marketing of their products. Each piece of clothing or household item produced utilizes hand-printed fabric and incorporates embroidery work; each item is unique and beautiful. Drawing on artistic traditions such as batik and block printing, the producers are considered artisans. The artisans are involved in decision making at every level; they help to design the products, and they are trained to check the quality of production at their respective units, as well as do quality control before the products are shipped overseas. The artisans also contribute photographs and stories to the catalogue. This involvement in the overall production process allows artisans to understand the entire production process, fosters a sense of empowerment, and leads to a sense of shared responsibility for the welfare of the whole organization.

The products produced by the artisans of MarketPlace India are developed with attention to the needs and skills of the workers. Some of the artisans choose to work at home, while tending to children, cooking, and dealing with other household responsibilities, so each article made includes some handwork, such as embroidery, crochet, or patchwork that can be done at home. Even the artisans involved in machine-sewing the items enjoy somewhat flexible work schedules depending on their personal situations. Some women bring their children to work with them or leave work to make the big midday meal. Sunanda's son had unexplained seizures, and she appreciates being able to bring him to work, *"At first, I was scared to leave my sick child at home, but then I was able to bring him to work and he stayed at the crèche."* The artisans' needs are taken into account in other important ways as well. Although every item includes hand stitching, care is taken not to choose small designs that can cause eye strain, or that the older women cannot do because of arthritis. Members of the coops appreciate the fair working conditions and living wage that working with MarketPlace India provides them, as well as the skills and leadership training, and the educational and social programs. But the benefits for members of MarketPlace India go beyond these tangible benefits—virtually everyone I interviewed thought of the coop as a supportive community, almost like an extended family. Kavita says, *"The coop is like a family. The first thing that came with the job is self-confidence, which I didn't have before because I never left the house and did not take public transportation."*

Women's Leadership

Many women who now work in one of MarketPlace's cooperatives did not leave the house before they worked there. In most cases, the women sought work because their husband's job was seasonal, or irregular, or he was unable to provide adequate support because of illness or alcoholism. Sometimes there was initial resistance from family members, most often husbands and mother-in-laws. However, because most families have no other viable means of support, and are living in poverty, the resistance is often short-lived, especially once the women begin to bring home their earnings. Often the resistance to women going out of the house and having a job is mitigated by the fact that almost all of MarketPlace India's members are women.

For many communities and castes in India, especially those from the villages, gender mixing (groups of men and women) goes against the grain of normal social relationships. So an all-women's workplace environment is viewed as less threatening to the traditional social order than a mixed-gender environment. Some women worked in mixed-gender environments before marriage, but after marriage acceded to their husband's wishes to stop doing so: "I had always worked at big companies. But when I got married, my husband wanted me to work at Pushpanjali because it was an all-women's group" (Littrell and Dickson 2010, 95–96). Working in an all-women's group allows some Muslim women an opportunity to work without breaking religious and cultural norms: "If Ashiana included men, I would not be allowed to work for them. It is essential that it is all women. Because it is only women, husbands trust Ashiana with their women and also allow the children to go on the picnics they arrange" (Littrell and Dickson 2010, 107). So for many of the women, working in an all-female cooperative opens up opportunities to work that would otherwise be denied.

It may sound like an all-women's cooperative simply supports male dominance over women by supporting patriarchal and religious norms of gender segregation. Ironically, however, this traditional gender segregation also serves to subvert traditional gender roles. Sharda observes, *"If we were a mixed-gender group, then men would have taken up all the responsibility, but because there are no men the women take on all the jobs, even the taxing [physically demanding] ones."* Women who are members of all-female cooperatives say that one of the benefits of being a member was that tasks were not assigned by gender. And when the women take on tasks that are typically done by men, they realize they can do things beyond the expected societal gender roles; this increases their self-confidence. This is echoed by a number of the women in all-female cooperatives: Asha points out, "If there were men, the job of collecting the fabric would have been given to them. We would not have the courage to go out and do it ourselves, but we are doing all the work." Her coworker Uma agrees, "I like it that all ladies can handle everything. If there were men, they would issue orders and the women would come to depend on them." And Sita, a member of another cooperative, says proudly, "We can prove that we don't need men to solve our problems. Whether they are small or big, we realize that they are OUR problems and we must make them better" (Littrell and Dickson 2010, 109). The majority of MarketPlace cooperatives are all women, and as we can see, this both supports and challenges current gender roles, ideologies, and customs. All-women's groups support the ideology of gender segregation whether because of religious custom or male authority within the family. But for some this allows them the opportunity to work outside the home, which would otherwise be denied; this brings with it a certain freedom of movement in public space and, of course, the economic advantage of earning one's own income. Moreover, within the all-women's groups, women engage in tasks and activities that go beyond their customary gender roles, spurring greater confidence in their own abilities and causing them to challenge gender roles that limit women.

Although most cooperative groups of MarketPlace are women only, three of the cooperatives include men as members. In these mixed-gender cooperatives, men usually take on the tasks typically viewed as "men's work"—heavy lifting, jobs that require more skill or may be dangerous, activities that require going out in public, or working at night: "men can do the difficult work like cutting, carrying heavy things, getting things done that require going outside, and they can work all night if they need to" (Littrell and Dickson 2010, 110). The women in the group also rely on men to problem-solve: "If we have any difficulties solving problems with the patterns, the men help out. And when the supervisor isn't there, the men help out with work problems" (Littrell and Dickson 2010, 110). From the perspective of challenging gender roles, and the social equality of women, the all-women's cooperatives may seem to have more impact. Nevertheless, the mixed-gender groups can play a role in the move toward gender equality. One woman in a mixed-gender group noted that the men in her group were like brothers to her. She is now more confident talking to men, and all the groups have an explicit commitment to gender equality. She says: "I have achieved equality with everyone. A lot of equality is maintained in working together" (Littrell and Dickson 2010, 111).

Moreover, the men involved in the MarketPlace cooperatives asked for their own discussion group where they could discuss the disconnect they felt between the gender equality within the organization and the dominant social norm of gender inequality. Originally only men, the discussion group now includes some of the women leaders in the cooperatives as well. A male group member shares his experience: "I have learned about gender bias and how patriarchal Indian society is. Exposure to all these new ideas has brought about a lot of change in my thinking and my attitude. But it is not all that easy to implement these thoughts, as you don't get support and encouragement from your relatives and from society. But one thing I can say now is that I have a better understanding of both my wife and all the women artisans working with me" (Littrell and Dickson 2010, 76). Involving men in the process of challenging patriarchy and working toward gender equality is important for achieving broad-based and sustainable social change. Social change involves structural transformation, including changes in institutions, opportunities, access to resources, and political power and representation, as well as shifts in attitudes and social relationships. I discuss the connections among these more throughout this book; here I want to note that these various arenas—economic, social, political, interpersonal, familial, and cultural—are interconnected.

As we saw, women in all-female cooperatives took on tasks normally done by men, and from this they gained both new skills and self-confidence. The women's newfound self-confidence results from the combination of the skills and abilities that they have achieved with relation to their work and the information and skills they have developed as a result of the social programs with which they are involved. Members of the coops not only make fabric, sew garments, and do hand sewing; they also run every aspect of the coop, from keeping accounts, to traveling, to picking up supplies. Many women had never traveled alone before, even on a local train or bus. Most of them had never been responsible for large sums of money. Some women knew only their local language and not Hindi, which is widely spoken, and at least one woman had never used a telephone before.

The expectation is that women are capable of participating in every aspect of running a cooperative, and each new experience adds to the women's sense of themselves as capable in ways that they had not previously realized. This newfound knowledge, that they are capable not only of earning a living but also of running a business, contributes to the women's self-confidence. And this, in turn, increases their agency. Kavita exclaims, *"Everything I did increased my confidence, including buying buttons. A woman can do everything. I have proved that there is nothing that women can't do."* This increased self-confidence, combined with their newfound earning power, allows them to change some of the conditions of their lives.

Many of MarketPlace India's artisans explicitly link these dramatic changes in their levels of self-confidence to their ability to deal with problems in their personal lives and in the communities to which they belong. For instance, Sunanda reports, *"I have been empowered in all the senses, for example, I used to give all my wages to my husband and he would spend it on drink. But now I only give him the money if he's sober."* One thing to note here is that although Sunanda gains power by earning money and contributing to the household, her ability to exercise that power and control her earnings to be used for food and household expenses, rather than alcohol, is a result of the confidence she feels in her own decisions.

In his research on women's NGOs in India, Patrick Kilby found that self-esteem and self-confidence allow "marginalized groups, particularly women, to assert themselves in a much wider range of social and political domains in their family and community lives" (2011, 124). One significant aspect of empowerment is personal agency, and Kilby's research corroborates my own by seeing a connection between increased self-confidence and a greater ability and willingness to act on one's own choices. Moreover, this has implications for women challenging entrenched gender roles and other societal injustices. His research, as well as my own, "supports the view that by facilitating women to work together in groups, NGOs can enable the social norms of gender, caste and other factors of exclusion to be challenged," whereas at the same time, it increases the range of decision-making domains in women's lives (Kilby 2011, 127). In chapters 2 and 3, I discuss further the relationship between access to resources, material conditions, agency, and social and political transformation. In chapter 4, I address issues of diversity and global justice through the lens of cosmopolitanism.

Respect for Diversity and Global Connections

MarketPlace India provides the structure and resources for each group to participate in workshops about health, parenting, social issues, global issues, and promoting social change. Sunanda states, *"After parasocial worker training, I feel able to help others, to respect other opinions."* Parasocial worker training helps to develop the women's leadership skills and their ability to help others. This is one of the many programs that actively encourage respect for a diversity of beliefs, backgrounds, and identity.

The religious affiliations of MarketPlace members reflect the religious diversity in India; three of the major religious traditions are represented among members: 66 percent are Hindus, 30 percent are Muslims, and 4 percent are Christians. Working together brings women from different religious traditions together who likely would not have formed relationships with one another: "Within the Mumbai slums, while the artisans may reside next door to each other, they formerly limited their daily exchanges to others of similar religious faith. Accordingly, for many women, the MarketPlace workshops provide the first opportunity to talk with and work closely among women with varying spiritual beliefs and viewpoints" (Littrell and Dickson 2010, 90). Like gender equality, this respect for religious diversity is encouraged and fostered within MarketPlace. Religion is an important aspect of life for many, if not most, of the women. Pushpika describes the way that one of the groups incorporated the importance of religion with the respect for religious diversity into their cooperative: "When I went to the workshop to see what had been done, I saw that they had put up a small altar where they had pictures of different gods and a light there. That's very important in Indian culture. Every home will have a small altar. And I felt very good that here this was part of showing their ownership that they had decided 'we want to have this altar because it's like our house' and they are going to represent different religions" (Littrell and Dickson 2010, 64). As Mary Littrell and Marsha Dickson note in their research study of MarketPlace: "Women . . . speak fondly of the social bonds of support they establish with other MarketPlace women from different religions and backgrounds" (2010, 85). Moreover, they found that their cooperative workplaces "provide a critically important psychological refuge where 'caste and religion do not matter'" (Littrell and Dickson 2010, 143).

While exposure to other religious traditions happens as a natural result of working alongside women from different backgrounds and communities, MarketPlace includes social programs that explicitly focus on dialogue and diversity such as the Global Dialogue program. MarketPlace members choose a current topic that relates to women globally, such as the imposition of the burka by the Taliban in Afghanistan, and discuss it. During the course of their discussion, they are able to share different opinions and gain insights into topics that affect women elsewhere while at the same time discussing their own differing religious beliefs and practices. MarketPlace India values and encourages respect for diversity, and women in the cooperatives often come from different religious, ethnic, caste, and community backgrounds. Forming relationships as coworkers and friends across these differences breaks down long-standing social divisions both within the cooperative group and outside it.

The Global Dialogue program also serves as a bridge between the artisans creating the clothing and their customers. Representatives from each cooperative meet monthly to discuss and select a theme for the MarketPlace catalogue. Themes have included celebrating strong women, redefining community, celebrating our differences, the power of identity, debating dowry, the meaning of beauty, and living in harmony with nature (Littrell and Dickson 2010, 152). The women contribute stories and pictures to the catalogue for each theme; some of these stories and pictures are also on the MarketPlace website. The Global Dialogue program promotes exchanges between the artisans in India and the women buying their products in the United States through the Global Dialogue program, one aspect of which is an exchange of letters via the Internet. The MarketPlace website includes several links to learn more about the members of MarketPlace India, from photos of daily life, to recipes, to updates on their social and political activism.

Women's Empowerment

The collaborative, participatory structure of MarketPlace India fosters women's leadership and encourages them to make changes not only in their personal lives but also in political and social structures that perpetuate social marginalization, gender inequality, and economic exploitation. One clear example of this capacity for social change at the community level is MarketPlace India's social action program. The social action program involves each individual coop choosing an issue that is important to them and their local community and developing a strategy for change and implementing it. One example of a successful social action program is the health education program. In one coop, all members went through an outside workshop on preventive health, with an emphasis on inexpensive traditional home remedies. After this coop went through the workshop, they put together an educational health program themselves. They created all the material such as posters, flip charts, and so on, and they ran peer workshops for the other coops. Significantly, both the type of information and the style of conveying it were tailored to the MarketPlace members. Because most members have limited education, and some are illiterate, information was shared through pictures and orally in a hands-on workshop. Additionally, the focus on inexpensive home remedies meant that women could apply the information they learned without added expense and without turning to a doctor or a clinic. Through these social action programs the women learn that they have the power to create positive change not only in their own lives but also in the community. Sharda proclaims, *"All the programs have had effects on my life, especially the social action program because I circulate the information in my mandel [cooperative group] and my neighborhood."*

Because the women in MarketPlace share their knowledge and promote change within their communities, the scope of change looks like an inverted funnel, starting with the group of women within the cooperative, but broadening out to include each woman's extended family, neighbors, and community. Focusing on particular, local issues helps each group to successfully set and reach their collective goals. With each small success, they are encouraged to tackle larger issues. Asha says, *"If tomorrow I see something happening in my neighborhood, I will fight for change."* For instance, in 2000, several of the cooperatives focused on the issues of community health and preventive health. The Pushpanjali cooperative was concerned about the fact that there were no covers on the raw sewage ditches in their neighborhood. Not only was this dangerous for children playing in the neighborhood and people walking, but also it contributed to significant health problems, both in terms of hygiene and because disease-carrying mosquitoes were breeding in the sewage water. Pushpanjali decided their social action project would be to get the city government to address this situation that so far had been consistently ignored. They educated city officials about the problem, conducted a door-to-door campaign in their neighborhood to elicit widespread support, and demonstrated at the offices of local politicians. Within a year, the problem had been addressed, and the sewage ditches were covered. This change in infrastructure has positive ramifications for everyone in the community, including a lower infant mortality rate, fewer breeding grounds for malarial mosquitoes, and a generally cleaner and safer environment. This is no small feat for a group of women, many of whom had never left the house or spoken in public before they started working in the coop.

MarketPlace members' work for positive social change includes larger scale action as well. They have successfully joined together and worked with other organizations to promote political and social change on the national level. In 2000, several coops undertook a social action program to call attention to the corruption in the distribution of government rations of rice and oil. The Government of India provides these rations for some of the poorest sectors of society; however, those distributing it were intentionally shorting people on their allotment so that they could sell the extra. In order to curtail this corruption in the distribution of food, the women worked in teams, some going in to claim their food, some observing, and some waiting outside with the police. This strategy worked at the community level, but the practice of shortchanging the poor on their food was so widespread that in May 2000, the women joined with 150 other organizations and demonstrated in the streets of Mumbai to bring widespread social and political attention to the situation. Ten thousand people showed up at Govandi, one of the largest slums in Mumbai, for the demonstration. After the demonstrations, the government intervened and improved the supervisory process of distributing rations. The success of this campaign and the support of a large number of other people made MarketPlace members aware of the power of working collectively for social and political change.

These examples of gaining self-confidence by learning new skills and doing new tasks, challenging gender roles, assuming leadership, and working together for social and political change illustrate the links between individual empowerment and collective empowerment. As the women gained self-confidence through training and their work in the cooperative, they were more able to speak up and to provide positive benefits to their families through their income and programs such as health training. They were also able to make changes in their neighborhoods, which benefit their communities beyond their cooperative group and their families, and to engage in large-scale political and social activism. MarketPlace India not only provides each individual with knowledge, skills, and a fair wage but also fosters a sense of solidarity and collective empowerment.

In the following chapters, I return to the themes raised here: the collaborative, participatory structure of cooperatives, challenging gender roles and gender norms through women's leadership and empowerment, and respect for diversity and global connections.

The Self-Employed Women's Association: Background

The success story of SEWA began with a struggle around economic issues, but it has grown to include many other issues. SEWA's primary focus is to organize women workers in the informal sector. Organizing women in the informal sector includes capacity building, leadership training, support to organize against police harassment and for fair wages, and access to sustainable income. From these economic issues, SEWA's work has grown to encompass a range of issues and projects, including Video SEWA, which trains poor, often illiterate, women to make videos to tell their stories. Throughout all of its work, SEWA employs a partnership model with poor women, responding to their needs and developing leadership from within the community. I learned about SEWA first-hand when I visited the SEWA office in Ahmedabad, Gujarat, in January 2006 as part of a Gandhi Legacy Tour focusing on social justice. Our group, led by Dr. Arun Gandhi, the fifth grandson of Mohandas K. (Mahatma) Gandhi, spent the day at the SEWA offices. We learned about the history and the mission of the organization, met many SEWA members, toured the office, sat in on a meeting, and heard a talk by SEWA's founder, Ela Bhatt. The next day our group had a free day, and most chose to go to a famous textile museum. I was so impressed with SEWA that I asked if I could return to their offices. I did so and spent another day learning about various SEWA programs, visiting the Video SEWA unit, and learning about an experiential immersion program where policymakers, both foreign and domestic, live with a rural family to learn about SEWA's projects and their impact on SEWA members. I spent time talking with SEWA's researchers who work closely with members and help to influence national and international policy with their research studies of SEWA's work.

I met more SEWA members, who came into the SEWA offices and bank and project units in an ever-flowing stream. Women laughed, talked, joked, worked, and drank tea. It was clear that everyone I saw felt comfortable, and that the relationships among them were easy and mutual. One indication of this is that regardless of role, rank, or caste, SEWA members would call each other "sister" [ben]; while this is a respectful form of referring to someone in Gujarati, it is not always done across divisions of caste and social hierarchies. The energy, excitement, and commitment to shared projects and goals were palpable. Before I knew it, I was discussing returning to learn even more about the amazing and powerful work in which SEWA was engaged.

I returned to Ahmedabad in October of 2006 to spend two weeks learning more about various aspects of SEWA's work. During that time I visited a number of cooperatives: dairy, midwives, vegetable vendors, textile, block printing, and craft. I also spent time in many offices, the main office, the research office, the video project office, the insurance office, a childcare center, and the publications office. During a recent visit in January 2017, I visited a SEWA project in the village of Ganeshpura outside of Ahmedabad. SEWA worked with the women in Ganeshpura to start a community radio station, grow plants, and develop vermiculture in order to enhance their own crops, and to sell the worms to others to provide natural fertilizer and aeration of the soil. Much of my information about SEWA comes from my time spent at SEWA in Ahmedabad and environs visiting cooperatives and projects, talking to the women involved in them, and observing. I also purchased a number of publications that document the vision and work of SEWA during my 2006 and 2017 visits; in addition to these sources, some of my examples and information come from two book-length studies on SEWA, as well as a number of articles that discuss SEWA's work.

I am not alone in finding SEWA an inspirational model for feminist work; a number of feminist theorists also refer to SEWA's work empowering women as exemplary (Nussbaum 2000; Mohanty 2004; Jaggar 2005; Narayan 2007; Ferguson 2009c). As already mentioned, Chandra Talpade Mohanty credits SEWA with doing "some of the most creative and transformative collective organizing" against Third World women's exploitation (2004, 164). In *Women's Studies International: Nairobi and Beyond*, Sara Stuart writes about SEWA's video project; she says that video can equalize or level relationships between literate and illiterate women and that this can "transform relationships, encourage a high degree of participation, and consequently have great impact" (1991, 81).

SEWA's impact is not just local; one of the many impressive aspects of SEWA's work has been its ability to move from the local to the global. After its local success, SEWA expanded across state borders and then across national borders, successfully making global alliances and founding international organizations. In the remainder of this chapter, I provide a history, background, and overview of SEWA's work. Like MarketPlace India, SEWA explicitly fosters women's individual and collective empowerment, and it uses a comprehensive model for transformative social change that sees economic issues as central but not singular.

Collaboration and Participation

The Self-Employed Women's Association, founded in 1972 by Ela Bhatt, was originally part of the Textile Labour Association (TLA), a labor union influenced by Mohandas K. Gandhi that emphasized mediation and negotiation to resolve disputes between labor and capital. The Gandhian principles that underlay the TLA also infuse SEWA, especially his ideas about the dignity of labor, the importance of human values, and nonviolence. Taken together, these principles indict poverty in several ways: "poverty is wrong because it is violent; it does not respect human labor, [it] strips a person of his or her humanity, and [it] takes away their freedom" (Bhatt 2006, 8). Ela Bhatt refers to economic security in terms of having basic needs met as the second freedom (political freedom is the first freedom); as I discuss later, political and economic freedoms are intertwined.

Organizing women around the issues of poverty and work proved to be extremely effective in India.

SEWA organizes women in the informal sector of the economy in India using a feminist model of participation and power sharing characterized by democratic practices and institutions. Jobs in the informal sector comprise over 90 percent of employment in India, and nearly 70 percent of those employed in the informal sector are women (Bhatt 2006; SEWA website 2015). The vast majority (94 percent) of women working for wages in India are employed in the informal sector, meaning wages and conditions of labor within this realm are very much women's issues (SEWA website 2015). Informal labor includes many activities, such as piecework, including tailoring, embroidery, cigarette rolling, and incense making. Informal laborers may also be street vendors; rag pickers/recyclers; gum collectors; salt makers; and construction workers. The common feature of informal labor is that there are no benefits and no steady salary. Workers are paid the bare minimum for their labor, always less than it takes to survive, and there is no job security. Often women working more than full time in the informal sector do not earn enough to provide for their basic needs, such as housing, food, and health care. Workers in the informal sector usually have little bargaining power, and women working in the informal sector often do not see themselves as workers in the traditional sense, that is, with a regular job, income, or workplace. Organizing women as workers productively brings together issues of gender and class without excluding other aspects of women's identities and social positions, such as caste, ethnicity, and religion.

According to *SEWA's 2015 Annual Report*, it has over 1.4 million members in India.[11] From its inception in 1972, SEWA grew rapidly; by 2004, it had become the largest union in India and the largest women's union in the world. SEWA's success relies on adapting to the needs and vision of its members and developing leadership from within local communities, which are often comprised of mainly poor women without much formal education. SEWA helps women workers to form cooperatives and unions, recognizing that the most effective gains for workers are made collectively. SEWA includes a range of services and benefits for its members, including a cooperative bank, health care and disaster insurance, childcare, literacy and computer training, and video-making classes. There are many SEWA groups in several different states in India, and the focus is on improving women's lives on a material and economic level and making women's voices heard locally, nationally, and globally. SEWA serves as a model for other organizations; in fact, a sister organization, SEWU (Self-Employed Women's Union) in South Africa, is modeled after it.

SEWA defines itself as a movement, not a program. SEWA's members define the goals of the organization. The common denominator is each member's desire to earn enough to help provide basic necessities for herself and her family. But SEWA's success lies not only in helping each individual achieve her goal but also in helping all members realize the power of acting collectively. As a workers' movement, SEWA stays close to its roots by facilitating the formation of cooperatives and unions. Both unions and cooperatives have a democratic, participatory structure that fosters empowerment of individuals within the organization as well as recognizing the power of group action and solidarity. As an all-female group, SEWA promotes and fosters the idea that women are powerful and capable. Within SEWA, women are able to take on positions of leadership, which are not generally available to poor women with limited education. The skills that they learn in these leadership roles—traveling outside their village, collecting information, public speaking, running meetings, and keeping accounts—increase their confidence and their status in the community. Along with these skills, the women benefit from increased security due to their affiliation with SEWA. At the time of my research, membership in SEWA cost only 5 rupees per year (the equivalent of twelve cents), and it provides the women access to SEWA's cooperative bank, health care insurance, disaster insurance, childcare, literacy classes, computer classes, transportation for raw materials and finished products, and so on. In addition to all these benefits, in many cases women's income improves as a direct result of SEWA's bargaining for higher wages and better working conditions.

Women's Empowerment

An early example of SEWA's success was organizing home-based workers in the Muslim community. One of the many occupations in the informal labor sector is making quilts from fabric scraps, called chindi, left over from clothing production. The fabric scraps are sold to a trader who picks them up from the mill, and who in turn sells them to women in the city to be stitched into quilts. It takes an average of two days to produce twelve quilts, often composed of sixty to ninety individual pieces. In 1977, each woman received only 60 paise per quilt—a total of 7.20 rupees (roughly equivalent to 20 cents) for two days of work. Not only was this not a fair wage for her work; it also did not account for the costs of production.

"By using her own workplace and providing her own sewing machine, electricity, vessels for washing, fuel for boiling water, cleaning products, and even the thread for sewing—all of which she paid for with her own money—she was in fact, subsidizing the trader" (Bhatt 2006, 60). Some women rented the sewing machines they used, increasing the cost of production even more for them.

Because the women were working hard, and yet earning very little, if any, money for their labor, they reached out to Ela Bhatt and the members of SEWA. SEWA leadership began their work by doing surveys to find out the issues and the problems of the community. When SEWA begins working on a new issue or in a new community, they use surveys to provide a deeper understanding from multiple perspectives; these surveys also help to identify potential leaders in the community. During a three-year period, the chindi quilters lobbied for a wage increase; they wrote letters, held demonstrations, and held meetings with the Ministers of Finance and Labor. However, their self-advocacy did not go unpunished; chindi traders retaliated by denying the SEWA members work for a period of several months (Bhatt 2006, 64). The quilt makers countered this by setting up their own cooperative through SEWA.

In the end, the workers triumphed. The successful outcome for the workers of a 100 percent increase in their income over a period of three years (from .60 rupees to 1.25 rupees per quilt) is clearly due to the strength of the quilt makers' collective bargaining power. Without the strength of six hundred other women behind her, an individual who demanded a rate increase would have found herself without any work. And without SEWA backing the women's demands, the temporary lapses in work for all six hundred women in the quilt makers' union might have had graver consequences. After the story of this community's success spread, other communities where women also stitched products from chindi expressed an interest in joining SEWA and organizing a union in their area.

Oftentimes one of the frustrations that the women express in the community meetings is not only the low wage for their work but also the lack of control over their working conditions. Usually the low wage is symptomatic of a lack of resources and choices in general and especially with regard to work. As SEWA's founder Ela Bhatt says, "To be poor is to be vulnerable. The condition of being poor, of being self-employed, and of being a woman are all distinct yet interrelated states of vulnerability. Poverty makes one the chronic victim of forces beyond one's control" (Bhatt 2006, 23). One health crisis or disaster, such as an earthquake, drought, or flood, can push an already struggling family deeper into poverty. Even under normal circumstances, poor families must borrow money from moneylenders to make ends meet. The moneylenders charge an exorbitant interest rate, and borrowers find themselves further indebted with each day, and with no way to pay off the interest, let alone the loan. This cycle of poverty is familiar, and barring access to credit for the poor, seemingly inevitable.

Banks that lend money to the poor, such as the SEWA Cooperative Bank, can be an important part of ending the cycle of poverty. SEWA was an early pioneer in recognizing that poor women need access to savings, credit, insurance, and other financial services. Its cooperative bank preceded the more well-known Grameen Bank, and it employs fundamentally different principles, discussed further in chapter 3. Significantly, the SEWA bank stresses savings encouraging women workers to save even small amounts and providing a mobile bank to collect the money. Having a savings account helps to empower women because it may be the only asset she has; generally, house titles and property are still in men's names. Ela Bhatt, SEWA's founder, has been an outspoken proponent of the importance of women having assets in their own name. She says, "We should encourage women to build up assets for two reasons. Because women's income is used mostly for *roti, capra*, and *makaan* (bread, clothes, and house), the more cash income which goes into her hands, the faster the family's quality of life goes up. And secondly, there is an increasing number of women headed households, and in times of crisis, assets are the only things which help them" (quoted in Rose 1992, 198). A savings account opens up further opportunities for SEWA members. They may be able to cover unexpected expenses with their savings, and when they cannot, they can borrow from the SEWA bank because they are members of it; usually people with no assets and without any credit history cannot borrow money. Other obstacles to accessing financial services for the poor include illiteracy, making it difficult to fill out forms; no bank in the area and no transportation; and no safe place to keep money. The SEWA cooperative bank introduced picture identity cards so that illiterate women could also have access to the bank, and it has set up local savings groups and mobile banks in villages and some areas of the city. Additionally, the SEWA bank offers a quick turnaround time between applying for and receiving a loan. This is especially important if the loan is going to be used to recover from a disaster, pay for emergency health care, or cover funeral expenses.

So far I have stressed the importance of economic issues and the role that SEWA plays in securing a livelihood for its members. But another important aspect of SEWA's organizing is the support and validation the women experience from their peers when they meet together in small groups to discuss the problems and issues they are facing. The community identifies leaders from within to be organizers and spokeswomen. Once the needs of the members of the community are identified, SEWA works with them to build the capacity to accomplish their goals. For instance, if the women in the community have embroidery skills, but live in a remote rural area where there is no market for embroidery, SEWA helps them organize into groups (cooperatives), and several cooperatives pool their resources to transport their goods to the city. Self-employment takes different forms in urban and rural areas: "[c]ooperatives offer better opportunities for self-employment [for rural women] by improving the women's skills through training and providing market links which result in an increased income" (Rose 1992, 207). Because each cooperative is an entity with collective resources, someone needs to be trained to keep the accounts of the group and to attend to administrative matters. As the women learn these new skills, their confidence grows.

This increased confidence is, in itself, positive, and it empowers women whose lives are difficult and whose work has been invisible. Gaining confidence can also play a direct role in women broadening their sphere of activity and engaging in social change. Lila Datania, a vegetable vendor, video maker, and SEWA member, speaks of the impact of video SEWA:

> More training should be given to uneducated women to make videos. When we make videos, and women like us watch them, we get confidence and try to make changes. When we see women like us who have done something brave and new, then we get the confidence that we can learn something new, too. When poor women see other poor women as health workers on the video, they say, "I can also learn about health and help solve these problems in my neighborhood." When other self-employed women see me, a vegetable vendor, making these films, they also have the confidence that they can do things which at first seem impossible. (Rose 1992, 158)

As Lila articulates so well, education and training foster self-confidence, and this self-confidence often translates into the ability to make changes in the women's personal lives, such as exercising more decision-making power in the family, tackling new projects, learning new skills, or even leaving an abusive situation.

Women's Leadership

This empowerment in their personal lives is directly related to the increased economic and political power that the women have by being members of SEWA's unions and cooperatives; as one's economic power increases, so does one's status in the family and the community, which often shifts the gendered power dynamics and gender roles. Some SEWA members call their new money-generated strength "powershakti." As Ela Bhatt reports, this "powershakti" has mixed effects on women's lives. Increased financial independence empowers women individually and "increases her value within the family and her standing in the community" (Bhatt 2006, 122). At the same time, disrupting the status quo in this way may spark hostility from family or community members. Nonetheless, facing these hostilities and resistances with courage can serve to increase a women's confidence.[12]

According to Dahiben, a member of the cleaning cooperative SSM: "Initially there was a lot of struggle and resistance from our men folk to the kind of work that I do, but seeing that I started getting a regular income and recognition as being part of SEWA Saundarya Cooperative gradually gained me respect both at home and in my immediate community" (Krishnaswami 2003, 12). SEWA anchors women's power firmly in a material and economic basis—as bank members, property holders, income earners, policyholders, and so on. But this individual empowerment remains inextricably tied to the women's membership in a larger group and their collective power to transform the conditions of their lives. By working together, the women are able to secure a decent livelihood, access to education, health care and insurance, childcare, and loans. They recognize that their success relies on the success of their SEWA sisters as they share resources and problem-solve together. Speaking of the success of organizing the *bidi* (cigarette) rollers, Godavaribehn says, "We have heard how good our voices sound *together*. We understand very clearly the more women we bring in to the union the stronger we will be" (Rose 1992, 129, emphasis in original).

Empowerment not only changes individuals' lives; it also transforms social relations in concrete, particular ways. For example, Puriben, an artisan with traditional embroidery skills, joined SEWA as a member, and she later became the leader of the SEWA group from her rural village. The village leaders [*panchayat*] felt that women leaving the village to go to SEWA meetings would destroy the local culture. They imposed a ban on women leaving the village, including attending SEWA meetings. However,

Puriben met with the village leader, reminding him that the women's work provided a steady source of income through drought and agricultural low seasons. The ban was lifted. At a SEWA meeting Puriben said that standing up for what she believed was empowering to her. Moreover, she is now respected in her village and community, as she says: "Now when I pass from the village, the village elders and children call me as 'Puriben' and not as wife of someone" (Nanavaty 2000, 3–4). In this case, the women's economic power of having the only consistent income increased their social power to meet with officials, and to ask for changes in the enforcement of traditional gender restrictions on mobility. They were not only successful in lifting the ban, which increased self-confidence, but also gained increased respect from community members for their social and political engagement. Economic power bolsters social power and increases self-confidence. In turn, this increased self-confidence fosters personal agency and political engagement.

During my research with both SEWA and MarketPlace India, I was struck by the connection between self-confidence, increased ability to maneuver in the public arena, and willingness to engage in political and social activism. As I discuss further in chapter 3, this link breaks down the division between empowerment as an individual sense or attitude versus a collective political engagement. It can be, and often is, both. Gauriben describes how this "growing self-confidence" affects her ability to "intervene in matters that affect" her life and the lives of the other women in her community (Bhatt 2006, 158). Women in Gauriben's community had to walk several kilometers every day to another village to fetch water because their village had no water tank. She and the other women fought to get the village to build one. This involved meeting with village and government officials. Gauriben notes, "We are not afraid to talk to men or with government officials. Very often we have to pull and push them to work with us. If a government official ignores me, I just go to his boss. If his boss does not listen, I turn to someone else until someone hears me out" (Bhatt 2006, 158).

This self-confidence and knowledge of how to navigate public, urban spaces often benefits their family members as well. When Kavitaben's husband, Shankerbhai, fell seriously ill, she insisted he go to a hospital in the city, against his wishes. They removed a tumor from his stomach, and his health improved. Kavitaben says, "Since then he never contradicts me. He has faith in whatever I say or do" (Bhatt 2006, 203). Thus, the women's increase in self-confidence, and consequently in their ability to act individually and collectively, garners them increased respect from family and community members. This increased respect is a shift in social relationships that devalue women.

Respect for Diversity and Global Connections

SEWA fosters values of economic and social justice, and it creates solidarity among poor women. This solidarity is not based on a common identity; rather, it is based on shared experiences despite differences. Solidarity for SEWA members is achieved by working toward a shared goal, but it is also created through the acknowledgment and recognition of vibrant differences among the women of SEWA: "The spirit and diversity of SEWA would presently be difficult to come by anywhere else. . . . Tribal, Hindu, Harijan, migrant, and Muslim women; tatooed Vaghari women, women in purdah; sinewed, muscular smiths; sun-darkened cartpullers and agricultural labourers; young, nimble girl bidi rollers with their mothers and grandmothers, progressively more thin and bent from sitting over their rolling work; street-wise and bawdy vendors alongside of women timidly emerging from homebound communities; all in different dress; speaking different languages and dialects; practicing different trades—all are coming together to generate strength" (Rose 1992, 20). This inclusivity is not accidental; like MarketPlace India, SEWA intentionally organizes women workers across religious, community, and caste lines.

After the Hindu-Muslim riots in Ahmedabad in 1985, SEWA members agonized over the fact that women in the same occupations and neighborhoods were separated into the relief camps that were segregated by religion, Hindu or Muslim. SEWA members from both religious communities had formed bonds through their struggles to attain better working conditions, so they spearheaded a meeting between the Hindu and Muslim communities in Ahmedabad. This was a first step in reconciliation and peace between the two communities. SEWA leadership also played a role in negotiating with officials to lift curfews, and in bringing the communities together to meet. Building connections and relationships among women of different religious communities helped to restore communication and to begin to heal the rift between those communities.

SEWA's commitment to inclusiveness, respect, and the human dignity of all helps to break down entrenched social and religious hierarchies through forming connections, relationships, and working toward social justice. "While always honoring a women's religious convictions and the skills imparted through her caste, SEWA has broken away from the traditional organizational hierarchy of the village. Every caste is represented in the union and cooperative leadership . . . Just as SEWA set the precedent by uniting urban women across community barriers, it deserves immense credit for its ability to organize across caste barriers in its rural work" (Rose 1992, 149).

The ability to both honor and challenge traditional beliefs, practices, and social relationships is essential to SEWA's methods and success. As I discuss in chapter 2, some feminist positions argue for a stark opposition between culture and gender equality, resulting in the imposition of a secular Western framework for addressing inequalities. Honoring religious convictions and traditional skills does not necessarily mean accepting egregious harms to women nor does it mean thinking that everything is acceptable "just as it is." Rather while working for global gender justice, sensitivity to local context and practices is a must. One of SEWA's staff members, Usha Jumani, feels that the focus on formal systems of work disregard what she sees as India's traditional work systems. She asks: "Why impose an alien culture on our culture and take that as a measure of progress?" She advocates self-employment and its reliance on verbal forms of communication (Rose 1992, 90).

One way that traditional work systems are maintained is by supporting traditional artisan skills such as embroidery, spinning, and weaving as well as textile skills such as batik and block printing. SEWA provides training, links to markets, and skills building to give women control over more of the process from production to sale. According to Renana Jhabvala, "The reason we [SEWA] support artisan production is because it is giving employment, and what else do artisans have to do? We want to protect what they have, and we want to increase what they have—their bargaining power, their skill levels" (Rose 1992, 232). One way in which the women workers are given more control is to help them control an entire process of production all the way to the point of sale. "For example, women block printers had been working on a piece-rate basis for a trader doing only the one step of the process they knew—the actual stamping of the dye onto the cloth, for very low rates. Once they were trained in how to make dyes, design blocks, prepare the cloth, and make more sophisticated designs and garments, they broke their relationship with the contractor, controlling the entire process and selling through the cooperative" (Rose 1992, 230).

Helping women gain control over the processes of their work and consequently their working conditions and wages, differs from dictating which work is valuable. One of SEWA's early challenges was getting home-based work recognized, rather than outlawed. Ela Bhatt addressed the World Labor Congress of the International Confederation of Free

Trade Unions, urging them to include home-based workers in legislation and also to provide them with access to training and collective bargaining. The resolution to recognize home-based work passed "radically altering the former western biased views that home-based work should be abolished" (Rose 1992, 97–98). This awareness of Western bias toward what counts as work, or how work should be done or valued is important both for arriving at solutions that work in local contexts and for respecting a range of beliefs, practices, and traditions. SEWA's approach to this is instructive for negotiating the tension between respecting cultural traditions and promoting gender justice; promoting gender justice can draw upon strategies of rights and equality while still respecting contextual, historical, cultural differences and diversity within groups.

SEWA's strategy of organizing women workers in the informal sector around the intersections of gender and class has proved very effective not only in addressing the needs of specific local communities but also in forging alliances across national boundaries. SEWA has organizations in fifteen states of India, as well as in several South Asian nations, such as Afghanistan, Bangladesh, Sri Lanka, Pakistan, Nepal, Myanmar, and Bhutan. Representatives of SEWA attended international meetings such as the International Labor Organization, where they took the lead in establishing HOMENET, an international network of home-based workers. Out of this effort came WIEGO: Women in Informal Employment: Globalizing and Organizing, an organization that documents the contributions of women microentrepreneurs to the global economy. SEWA also has a sister organization in South Africa, called SEWU, the Self-Employed Women's Union, founded by Pat Horn, who modeled SEWU on SEWA after her visit there. Additionally, SEWA participates in the global coalitions STREETNET, a worldwide network of street vendors; and GRASSNET, an international network of grassroots handicraft workers and the Global Trading Network of Grassroots Entrepreneurs. While SEWA always begins with specific issues in local communities, such as police harassment of street vendors, the organization also allies itself with others who may face similar issues in different contexts and countries. Members forge connections at international meetings and then continue the transnational organizing through the Internet. SEWA has been very effective in building alliances and solidarity across borders while staying grounded in local communities and facilitating significant change in women's daily lives.

Feminists have much to learn from SEWA's success. SEWA's training and collective capacity building improve women's situations within their household and community; and SEWA's international activism around gender and labor issues helps to mitigate the negative effects of globalization by providing sustainable and dignified wage labor for women. SEWA provides an example of comprehensive feminist social justice in action through its commitment to participatory, democratic structure; the individual and collective empowerment of women; economic empowerment through labor organizing, job creation, unions, and cooperatives; social empowerment, including developing self-confidence and challenging gender roles and women's inequality and oppression; and their respect for diversity and global solidarity.

Conclusion

Feminists concerned with women's status and social justice issues internationally can learn several useful things from the story of MarketPlace India and SEWA of India. In order to resist some of the pernicious effects of globalization, we need strong global labor alliances. As global capital moves into developing countries, too often poor women lose out. For example, much of the informal economy in Ahmedabad, India (where SEWA began) relied on the textile mills that produced cotton for garments. As the influence of Western values and fashions, and the influx of ready-made garments from synthetic fiber became predominant, the textile mills closed down, and the women who made chindi quilts had to find other work. The processes and effects of globalization are complex, but those without education, marketable skills, or property have the most to lose. In countries such as India where the majority of people live in rural areas and eek out a subsistence existence, the placement of a factory or a dam in their community may mean loss of arable land and, consequently, food insecurity rather than a new job or electricity (Roy 1999). Women in the global South are particularly vulnerable to these changes because they often still have less education and less cultural and political power than men. Without the possibility of earning a livelihood, women are subject to the whims of others. However, earning a livelihood is just one aspect of the comprehensive social change advocated by MarketPlace India and SEWA. Their capacity-building and leadership programs empower women to change the social and political conditions that oppress and marginalize them.

Both MarketPlace India and SEWA have developed very successful models for empowering women and improving their quality of life in a variety of ways: their economic status improved, their health improved, they developed political skills and participated in changing laws and policies that were detrimental to them, they developed their own voices, and they began to take on leadership roles in their communities and families, breaking down strict gender hierarchies and gaining respect as women. The challenge is to learn from their activism how to develop a more comprehensive theoretical framework for feminist social justice that is multifaceted and addresses individual empowerment and institutional and social change; that is my project here.

CHAPTER 2 | Women's Rights as Human Rights
Feminism and Universal Human Rights

We never talk to the women about rights.

—SUCHIRA, staff member at Marketplace India

SOME FEMINISTS BELIEVE THAT, in light of the many challenges of globalization, "generating effective responses to contemporary challenges and crises 'as if women matter' requires that all such issues are viewed through a gender lens that is centrally concerned with validating women's concrete experiences, and with promoting and protecting women's human rights broadly defined" (Reilly 2009, 2). Yet other feminists caution against using rights discourse for feminist gains. They believe that rights talk reflects a hegemonic Western, liberal political view and closes off emancipatory possibilities: "To remain invested in the liberal humanism of human rights and some semblance of the illusory pre-given subject is to remain invested in a project that can take us no further in the direction of freedom and happiness" (Kapur 2014, 43). Can these two seemingly contradictory views be reconciled? What on-the-ground strategies have grassroots women's groups used to successfully advance women's equality and liberation? What are the benefits of using the framework of universal human rights for transnational feminist work? And what are its limitations? Following the methodological thread discussed in chapter 1, that looking at the struggles of Third World women workers can productively inform feminists both about how to build solidarity movements and about the limitations of certain theoretical approaches, in this chapter I draw upon the experiences of SEWA and MarketPlace members to examine both the achievements and the limitations of using universal human rights for feminist aims.

In many international fora over the past forty years, feminists have struggled to get women's rights on the agenda. Over forty years ago, the United Nations Conference on Women ushered in the Decade of Women (1975–1985) followed by several conferences assessing the progress made on international conventions such as the Convention on the Elimination of All Forms of Discrimination Against Women (CEDAW). The United Nations also offered new goals for the millennium, including a focus on the health and well-being of women and girl children, whose specific needs around reproductive health and gender-based violence had previously been neglected under the "one-size-fits-all" rubric of international human rights discourse. Feminists who hold the perspective that "women's rights are human rights" advocate for the extension of universal human rights to include women and the broadening of universal human rights to include gender-based violence. Including violence against women as a human rights violation brings recognition to wartime rape, domestic violence, and sexual violence as human rights violations disproportionately experienced by women, and often overlooked by gender-neutral policies. In this respect, the "women's rights as human rights" approach has been very successful.

However, using the universal human rights framework for transnational feminism has some serious limitations. The "women's rights as human rights" approach privileges legal and political rights, allowing scant attention to economic and social rights. As I argue, feminists cannot afford to neglect economic and social rights because women are the largest majority of impoverished people, and because the lack of social rights to health, education, and childcare affect women more negatively than men. Even when the rights framework is broadened to include economic and social rights, problems remain. Feminists from a range of approaches fault the liberal framework associated with rights as difference-blind by failing to take cultural, social group, or religious differences seriously.[1] Many feminists also challenge the individualistic assumptions of the rights framework; for example, care ethicists argue that selves are relational. And some postcolonial feminists challenge the underlying metaphysical assumptions of the individualistic self (Kapur 2014). Relatedly, some postcolonial feminists criticize the very concept of rights, sometimes calling for rejection of rights as an imperialist, Western-biased concept.

In this chapter, I begin with an overview of the "women's rights as human rights" movement and strategy for transnational feminist advocacy.[2] Then I address the criticisms: the focus on legal and political rights; the assumption of individualism underlying the rights framework; the abstraction from cultural, social, historical, and religious context; and the cultural imperialism. As I successively move through these criticisms, I show how some of them can be accommodated within liberal rights theory. For instance, the focus on legal and political rights can be countered by including economic and social rights, while neglect of cultural, religious, and social identities can be accommodated by challenging the abstract individualism of rights discourse, and sometimes by recognizing group rights. But challenges to the theoretical underpinnings of rights discourse, such as its commitment to individualism, and the claim that the rights framework is imperialist, are not so easily accommodated within the liberal rights framework.

I therefore conclude that if feminists adopt rights discourse for transnational feminist advocacy, we adopt it critically and strategically, mindful of its limitations and problematic history. Advocating for universal human rights has served as the primary strategy for advancing transnational feminism, and women's issues, but it deserves critical scrutiny. As I discuss in chapters 3 and 4, the framework and assumptions underlying the universal rights framework also undergird economic neoliberalism and universalist cosmopolitan approaches—namely, the assumptions of atomistic individualism; of freedom as noninterference; and of abstract universalism. I argue that we need a broader, more inclusive framework than the individualist rights paradigm, which is often abstracted from material circumstances; I advocate replacing the rights framework with a feminist social justice framework

The structure of this chapter is as follows: There are three main sections, "Feminism and Universal Human Rights," "Feminist Challenges to the Human Rights Framework," and "From Rights to Social Justice: a Complex, Multi-dimensional Feminist Approach;" the first two sections are divided into subsections, and a brief Conclusion follows the third section.

In "Feminism and Universal Human Rights," I discuss the genesis of the women's rights as a human rights movement, noting its successes and its limitations. Then, I discuss the importance of economic and social rights. One of the weaknesses of the universal human rights approach is that at the international level it has focused on protecting and promoting legal and civil rights, rather than on securing economic and social rights. As I discuss, all of these rights are important and are, in fact, interrelated. Through the example of dowry, I illustrate that economic issues play a role in what is often believed to be a cultural practice; and that legal changes alone are not sufficient for making changes toward gender equality. Economic policies and practices that support legal changes must also occur.

In "Feminist Challenges to the Human Rights Framework," I address feminist criticisms of "women's rights as human rights." I look at feminist criticisms of the universalism of rights theory, and of the concept of the self at its core, as abstracted from all social relations and historical context. Then I discuss feminist criticisms of cultural imperialism and the ways that these criticisms reinforce other feminist criticisms from completely different perspectives; both care ethicists and postcolonial feminists take issue with the abstract self and the hyperindividualism at the core of liberal political theory. After discussing the ways that religion and cultural and social norms play a role in our lives, I use SEWA's response to the sati of Roop Kanwar to illustrate that acknowledging the significance of culture need not result in accepting gender oppression.

In the third main section, "From Rights to Social Justice: A Complex, Multidimensional Feminist Approach," I use an extended example to show how a feminist social justice approach can address the social, economic, and cultural aspects of women's oppression, and I argue that this provides a more comprehensive framework for negotiating the complex relationships among gender, class, religious, and racial and ethnic identities and oppression than a human rights framework.

My criticism of the rights framework contributes to the overall argument of the book—that a feminist social justice approach provides a more comprehensive framework than a rights framework because it addresses material deprivation as well as the social oppression and economic exploitation at the heart of continuing systemic inequalities. Without addressing the fundamental causes of injustice and inequality, we cannot hope to eradicate them.

In this chapter, I demonstrate that although human rights has been an important tool for addressing many of the inequalities among persons and violations of human dignity, it has both practical and conceptual limitations. While some of its limitations have been addressed within rights theory—abstract individualism is countered by group rights; atomism is countered by theories of relational rights, relational autonomy, and relational freedom; and emphasis on legal and civil rights is countered by theorists who argue for the primacy of social and economic rights and theorists who argue for the indivisibility of rights—other limitations cannot be addressed within rights theory alone. Notably, rights theory lacks a power analysis that articulates social relations of domination, oppression, and exploitation. Without a power analysis, such as that found in feminist theory, Marxist theory, and postcolonial theory, systemic inequalities and unequal social relations grounded in social, cultural, economic, and political power differences remain difficult to identify and address.

In spite of the different foci of these two approaches—the rights approach aims to protect legal and political rights, while the feminist social justice approach questions the material and economic background conditions within which these unequal rights arise—both approaches aim to protect and promote human dignity. Human rights has been the primary vehicle by which inequalities have been addressed and remedied in the twentieth century, so it is not surprising that feminists adopted this powerful and effective strategy to argue for women's rights and equality. However, social justice may be a more promising approach for the twenty-first century.

Human rights discourse developed in the twentieth century through a number of international declarations and conventions, most significantly the United Nations Universal Declaration of Human Rights (1948), the International Covenant on Civil and Political Rights (1976), and the International Covenant on Economic, Social, and Cultural Rights (1976); taken together, these three documents comprise the International Bill of Human Rights. Since its emergence in the mid-twentieth century, the idea of universal human rights discourse has been mobilized in the international arena, and successive United Nations Declarations on the Rights of Indigenous Peoples, on the Rights of Persons with Disabilities, and the Rights of Peasants show an increasing move toward inclusivity.

The concept of universal human rights that the International Bill of Human Rights articulates helps to provide the moral grounding to make political claims that promote equality within nation-states. The notion of universal human rights is based on the assumption of the equal worth and dignity of each human being. Rights discourse is a powerful tool for making governments accountable for the treatment of their citizens, often preventing or inhibiting violations of human rights such as false imprisonment, forced labor, torture, lack of due process under the law, and restriction of civil liberties. Understandably, feminists have adopted this powerful discourse to help secure women's rights. In many cases, such as false imprisonment or a lack of due process under the law, securing women's rights simply means ensuring that women are fully included in the group to whom the right of due process is extended. In other words, protecting women's civil and political rights is on par with the protection that men enjoy. In this case, we see the powerful positive force of universal human rights discourse; it views all as equal and equally deserving of the protections and opportunities that rights can afford.

One of the basic advantages of universal human rights is that it advocates equal treatment without regard to sex, gender, cultural, racial, ethnic, and other features. This "difference-blind" approach can be useful. Obviously, women's equal treatment under the law is preferable to being denied basic civil and political rights. All too often women are systematically disadvantaged in the law when it comes to owning property, inheritance, marriage and divorce, reproductive issues, and equal access and opportunity to jobs and education. Because of this, many feminists advocate the view that "women's rights are human rights" (Cook 1994; Peters and Wolper 1995; Bunch 1995, 1996; O'Reilly 2009).

"Women's rights are human rights" advocates believe not only that women should be included in the purview of existing human rights, but also that the notion of human rights needs to be broadened to include such issues as sexual violence, domestic violence, reproductive issues, and gender-specific violence. Including gender-based and sexual violence as human rights violations is an important step in recognizing women's human dignity. However, in the international arena the inclusion of gender-specific violence often focuses on issues such as honor killing, female genital cutting, and dowry murder. When Western feminists focus on these issues as the most significant issues in "other" cultures and attribute these violations of women solely to culture, this contributes to a Western bias toward non-Western cultures. This, in turn, legitimates postcolonial feminist criticisms that imposing universal human rights, specifically to promote gender equality cross-culturally, is culturally imperialist.

How can feminists both advocate for women and gender equality transnationally and recognize the diversity among women in terms of culture, class, nationality, religion, sexual identity, caste, ethnicity, and ability? As I shall argue, human rights has been an important, though limited, strategy internationally. It at least provides a moral minimum in terms of protection from state violence, and it bolsters women's claims to pass and enforce state laws that make it illegal to discriminate against women. My aim here is to illuminate some of the complexities of using universal rights discourse to advance a transnational feminist agenda, recognizing both its limitations and its benefits.

Feminism and Universal Human Rights

Women's Rights as Human Rights

In the last quarter of the twentieth century, women's rights emerged as an important issue in international forums and conferences. As a strategy for gender inclusion, rights has been very successful. The success of the "women's rights as human rights" movement is two-pronged: first, it draws on the accepted language and conceptual framework of human rights to promote gender equality through women's inclusion as full human beings who have human rights. Second, as discussed later, feminists challenged the traditional split between public and private and broadened rights to include issues that primarily affect women, such as domestic abuse, sexual violence, and reproductive rights. Both moves—the move to make human rights more inclusive and the move to change what counts as a human right—build upon past successes of human rights struggles as well as the increasing codification, infrastructure, and acceptance of universal human rights internationally. However, rights discourse also presupposes particular conceptions of self, freedom, and happiness. Specifically, rights discourse emerged out of the Western Enlightenment framework of liberal political thought and carries with it some of the ideological presuppositions characteristic of liberal rights discourse, namely hyperindividualism, a negative conception of freedom as noninterference, and the ideal of the abstract self. Postcolonial feminists challenge the appropriateness of rights discourse, noting the historical connections between liberal humanism and colonialism, the bias toward secularity and abstraction in rights discourse, and its staunch individualism.

Internationally, women have pushed for recognition of their human rights. At the first United Nations Conference on Women in Mexico City in 1975, women from all over the world gathered together to discuss how to improve the quality of women's lives both in their respective countries and globally. One of the primary strategies for improving women's lives has been via improving women's status legally and politically. This strategy can be realized through holding individual countries accountable to international standards, and it can be monitored through changes in the law and by promoting women's right to political representation and access to public life.

At first, women's rights agendas often focused on civil and political rights, such as equal opportunity in education, employment, housing, and credit. Before the women's rights as human rights movement, gender-specific issues, such as reproductive health care and protection from rape and domestic violence, were viewed as a special interest agenda and were marginalized in favor of mainstream human rights issues (Peters and Wolper 1995). For instance, for many years prior to the women's rights as human rights movement, well-established international human rights organizations, such as Amnesty International and Human Rights Watch, had some success in documenting and bringing to international attention human rights abuses, especially human rights abuses perpetrated by the state. Often this publicity, media attention, and pressure from the international community, including governmental sanctions against offending countries, resulted in changes. With evidence of this success in mind, it is no wonder many feminists advocate a strategy that includes women and gender issues in the scope of human rights rather than criticize rights as a framework for change.[3] Working for legal and political reform within countries remains an important aspect of the project of securing justice for women. However, the strategy of inclusion of women into traditional human rights categories and frameworks does not go far enough. Simply focusing on extending human rights to include women, particularly with the emphasis on civil and political rights, leaves in place the division between the public and private sphere characteristic of political liberalism.[4] Advocates of the "women's rights are human rights" position challenged this division and focused on broadening the scope of rights to encompass the private sphere as well as the public sphere (Cook 1994; Bunch 1995; Peters and Wolper 1995). During the 1980s and 1990s, feminists argued that gender-specific issues ought to be included in the purview of human rights whether in the public or private sphere, summing up this claim as "Women's rights are human rights."

Much of the work of the women's rights as human rights movement took place in international conferences and United Nations meetings; since 1975, there have been four United Nations Conferences on Women, preceded by a Non-Governmental Organizations Forum on Women (1975, Mexico City; 1980, Copenhagen; 1985, Nairobi; 1995, Beijing). These international conferences brought visibility to women's issues, and feminists advocated for the recognition of women's rights. Clearly, advocacy for recognizing women within the frame of human rights was needed. Prior to feminist advocacy, mainstream international human rights organizations operated as if rights were gender neutral; for example, Human Rights Watch only established its Women's Rights Project in 1990, a full twelve years after the group was founded in Helsinki. The inclusion of gender issues and women's issues in international politics, policies, and nongovernmental organizations (NGOs) represents an important achievement of various women's struggles and the international impact of feminism. While the women's rights as human rights position advocates for the inclusion of women in legal and civil rights in the public sphere, it simultaneously challenges the public/private distinction by including sexual and gender violence in the private sphere as human rights abuses, such as domestic violence and marital rape.

The United Nations Conferences on Women, and the NGO Forums that preceded them, brought international attention to a wide range of women's issues globally and allowed women activists and policymakers to network. While these conferences had a broad focus, one of the most significant results of the "women's rights as human rights" movement was the recognition of many forms of violence against women as a violation of human rights in the wake of testimony at the Vienna Tribunal on Human Rights in 1993. At this international UN conference on human rights, academic and activist feminists from around the world brought attention to the many forms of violence that primarily or at least differentially affect women. Moving testimony from elderly Korean comfort women forced into prostitution by the Japanese during World War II, Bosnians raped as a tactic of war and ethnic cleansing, women political prisoners raped as a form of torture, and a young female incest survivor from the United States got the attention of the primarily male UN representatives and resulted in the Vienna Declaration on the Elimination of Violence Against Women (1993).[5]

The Vienna Declaration on the Elimination of Violence Against Women goes beyond the traditional conception of human rights, which serves to protect women from state-sanctioned violence and abuse, to articulate a new framework for human rights that addresses the private sphere where most violations of women's rights take place:

> Traditional human rights standards categorize violations in ways that exclude women, eliding critical issues. While men may care about reproductive freedom, their lives are not actually threatened by its absence; for women in areas of high maternal mortality, full reproductive freedom may mean the difference between life and death. Likewise, while asylum law protects those with a "well-founded fear of being persecuted for reasons of race, religion, nationality, membership in a particular social group or political opinion," it rarely protects those persecuted for reasons of gender [. . .]. And while men may be the victims of private violence, such violence is not part of a pattern of gender-based abuse. (Peters and Wolper 1995, 2)

Promoting human rights for women means not only granting and protecting women's political and legal rights on par with those of men; it also means addressing issues that differentially affect women, such as rape (as a form of torture and as a weapon of war), domestic violence, sexual slavery and exploitation, honor killing, dowry murder, and reproductive issues, including sex-selective abortion.[6] Violence against women, broadly construed, characterizes many of the ways that women's human rights are violated. The power of the "women's rights as human rights" movement stems partially from its reliance on the already existing framework of international human rights, yet the recognition of sex-specific violence broadens the definition of human rights.[7] As a result of feminist activism, major international human rights groups have recognized women's human rights as a distinct category within human rights.

The international movement for women's rights as human rights was a result of activism, pressure from NGOs, and the engagement of some academic feminists. Significantly, this effort resulted in the inclusion of women's rights in mainstream human rights organizations, as well as the recognition of sexual and gender-based violence as human rights violations. Feminists were wise to mobilize the discourse of human rights in the 1990s; "because human rights is a language that has legitimacy among many individuals and governments, the appeal to human rights agreements and international norms can fortify women's organizing" (Bunch and Fried 1996, 204).

The inclusion of sexual and gender-based violence broadens rights to recognize violations of human rights in the private sphere; this challenges the long-standing division between public and private that undergirds the thinking of traditional liberal political theory. Challenging the division between public and private shows how the strategic use of human rights discourse can challenge political and legal norms, and correlatively, broaden the conceptual underpinning of human rights theory. Historically, human rights theory and activism has been concerned with state violations of individuals' rights in the public sphere. Including gender-based violence, such as domestic violence, rape, and female genital mutilation, changes this focus in three ways; it includes violations in the private sphere; violations by individuals; and violations endorsed and supported by cultural and social norms.

Yet this challenge to the public/private dichotomy still leaves in place the ideologies of individualism, private property, the notion of freedom as "freedom from constraint," and the idea of equality as based upon similarity, which are legacies of the European Enlightenment tradition and liberal political theory. A further limitation of the rights framework is that it is tied to the state in an era during which state power has eroded: "the fixed notions of the sovereign state and subject are mocked in an era of globalization, migration, and the emergence of new forms of nonstate power— the World Trade Organization, nongovernmental organizations, and even terror networks" (Kapur 2006). Additionally, legal and political rights not only rely on states for their legitimacy; they also require a strong state for enforcement. For example, Kirti Singh claims that one of the obstacles to women's rights in India is the unwillingness of the state and government to abide by India's Constitution; this inhibits legal reforms that would promote women's equality (Singh 1994).

Because of their emphasis on the individual, rather than on structures and systems, human rights approaches grounded in liberal political theory fail to challenge fundamental systemic inequality and oppressive social, economic, and political structures. In short, a human rights approach seeks to make changes within the existing system, rather than changing the system. Moreover, it fails to challenge deeply embedded theoretical and conceptual assumptions, including the legacies of colonialism, which privilege individuals and abstract them from social, political, and economic systems.

These legacies of colonialism reappear in the project of neocolonialism now implemented through neoliberal economic policies; women in the global South living in conditions of poverty are more vulnerable to the negative impacts of global neoliberal economic policies, so ignoring social and economic rights contributes to the ongoing structural injustice they endure. Many feminist organizations from the global South focus on poverty, inequality, and basic needs while the majority of feminist organizations from the global North are primarily concerned with extending women's civil and political rights. For example, the Self-Employed Women's Association aims to organize women for self-reliance and full-employment. Its eleven-point program includes employment, income, nutritious food, health care, childcare, housing, asset[s], organized strength, leadership, self-reliance, and education. SEWA's primary mission is organizing women workers in the informal labor sector so they can earn a living wage.

By contrast, the most visible and mainstream women's organization in the United States is the National Organization for Women, whose focus has been on women's political and legal rights and equality. The focus on political and civil rights championed by liberal Western feminists reinforces a Western, global North perspective on rights that reflects its dominant position through normalizing a postindustrial, elitist perspective emphasizing civil and political rights while virtually ignoring social and economic rights.[8] This difference in emphasis not only underscores a difference in priorities but also reveals the systematic domination of the global South by the global North through processes of colonialism and neocolonialism. These processes have systematically underdeveloped the resource-rich global South, both through enslaving people and shipping them to the colonizing country, and through expropriating nonhuman resources. For women, who globally are among the poorest, this perspective that devalues economic and social rights is especially harmful.

Without devaluing the important accomplishments of the women's rights as human rights movement and approach, I turn next to three main feminist criticisms of human rights. First, the strong association of the human rights framework with civil and political rights too often leaves social and economic inequalities unaddressed. Second, many feminists take issue with the individualistic focus of rights. Third, universal human rights are often characterized as Western or Eurocentric; this makes them especially problematic in the context of cross-cultural application. I argue that these challenges indicate that it is time for a new discourse and strategy for transnational feminism: social justice.

Economic and Social Rights

Since its inception as an international guideline, universal human rights have included economic and social rights. The United Nations Declaration of Human Rights includes social and economic rights, along with political and legal rights (Articles 22–26). Social, economic, and cultural rights are further elaborated in the International Covenant on Social, Economic, and Cultural Rights (ICSECR). But as we have seen, many Western feminists seem to be more concerned with issues that fall within civil and political rights, such as equality and nondiscrimination. A focus on these issues reveals a class bias as well as a narrow focus on industrialized countries; middle-class and elite women in any society do not generally worry about daily subsistence. Economic rights include the right to decent work, to unionize, to social security or social insurance, to parental leave, and to an adequate standard of living. Social rights include the right to free education and the right to health, including reproductive health. Social and economic rights provide a baseline of economic security that ensures people do not die from preventable diseases or malnutrition. Obviously, the lack of these rights has a greater impact on poor people and upon those in less wealthy nations. And, indeed, in the United Nations the rights included in the ICSECR are associated with development goals and attaining an adequate standard of living for the majority. In spite of its claim of defending human rights, the United States has not yet ratified the ICSECR, in part because endorsing it implies the need for universal health care. Wealthy nations with a strong history of individualism and independence often view social and economic rights as an impediment to individual rights. Not surprisingly, feminists from wealthy countries also focus on legal and political rights. Legal and political advances are certainly necessary for women's full recognition and participation in public domains. However, the granting of rights is not the same as the ability to exercise them. The work of feminists fighting for women's rights to be free from violence and gender discrimination of all kinds remains central to the project of realizing equality for all women. But political and legal rights are intimately connected to social and economic rights; thus, feminists need to also argue for increased economic opportunities for women.

A compelling criticism about the differing priorities of feminists from the global North and the global South comes from Amrita Basu: "Even when they agree on the importance of an issue such as human rights, women from various world regions frame it differently. While Western women traditionally have based their human rights struggles on issues of equality, non-discrimination, and civil and political rights, African, Asian and Latin American women have focused their struggles on economic, social and cultural rights" (2013, 70). Given inequalities of wealth among and within countries, and the stark inequality of wealth between industrialized countries in the global North and poorer countries in the global South, this difference of priorities reflects the privilege of those who can leave aside questions of basic survival. Basu's criticism underscores the bias of the rights framework, which tends toward legal, rather than economic solutions. Her criticism focuses on the way in which human rights discourse has been implemented in United Nations conferences and documents, rather than on the conceptual limitations of human rights discourse. Basu is not alone in her observation that Western perspectives and voices have been advantaged in discussions about women's rights internationally. Celina Romany claims that the process of securing international human rights for women privileges agendas and organizations from the global North and from Western nations. She notes that greater "financial and informational resources of northern NGOs determined their leadership role in feminist reconceptualization of human rights"; additionally, she criticizes the Vienna Declaration and Programme of Action for failing "to address the intersection of gender, class and ethnic subordination in its definition of discrimination" (Romany 1995, 547).

As I have argued, when feminists continue to focus on civil and political rights rather than social and economic rights, they perpetuate the dominance of the global North. Feminists must prioritize economic and social rights because these are inseparable from gender, the sexual division of labor, and women's material position. Moreover, we must prioritize them in order to achieve social justice, given the inequalities of wealth among and within countries, and the stark inequality of wealth between wealthy industrialized countries and poor countries in Africa, Asia, and Latin America.

Focusing on social and economic issues is not only a difference of priorities but also of perspective. In her report on the 1995 United Nations Women's Conference in Beijing, Esther Ngan-ling Chow notes: "While sharing some common ground, women from the North were primarily concerned with equality and a better quality of life, and women from the South with issues of basic rights and needs, poverty, development, and human security. In the latter case, the struggle of women from the developing South *should also be understood in the context of each countries [sic] experience under the domination of imperialism, colonialism and neocolonialism and against 'a background of nationalist struggles aimed at achieving political independence, asserting a national identity, and modernizing society'*" (1996, 18, my italics). Chow mentions not only the difference in emphasis between feminists from the global North and feminists from the global South—equality versus meeting basic needs and ameliorating poverty—but she also notes the differences in historical, political, and social context, as well as power differences such as the continuing domination from the global North through the legacies of colonialism. Ratna Kapur points out the colonialism often present in human rights discourse: "Human rights advocates, including feminist scholars, have failed to adequately centre and interrogate the colonial trappings and 'First World' hegemonic underpinnings of this project, and frequently ignore or exclude the non-west from the conversation. Analysing human rights from a postcolonial perspective provides an enriched perspective of how the terrain has operated and the politics of inclusion and exclusion that it has sustained and even justified" (Kapur 2006, 684). I concur with Kapur that although human rights discourse has been effectively mobilized, we still need to examine and interrogate its assumptions, and who the discourse may exclude. I discuss the importance of analyzing human rights from a postcolonial perspective further in the section "Feminist Criticisms of the Imperialism of Human Rights."

Feminists and the Indivisibility of Rights

As we have seen, several feminists, such as Basu, Romany, Kapur, and Chow, attribute a difference in priorities between feminists from the global

North and the global South. Rather than prioritizing one set of rights over another, some feminists argue for the indivisibility of rights. In her essay "Transforming Human Rights from a Feminist Perspective," Charlotte Bunch, who has been instrumental in the women's rights as human rights movement, notes the importance of social and economic rights, and their connection to civil and political rights: "Much of the abuse of women is a part of the larger socio-economic and cultural web that entraps women, making them vulnerable to abuses that cannot be delineated as exclusively political or solely caused by states. *The indivisibility of rights and the inclusion of the so-called second generation (or socio-economic) human rights to food, shelter and work (clearly delineated in the Universal Declaration of Human Rights) is therefore vital to addressing women's concerns fully*" (Bunch 1995, 14, my italics).

As I have argued, legal and political rights alone cannot fully address the many interconnected ways that women are disadvantaged and marginalized. They are only one part of a larger strategy that must include socioeconomic change and changes in cultural institutions, practices, and attitudes. Moreover, women's rights to food, shelter, and work depend on changes in social institutions that are not simply transformed by new laws that allow women to vote or protect women from employment discrimination. Protection from employment discrimination is meaningless if there is a lack of decent work in your village or city, or if you are prevented from pursuing the education or training that would qualify you for available work. Legal and political rights provide a formal structure for women to challenge gender inequality, but more is needed in order to address women's needs, especially if they also suffer material deprivation, as do many working-class and poor women.

For instance, used-garment workers in India face a variety of challenges from food insecurity, to police harassment and social discrimination. Most used-garment dealers in India are women, and most are from historically marginalized social groups, called "backward castes" by the government. Used-garment trade is quite common in India, but it is illegal. This illegality presents many interrelated social and economic problems for the trader. For instance, "Chanda [a Vaghari garment trader] related to Elabehn [founder of SEWA] the difficulties of the garment trade fraught with debts and police harassment, juggled between feeding the family, pregnancies, and the problems of family life in the slums. British laws are still found in Indian books which relegate small traders to the ranks of illegal encroachers, even though it is the most widespread and traditional way of trading" (Rose 1992, 43).

Because informal trading is illegal under laws held over from British colonialism, the traders are subject to arrest and fines. When they are arrested and fined, they lose income and must take loans from moneylenders at high interest rates to pay daily expenses as well as the fines. In this case, legal changes would help them if changes were made in the laws imposed during British rule that made their livelihood illegal. But more than legal changes are necessary in order to stop the cycle of poverty these women face and to combat their social marginalization. In the case of Vaghari women garment traders, in addition to engaging in a traditional occupation that is illegal, they face other pressing issues such as social oppression and economic marginalization, police harassment, and having enough money to meet their family's basic daily needs. In this example, we can see the interrelationship among legal, social, and economic rights. Because of this interrelationship, some feminists have argued that legal, political, economic, and social rights are indivisible.

Feminist political theorist Rosalind Petchetsky makes a compelling argument for the indivisibility of rights with respect to reproductive rights. She claims that the women's movement has become issue driven, working on such issues as violence, reproductive rights, sexuality, women in development, and women and work; and that this results in a type of fragmentation that goes against promoting the indivisibility of human rights. As I have been arguing, she also believes that without so-called second- and third-generation rights, first-generation rights cannot be exercised. For example, she says: "[P]ractically speaking, it [the indivisibility of rights] has to do with the real-life fact that a woman cannot avail herself of her 'right to decide freely and responsibly the number, spacing, and timing of her children' (ICDP Programme of Action, 7.3) if she lacks the financial resources to pay for reproductive health services or the transport to reach them; if she cannot read package inserts or clinic wall posters; if her workplace is contaminated with pesticides or pollutants that have an adverse effect on pregnancy; or if she is harassed by a husband or in-laws who will scorn her or beat her up if she uses birth control" (Petchetsky 2002, 75). In this example we see very clearly the relationship between the complete package of political and civil, social and economic, and self-determination and self-development rights, and why they are indivisible. One cannot exercise the right to family planning without economic resources, a level of education that results in literacy, environmental protections, and changes in a society and culture that allows the harassment of female family members. Moreover, the ability to access health care also often depends on larger social and economic issues such as having an adequate infrastructure, including public transportation and roads to get to clinics and hospitals from rural areas.

Many of Petchetsky's examples of the importance of the indivisibility of rights in health and reproductive issues are from outside the United States. However, the same principle of indivisibility of rights holds within the United States. In order for the right to health to be realized, social and economic rights would need to be recognized, and institutions, policies, and practices changed so that everyone regardless of class or personal resources had access to free health care. The interconnection of legal, political, economic, and social rights illustrates the indivisibility of rights.

But a comprehensive framework for social justice goes beyond even the indivisibility principle (the recognition that social and economic rights are inseparable from legal and political rights); it includes attention to context and material circumstances as well as challenging oppression and structural inequality. Women of color in the United States founded the *reproductive justice* movement; they make a powerful argument that a *reproductive rights* framework is individualist and does not account for structural inequality, oppression, and social and economic inequalities (Asian Communities for Reproductive Justice 2010).[9] They clearly articulate the limitations of the (reproductive) rights framework and argue for a model founded on a more comprehensive view of social justice, advocating a reproductive justice model. "Reproductive liberty must encompass more than the protection of an individual woman's choice to end her pregnancy. It must encompass the full range of procreative activities, including the ability to bear a child, and it must acknowledge that we make reproductive decisions within a social context, including inequalities of wealth and power. *Reproductive freedom is a matter of social justice, not individual choice"* (Roberts 1997, 6). Likewise, SAMA, a women's health advocacy network in India, questions the focus on individualistic rights and choice as the framework for achieving gender justice. They ask: "Why a choice in contraception alone? Why shouldn't women be given choices in employment, food, education, access to health care, civic amenities, or, at a more basic level, to have equal rights as men in the family and society or to not be killed in the womb?" (SAMA 2003, 7).

The reproductive justice framework shifts concerns from freedom and choice associated with negative freedom to concerns with a larger context that supports reproductive health, such as prenatal and maternal health care, adequate nutrition, and an environment free from violence. This shift to adequate material conditions and a context that supports the choice to have and raise a healthy child necessarily includes a shift to the so-called positive rights: social and economic rights. SAMA's insight that reproductive choice cannot be promoted in the absence of other choices for women is crucial, echoing Dorothy Roberts's claim that reproductive choice cannot merely be seen as an individual issue but must be viewed as a matter of social justice. Furthermore, SAMA sees choice itself as an ideological smokescreen that fails to address the material conditions in which choice is shaped. "Also, an urgent need has been felt to demystify the concept of choice, which has worked to promote ARTs [artificial reproductive technologies]. Since these technologies are propagated within the parameter of choice, it is critical to evaluate the concept of choice itself. For example, it is difficult to distinguish between latent choice and social choice shaped by family, market, and other agents" (SAMA 2006, 101).

The insights from the reproductive justice movement can inform a broader criticism of abstracting freedom, choice, and rights from their social context and material circumstances. Inequalities of wealth and power pervade society and are becoming more pronounced. Any framework that hopes to successfully achieve justice for all must take social and economic factors into account. Moreover, as I discuss in detail later, abstracting practices from their social, political, and historical context distorts and simplifies complex issues. As Uma Narayan notes, feminists should avoid replicating a colonialist stance that abstracts from historical and cultural specificity (Narayan 1997). For example, feminists may criticize the practice of dowry as a form of gender inequality and call for laws banning it. But in many cases the issues of legal and economic reform cannot be easily separated. Kirti Singh mentions that positive changes in dowry laws without corresponding changes in property and inheritance laws do little to improve women's condition: "All this [these legal changes] makes her financially dependent on her husband and makes it extremely difficult for her to opt out of a violent home" (Singh 1994, 392). Here she is specifically discussing the amendment to the dowry prohibition act that is supposed to aid in its enforcement by providing officers to ensure that the laws prohibiting dowry were followed. However, there has been little follow-through at the state level and so the practice of dowry continues in spite of its illegality. When dowry was legal, it was seen as the women's property, but now that it is illegal, it goes unacknowledged. Because property and inheritance laws in India still favor men, this leaves women without any financial resources of their own. As Singh notes, women's increased financial dependence on their husbands leaves them without options even in the face of domestic violence. This financial dependence could be lessened by further legal changes in inheritance and property laws, and also by access to economic resources for women. As is true anywhere, if women are completely dependent on husbands or male relatives for their livelihood, this leaves them vulnerable to domestic violence or abusive family dynamics.

As we have seen in chapter 1, providing women with opportunities to earn a living wage and contribute to the support of their families can serve to increase their status within the family and allow them to exercise more control over the resources of the family, as well as opt out of a bad family situation, if necessary. But those without much formal education are unlikely to get skilled or professional high-paying jobs. Moreover, when girls receive less education than boys, the cycle of gender discrimination continues. The women at SEWA and MarketPlace India recognize that their own life chances and economic opportunities are tied in part to their level of education. They are determined to provide more opportunities to their daughters than they had, and to intentionally intervene in a cycle of gender discrimination that privileges boys' education over girls'.

The majority of the women that I interviewed at Marketplace India were using part of their earnings to send their daughters to school past the eighth grade, which was the mothers' average level of education. In contrast, the average level of education for boys in this group (poor, and originally rural, but now living in and around Mumbai) was tenth through twelfth grade. Supporting girls' education has far-reaching consequences, as higher levels of education for girls and women results in a higher income and correlates with a higher quality of life for their families (PCI 2004). Higher education for girls can also disrupt discriminatory gender norms and social practices, such as arranged marriage and dowry. For example, one artisan from MarketPlace India describes her daughter's marriage situation:

> When my daughter was sixteen years old she began a job and also studied computers. When she was twenty she "met" a boy in Bangalore through the internet. When they decided to get married, I told his family that my husband had left me and I worked very hard to bring up my two children myself. I wanted them to know the truth. I am very proud that my daughter found her own husband. Between her earnings and mine we paid for her wedding. I did not pay any dowry. I am proud of my daughter. She is educated and her husband knows that what she brings to the family are her accomplishments and values—which are more valuable than any dowry. (Littrell and Dickson 2010, 148)

Here we see that access to decent work and economic resources through working at MarketPlace India not only allowed the MarketPlace member to raise her children as a single mother; it also provided her daughter with an education that gave her options as well, including the option to choose her own husband and not provide dowry. In this way we can see how economic resources play a role in women's independence and also enlarge her range of options.

Without the constraint of financial dependence, women and girls may challenge gender norms helping to create new social norms. There is a generational effect: when mothers have the financial resources to educate their daughters, then this education opens up more opportunities for their daughters to earn their own livelihood. Kavita, a Marketplace India member, affirms, *"It is important for women to get educated, because otherwise men will still be seen as superior. Because I was less educated, I could never voice my opinions."* Economic opportunities for women translate into a better quality of life for them and their families, including higher educational attainment. As evidenced in Kavita's quote, educational attainment may, in turn, encourage women to speak up, explicitly challenging gender bias, as well as simply contributing to the ongoing change in societal gender perceptions by adding more women's voices to the public dialogue.

Contrary to some Western feminists characterizing dowry as a regnant cultural practice still widely supported in contemporary India that can only be rectified with diminishing the role of culture and its influence on women's lives, dowry is a complex phenomena with economic, kinship, gender, and sociocultural components. Like other presumably "cultural practices," it was codified and standardized under British rule. But it was made illegal in two states (Bihar and Andra Pradesh) in the 1950s soon after India's independence. As we have seen, illegality alone has not eliminated the practice of dowry. However, opening up economic and educational opportunities for women can contribute to phasing out this practice.

As we have seen, human rights, as it is currently discussed and applied, emphasizes legal and political rights at the expense of social and economic rights.[10] However, this criticism can be remedied by the indivisibility of rights approach, which sees political and legal rights as inextricable from economic and social rights. And we have seen how political, legal, economic, and social rights are in fact indivisible, for instance, in Petchetsky's example of reproductive health. Unfortunately, the crucial importance of economic and social rights sometimes remains invisible to those in economically privileged positions. Nonetheless, the objection that rights discourse tends to privilege legal and political rights can be countered by including economic and social rights, or by ascribing to the indivisibility of rights approach. Equally acknowledging the importance of legal, political, economic, and social rights or viewing them as indivisible still remains wedded to a human rights approach that accepts the theoretical framework and assumptions behind human rights. In the next section I address criticisms that challenge the theoretical grounding of universal human rights.

Feminist Challenges to the Human Rights Framework

Feminist Challenges to the Individualism of Rights

While the feminists who advocate for women's rights as human rights, such as Julie Peters and Andrea Wolper, challenge the long-standing separation of the public and private spheres, which is central to liberal political theory, they do not challenge the individualism of liberal rights theory, nor its focus on political and civil rights. Feminist care ethicists criticize the liberal conception of rights and autonomy as individualistic and as abstracted from social context. Carol Gilligan introduced the idea of a care ethic in the early 1980s when she pointed out the male bias in Kohlberg's theory of moral development.[11] Additional studies in psychology revealed that Kohlberg's scale of moral development, which mirrors deontological moral theory, was not merely gender biased, but also racially, culturally, and class specific.

Gilligan's work impacted a variety of fields because it challenged the normative notions of the abstract self, hyperindividualism, and abstract reasoning, all of which are central to mainstream moral theory. Subsequently, Gilligan's own work was both criticized and extended. One line of criticism of her work is that it focused on gender differences but did not include racial, ethnic, or cultural differences. What was presented as universal moral reasoning in most psychology studies was based on a specific subset of people—White, Educated, Industrial, Rich, and Democratic—a group known as the "WEIRD" subjects (Heinrich, Heine, and Norenzayan 2010). What was considered to be a universal scale for assessing moral reasoning was shown to be racially, ethnically, culturally, class, and gender biased. In a parallel move, the presumed universality of mainstream philosophical theories has been criticized as simply reflecting the dominant group. I focus on feminist challenges to the assumptions undergirding some Enlightenment political and moral theory from two very different sources: care ethics and postcolonial feminists. Both challenge the individualism and the abstraction from context of rights theory, which is grounded in certain conceptions of liberal political theory.

Care ethicists argue that the abstract self is removed from social context; it does not account for those who are dependent or vulnerable (Held 1987; Tronto 1993; Kittay 1999). Conceiving of the self as abstract also reinforces hyperindividualism by not recognizing the role of the family in providing the context for the development and growth of children to adulthood. More specifically, it ignores women's fundamental role in nurturing and socializing children. Care ethicists point out the male bias of rights theory; this male bias is evidenced by ignoring social context, by emphasizing individualism, and by privileging an abstract and rationalistic model for social and political interaction. Counter to these assumptions of a self independent of material conditions embedded in liberal political theory and deontological moral theory, care theorists argue that the facts of human dependence and interdependence must be accounted for. Given the inevitability of dependence at the beginning of the life cycle, and the frequent dependence at the end, assuming the radical independence and separateness of persons ignores the actual social conditions of human life. Notably, the assumption that human beings magically appear as fully mature, independent adults discounts the work of mothering. Challenging the predominant view of moral and political subjectivity as isolated and completely independent individuals, feminists developed alternative views that accounted for dependency, mothering, embeddedness in and attention to relationships, care, and the importance of social context (Kittay and Meyers 1987; Ruddick 1989; Meyers 1994; Held 2006). Feminists argue that the work of caring for those who are young, elderly, disabled, sick, or vulnerable is rendered invisible by the classic liberal account of people as atomistic independent individuals. Acknowledging the fact of dependency during the course of a human life leads us to acknowledging the reality of interdependence. Each of us lives in a web of social, economic, familial, and political relationships. In the conclusion to this book, I advocate a shift from viewing the self as independent (or dependent) to an acknowledgment of interdependence.

Since Gilligan introduced the idea of a care ethic, feminists have explored its theoretical import and its applications. Subsequent feminist theory develops Gilligan's initial insights to argue that relationships, social context, and particularity play important roles in moral reasoning.[12] Viewing social context and relationships as the basis for moral reasoning, rather than as an impediment, feminists refigured agency as a competency of a subject enmeshed in (but not determined by) social relationships (Benhabib 1987, 1992; Meyers 1994; Friedman 2003; Nedelsky 2011).

Other feminists extend care ethics into the political sphere and look at its implications and applications for transnational feminism, including applying care ethics to care work, such as childcare, elder care, and caring for the ill, mothering, welfare, and women's immigration and transnational domestic labor. For instance, Joan Tronto discusses the ways that care work is devalued and unfairly compensated in the public sphere; Eva Feder Kittay explores relations of care and dependency at home and abroad, looking at the ways that those doing care work are often rendered dependent on a government system that infantilizes them (Kittay 1999). Transnational feminist theorists have introduced the term "global care chains"; global care chains refer to the transnational character of care work, typically performed by women (Hochschild 2002; Weir 2008).[13] The transfer of care work, once taken on by female family members, is now often paid work performed by immigrant women. The outsourcing of care work results in a moral harm because the relationships developed from it are not fungible. For example, a mother from the Philippines who leaves behind her own children to raise someone else's children in the United States is harmed by being deprived of an opportunity to develop a relationship with her own children, especially since developing a relationship with someone else's child cannot substitute for that (Kittay 2014).

As work by care theorists demonstrates, relations of care and dependency extend far beyond the private realm of the family, blurring the public/private split and reaching across borders. Acknowledging our interdependency and recognizing the self as relational and socially, historically, and culturally situated is at odds with the fundamental assumptions of liberal political theory that underlies the rights framework. These feminist criticisms cannot easily be accommodated by the rights framework, which is premised on atomistic/ontological individualism.

As I discuss in chapter 5, Iris Young's social connection theory of responsibility complements the relational feminist approach by emphasizing our interdependence and our material social relations as consumers and producers. The criticisms raised by feminist care theorists strike at the heart of underlying assumptions about conceptions of the self, social and political theory (and reality), and social relations. These criticisms therefore challenge the validity of a social and political theory, such as classical liberal political theory, which is based on rights and justice and an abstract individualist conception of the self. Feminists offer an alternative account of the self-in-relation, and of correlative notions of relational autonomy, as well as relational freedom.[14] In chapter 4, I develop a "relational cosmopolitanism."

Challenges to liberal individualism come from postcolonial feminist theorists as well as care theorists. For instance, in an insightful critique of the liberal paradigm, Ratna Kapur discusses the differences between the self of liberal theory and the self in Advaita philosophy: "In Advaita the reflective self that surfaces is not the rational subject who exists *a priori* to social relationships. It is a self that cannot be captured within a liberal imaginary" (Kapur 2014, 43). She argues that human rights is based on a liberal humanism that presupposes particular conceptions of happiness and freedom, as well as the self, that are not universally shared. In the next section, I discuss the postcolonial feminist charge of Western imperialism to rights discourse and liberal theory.

Feminist Criticisms of the Imperialism of Human Rights

As care ethicists have pointed out, the use of rights discourse privileges certain notions of the person, namely abstract, atomistic individualism. This means that not only are rights possessed and exercised by the individual, but this notion of rights also asks us to abstract from all the particularities of a person, such as her culture, religion, social class, ethnicity, race, sexual identity, and nationality. This very conception of rights as inhering in individuals already precludes other conceptions of identity, self, autonomy, and freedom. Moreover, the discourse of liberal rights assumes a framework of progress and specific notions of happiness tied to an Enlightenment belief in progress, as well as to hegemonic ideas about the market and capitalism (Kapur 2006, 2014).

While care ethicists often cite male bias as one of the problems with the atomistic conception of self underlying the rights-justice framework, postcolonial feminist criticisms center on the idea that rights are assumed to be a fundamentally Western liberal notion and therefore the application of rights to other contexts without an understanding of those contexts belies a Eurocentric and biased view (Mohanty 1991a, 1991b; Bulbeck 1998; An-Na'im 1999; Spivak 2003; Menon 2014; Kapur 2014, 2015). One of the features of rights discourse is its claim to universality; and it is precisely this claim that is challenged by postcolonial feminists. For example, Ratna Kapur argues: "The critiques [of rights by Third World, postcolonial, and feminist legal scholars] expose the discursive operations of rights as a governance project primarily concerned with ordering the lives of non-European peoples, rather than a liberating force; and that the pre-given rational subject of human rights is contingent and one of the prime effects of power" (Kapur 2014, 25). By not acknowledging the origin of rights within a particular social and historical context, and thus its specificity as a discourse, theorists who apply rights cross-culturally without attention to context run the risk of Western cultural imperialism. In spite of feminism's attention to diversity, Western feminists sometimes reproduce cultural imperialism in our attempts to apply Western standards cross-culturally and when making claims about women as a group. Uma Narayan notes: "Ahistorical and apolitical Western feminist understandings of 'Third-World traditions' continue to appear, for instance in more contemporary work on issues such as sati and dowry-murder, and in discussions relating to human rights-based interventions into 'cultural practices' affecting Third World women" (Narayan 1997, 43).

Postcolonial feminists and feminists of color warn against representing the other and to avoid falsely essentializing women by assuming that all women have common interests.[15] Arguing on behalf of women obscures differences of class, caste, race, ethnicity, and religion even among women within the same society. Moreover, white Western feminists who promote women's rights cross-culturally may inadvertently bring their own biases to bear on the situation, including isolating gender oppression from other aspects of oppression such as caste, class, racial, and ethnic or by pursuing a human rights agenda without understanding the complex history and politics of cultural or religious traditions.[16]

When reflecting on the role of culture and cultural traditions in people's lives, it is easy to err on either side—on the side of embracing tradition uncritically, or on the side of dismissing tradition as insignificant. On the one hand, we may view traditions and cultures as static, unchanging, and outside of history and politics, consequently reifying and essentializing them. On the other hand, we may completely dismiss the role of culture and religion on people's identity and values. This second error is often associated with Western liberal bias: the idea that culture, religion, and tradition can easily be left aside in favor of (abstract) individualism devalues the significance of culture and its impact on identity. When Western feminists assume that the liberal view of rights can be applied universally, they call into question the deep significance of culture, tradition, and religion in peoples' lives. Susan Moller Okin holds such a view of rights, one that is in conflict with other aspects of identity and values: "Many violations of women's basic human rights both occur within families and are justified by reference to culture, religion or tradition. So recognizing women's rights as human rights means looking at the institutions of family, religion, and culture or tradition in a new light" (2000, 33). Rather than assuming that the rights framework can automatically trump considerations that are local or contextual in issues of justice, a more modest approach would be to interrogate both rights and local contexts, traditions, and values to see points of overlap and disjuncture. Simply assuming that cultural traditions are opposed to rights without historical context and specificity replicates what Narayan calls the "colonialist stance" and "colonialist representations," both of which involve simplistic views of "cultural traditions." She notes that anyone can produce a colonialist representation, including Third World men or women. Colonialist representations replicate "problematic aspects of Western representations of Third World nations and communities, aspects that have their roots in the history of colonization" (Narayan 1997, 45). Thus, both devaluation and distortion of culture reinforce the dominance of the hegemonic Western view. As Oyeronke Oyewumi says, "one cannot assume the social organization of one culture (the dominant West included) as universal or the interpretations of the experiences of one culture as explaining another one" (Oyewumi 2008, 169). Many feminists engaged in cross-border theorizing and activism share Oyewumi's view that categories and concepts cannot simply be extrapolated from one culture to another. If culture provides a set of social meanings through which we make sense of ourselves and the world, then it should be taken into account as we work toward developing approaches for transnational work for gender justice.

Susan Moller Okin's provocative essay "Is Multiculturalism Bad for Women?" captures well the conflict that arises when one assumes that gender equality and culture clash. One of the primary reasons for this conflict, according to Okin, is that gender equality relies on a strong sense of individual rights, whereas respecting cultures often means acknowledging group rights. Because she opposes individual rights associated with gender equality to group rights associated with respect for culture, she argues that, in fact, multiculturalism *is* bad for women. She makes a strong argument that most cultures, because they are patriarchal, are antithetical to women's rights, and thus in order to achieve gender equality, these cultures must be abolished. For instance, Okin states, "[M]ost cultures have as one of their principal aims the control of women by men" (Okin 1999, 13). The reason for this is that according to Okin, and other feminists such as Charlotte Bunch, patriarchy and culture are inseparable. For instance, Bunch states, "Most cultures as we know them today are patriarchal" (Bunch 1993, 251). Okin even goes so far as to claim that women and girls in minority cultures might be better off if their culture became extinct and they were fully integrated into the majority culture (Okin 1999).

The distinction between minority and majority culture here is telling. Significantly, her focus and examples of "problematic" cultures are all non-Western cultures. To Okin, and many other Western feminists, the faults of the majority culture are invisible. Majority culture is assumed to be neutral, when in fact it is Western, white, heterosexual, and secular. Moreover, majority culture here is associated with Enlightenment liberal ideas of equality, justice, and progress and is contrasted with minority cultures, which are characterized as having distinct cultural traditions embedded in a history and belief system specific to its members. Understandably, many feminists respond by defending the ubiquity of and importance of culture both to their own identities and for international feminist discourse and activism. Following Narayan's lesson, to complicate the notion of cultural tradition provides an important point of intervention in the liberal-multiculturalist debate around gender and women's issues. Narayan points out that many feminist criticisms of "cultural traditions" that harm "Third-World" women rely on a simplistic view of cultures as unchanging and monolithic (Narayan 1997, 50).[17] Moreover, as Narayan notes, "Traditions/Religions/Cultures" are seen as synonymous without attention to their differentiation much less the complex history and internal variation of each (Narayan 1997, 50).

Okin argues against multiculturalism and for liberalism because she believes that multiculturalism—which takes seriously cultural norms and values, and supports the idea of group rights—harms women. She brings up a number of examples, such as honor killing, dowry murder, sati, and female genital mutilation. She attributes all of these to culture or religion, exemplifying the error of seeing these as synonymous. Her use of examples of gender violence that she attributes to culture positions liberalism as the bastion of women's protection in postindustrial Western societies and reinforces the view that the liberal rights and equality framework serves to single out violence against women in non-Western countries. She does not discuss the ways in which Western societal norms may contribute to violence against women; for instance, the lack of an extended family structure in the United States isolates women as part of a nuclear family and makes them more vulnerable to domestic violence and economic dependence on their spouse. Additionally, Okin is vehemently secular, noting that all three of the major religions—Islam, Christianity, and Judaism—are patriarchal. Her outright rejection of religion as patriarchal ignores the multiplicity of religious traditions, the many feminist reinterpretations of the major religions she lists, and the fact that secularism is not immune to patriarchy. Moreover, enforcing secularism ignores the many women globally who have deep religious commitments.[18] She views both culture and religion as monolithic and homogenous and as primarily a vehicle for gender subordination; here again, she exhibits a colonialist stance by blaming culture and religion for gender inequality while not distinguishing between them, or providing a nuanced view of either one. A more nuanced view of culture reveals the overlap among cultures, the heterogeneity within them, and the ways in which culture can enlarge—and not merely diminish—women's lives and agency.[19]

Okin herself highlights one aspect of the heterogeneity within cultures when she worries that the multiculturalist's support of group or cultural rights may perpetuate existing unequal power relations, specifically privileging voices of males and elders. Heterogeneity and power differences among members of a group are important issues to address while defending group rights; left unaddressed, these power differences could easily leave more vulnerable group members, often women and girls, at a disadvantage or open to abuses of power by other group members. Unfortunately, Okin did not extend her analysis of the heterogeneity and power differentials within groups to examine the heterogeneity and power differences among women. Extending the analysis in this way opens up the space for understanding that not only are women differently situated than men in, for instance, a cultural or religious community or with respect to race and ethnicity but also that our locations in these communities and social groups means women are situated differently from one another in significant ways.

Okin's position, which pits women's rights and gender equality against cultural tradition and religion, exemplifies the colonialist stance by seeing "tradition/culture/religion" as unified, simplified, ahistorical, and apolitical. This distorted view of cultures, traditions, and religions plays into a simplistic opposition between modernity and cultural tradition, where human rights falls on the side of modernity, and culture must be excoriated (and in some cases, exterminated) in order to achieve gender equality. Okin is not alone in adopting the colonialist stance; much of the literature on women's rights as human rights reads like a laundry list of horrific violations to women occurring mainly in countries in the global South:

> In India, a ten-year-old girl boards a flight for Saudi Arabia; her companion is a sixty-year-old businessman who has married the girl after purchasing her from her parents. In a U.S. suburb, a woman kept under "house arrest"

is beaten if she tries to contact friends or relatives; her "jailer" is her husband. In a Sudanese village, a group of little girls is taken to an unfamiliar place where a woman cuts away their genitalia using an unsterilized piece of broken glass. In Peru a woman is arrested after inquiring about her husband, who has not been seen since he was questioned by soldiers several days earlier. In Burma, a twenty-two-year-old woman and her eleven-year-old niece are taken into custody as they hurry home just after curfew; the young women is raped by six soldiers, the eleven-year-old by seven, including the unit commander. (Peters and Wolper 1995, 1)

Although this introductory paragraph to the *Women's Rights, Human Rights* anthology includes one example from the United States, all the other examples are from countries in the global South. Drawing the majority of examples of violations of women's human rights from the global South justifies the criticism that human rights discourse is an extension of Western imperialism because of its presumed focus on cultural causes, rather than economic issues or other forms of structural injustice. I have discussed the damage that attributing violence against women to culture can do without a thorough examination of the historical, political, economic, and social context. Feminists can and should be concerned about practices that harm women without simply attributing them to culture. Moreover, a feminist analysis that looks at practices that harm women needs to address the variety of practices in both the global North and the global South. Often when feminists argue that women's rights and gender equality must take precedence over culture and tradition, because the latter are patriarchal, they rarely, if ever, explicitly cite examples from Western culture. All too often Western feminists are oblivious to their own culture, assuming cultural neutrality in the West, and implicitly using it as a benchmark for other cultures to aspire to. This ethnocentrism contributes to misrepresenting non-Western cultures, leading postcolonial feminists to criticize the rights framework as ethnocentric and Western biased. If feminism aims to be inclusive, it must be culturally and historically sensitive and not impose ethnocentric views from the dominant West.

As Uma Narayan points out in her book *Dislocating Cultures*, attributing violence against women to cultural factors is much more likely to happen when white Western feminists describe the situation of women of color in the non-Western world. As she explains, attributing practices like sati and dowry-murder solely to culture relies upon a view of culture as static and ahistorical, and a view of non-Western cultures as radically Other. This skewed view of culture results in drawing sharp differences among cultures, as well as overlooking differences within cultures, thus homogenizing them. Significantly, this homogenizing of cultures in the global South obscures the critical, resistant forces within the cultures, such as indigenous feminist organizations. This, in turn, sets up a false and harmful dichotomy between "the West and the Rest," with the West playing the role of modernizing liberator for "the Rest."

Understanding issues in their historical and cultural context can provide important insights, as we shall see in the specific examples of dowry and sati discussed later. Feminists uniformly condemn cases of gender-specific violence, such as dowry murder and sati. But looking at it as solely a cultural issue, rather than as an economic one, distorts and sensationalizes it (Narayan 1997). In reality, dowry murder is not sanctioned by tradition or culture any more than killing one's wife for the life insurance money is sanctioned in US culture. Both happen primarily for economic reasons, in the context of a host of other issues, including structural inequality between men and women. Assigning the blame for dowry murder to culture, rather than looking at it as a fairly rare occurrence that is nonetheless serious because it is part of the larger problem of violence against women, contributes to the Othering of non-Western cultures. Narayan reminds us that the motivations for supposed "cultural practices" such as sati are complex, including political, economic, community, and familial factors. Viewing dowry murder as some exotic cultural practice sanctioned by tradition serves to simultaneously vilify and justify it as something totally outside the scope of non-Indian experience. But perhaps more important, this type of reductive analysis can impede solutions, which need to take cultural, economic, historical, and political factors into account. Moreover, notions of cultural authenticity are contested, and often tied to other issues, such as religious fundamentalism and nationalism (Narayan 1997).

Understanding culture as dynamic rather than stable, heterogeneous rather than monolithic, and porous rather than isolated goes some way toward ameliorating the sharp conflict between the multiculturalist view and the liberal view.[20] Moreover, understanding the formation of cultural traditions and cultural authenticity in the context of colonialism, nationalism, religion, and other factors provides a more nuanced view. Seeing cultures as complex—shaped within multiple domains of economics, nationalism, religious influences, and political struggles—as well as internally contradictory, opens up the possibility for internal cultural critique of gender oppression as well as other forms of oppression.

Many feminists, such as Chandra Talpade Mohanty, Lila Abu-Lughod, and Gayatri Chakravorty Spivak, point out the similarities between the contemporary discourse of equality, freedom, and rights and earlier colonial discourse about Third World women. As Abu-Lughod notes, historically the West has justified its intervention into other cultures by seeking to "protect" women (Abu-Lughod 2002). In her essay, and a recent book of the same name, "Do Muslim Women Really Need Saving?" Lila Abu-Lughod examines the ways that the rhetoric of protecting Muslim women from practices characterized as oppressive by the dominant West, such as veiling, has been used to justify US military intervention in the Middle East (Abu-Lughod 2013). This rhetoric of protecting or saving women of color from men of color is not new, as Gayatri Spivak puts it; history is full of examples of "white men saving brown women from brown men" (Spivak 1988, 296). While Spivak is referring to white men's historical role in colonialism, well-meaning white feminists may inadvertently undermine a woman's cultural or religious identity in the name of gender equality. One contemporary example of feminist disagreement is over the issue of veiling. As Abu-Lughod and others point out, not only does the practice of wearing the veil differ from country to country, but its meaning varies with respect to nation, history, and politics. Viewing the practice of veiling solely as a sign of women's oppression decontextualizes the many meanings it has had; for instance, as a symbol of resistance to colonialism. Instead, the practice of veiling (and other cultural and religious practices) must be understood and addressed in their specific historical and cultural context. Imposing dominant conceptions of secular liberalism can contribute to women's oppression, especially if they are members of minority communities: "Women in religious minority communities are constantly renegotiating the boundaries and contesting the meaning of equality, understandings of secularism and the right to religious freedom, attempting to delink their meanings from their majoritarian moorings or capture by Hindu nationalists. These engagements attest to the importance of challenging the unhelpful dichotomies between religion and rights, the complex and contradictory nature of the human rights terrain, and why the meanings of rights need to be constantly monitored, revisited and interrogated" (Kapur 2006, 687).

Western feminists should not assume that justice and equality must be the primary values of women everywhere. Abu-Lughod raises the question: are emancipation, equality, and rights part of some universal discourse of justice to which we must all subscribe? On the contrary, she suggests that there may be other values, such as closeness with family and cultivation of piety, to which women in different parts of the world may give greater priority. She reminds feminists engaged in transnational work that "We may want justice for women, but can we accept that there might be different ideas about justice and that different women might want, or choose, different futures from what we envision as best? We must consider that they might be called to personhood, so to speak, in a different language" (Abu-Lughod 2002, 787–788). Abu-Lughod cautions that assuming that ideas of individual freedom, individual rights, and an abstract equality as universal simply ascribes dominant Western liberal values to other cultures. Universalizing particular conceptions of freedom, equality, and rights does not serve feminists well in working toward transnational solidarity. Saba Mahmood explicitly makes the connection between liberal thought and the devaluing of a nonsecular perspective. During her study of the piety movement in Egypt, she explored the pietists' notion of subordination to God as freedom. As she notes: "The account I have presented of the mosque movement shows that the distinction between the subject's real desires and obligatory social conventions—a distinction at the center of liberal, and sometimes, progressive thought—cannot be assumed, precisely because socially prescribed forms of behavior constitute the emergence of the self as such and are integral to its realization" (Mahmood 2005, 149).

SEWA recognizes that cultural values can play an important role in struggles for social justice. SEWA follows a Gandhian model of struggle against exploitation combined with social and economic programs (Gandhi called these "constructive programs") that provide dignified and sustainable work, and meet people's needs for food, shelter, education, and health care. This Gandhian model prioritizes nonviolence, mediation, and self-help. Kalima Rose connects SEWA's philosophy of struggle to femininity: "It is an especially feminine philosophy which adheres to non-violence, to arbitration and reconciliation, and most importantly, to a quiet, fiercely determined resistance to exploitation" (Rose 1992, 31–32).

Note that resistance to exploitation, rather than equality or rights is cited as the goal. As I have been arguing, the discourse of rights assumes individualism and privileges freedom as noninterference. In contrast, methods of nonviolence, mediation, and arbitration recognize the value of relationships and our interdependence far more than antagonistic methods. And, contrary to advocates of universal rights who worry that without human rights as the universal standard we will lapse into a type of anything-goes relativism, resistance to exploitation provides a broad-based platform for addressing legal, sociocultural, and economic harms. Finally, SEWA provides a model of a strategy for empowering women that rejects colonialism and encourages internal cultural criticism: "SEWA is constantly challenging the relics of colonialism and western influence which marginalize Indian ways of life and work, and demanding that society at large also examine its policies and priorities" (Rose 1992, 30).

As many postcolonial feminists point out, when the West is privileged as the standard and is taken to be normatively neutral, this delegitimizes and devalues non-Western theories, histories, practices, and cultures. When Western culture is presumed to be neutral, it denies the plurality of cultural values, and it obscures the particularity of its own values. This presumption of Western cultural neutrality contributes to the reductive view of non-Western cultures as isolated and homogeneous. Many non-Western societies have indigenous conceptions of human rights, and histories of dissent and protest. Recognizing indigenous versions of human rights that arise from non-Western cultural contexts and outside of Western European histories is often mischaracterized as acceding to relativism.[21]

I do not have the space here to revisit the universalism-relativism debate, but I think that there are a variety of ways to recognize value pluralism as well as acknowledge power relations, and local, historical contexts without lapsing into relativism. In her book *Globalizing Democracy and Human Rights*, Carol Gould offers a distinction between abstract and concrete universality, where concrete universality emerges out of dialogue and consensus. Her approach is similar to other feminist approaches that recognize dialogue and struggle as central to forming any type of coalition. In my analysis, I articulate a form of feminist resistance that is based on women's actual struggles for justice, which begins from their resistance to economic exploitation and social oppression. Their struggles for justice begin from their specific situations, and they do not rely on appeals to abstract rights, but rely instead on changes to systems and structures that create and maintain their exploitation and oppression. As we have seen, they view the imposition of Western values in conceptions of work, culture, and secularism as culturally imperialist. Resistance to economic exploitation, social oppression, and Western imperialism offers a platform for justice that is not based on political liberalism but is not relativist. One can argue that a universal application of rights without attention to the historical, political, cultural, and social particularities of a society is imperialist, while still acknowledging indigenous conceptions of rights, dissent, and protest that appeal to a normative framework.

Universal human rights are a specific strategy and discourse with a particular history. There are plenty of examples of the universal application of human rights imposing Western values in the place of local values, and serving as a measure of modernity and even civilization for other cultures: "The universalization of human rights cannot be dissociated from the complex historical process spreading Western Christian civilization to other regions" (Kobila 2003, 105). Given its association with colonization and the "civilizing mission of White Christianity." we must acknowledge that the universal application of human rights can be, intentionally or unintentionally, a neocolonial imperialist strategy. All too often, the wealthy nations of the global North accuse nations in the global South of rights violations, and not vice versa: "Human rights have become another weapon in the arsenal of western countries in their efforts to bring recalcitrant Third World nations to heel in their 'New World order.' Western nations are increasingly using the very narrow interpretation of human rights as a yardstick with which to judge Third World governments" (Aziz 1999, 39). Used in this way, human rights discourse simply shores up the position of world powers and their economic power: "The US as global champion of universal human rights cannot but be seen in this context, with its selective regime of sanctions and human rights conditionalities protecting the interests of American and multinational corporations all over the world" (Menon 2002, 164).

In chapter 3, I develop this claim in the context of globalization, global inequality, and the gender gap in economic resources. Drawing on my experience with women's organizations in India, I illustrate how economic, social, political, cultural, and religious factors work together both in forming webs of oppression and in transforming them. I argue that a feminist social justice approach better accommodates the range of issues women deal with, particularly identity issues, oppression, and structural inequality, than the rights framework does.

From Rights to Social Justice: A Complex, Multidimensional Feminist Approach

In order not to perpetuate cultural imperialism, Western feminists engaging in international, cross-cultural work need to be reflective about the ways that we include cultural considerations in our work, and to recognize our own specific cultural location. Simply applying rights without addressing these concerns can actually serve to undermine feminist and other causes that rely on a different paradigm for political action and social change. Taking cultural difference seriously complicates any attempt to promote a transnational feminism. As discussed earlier, feminists have made great strides in the past forty years in getting women's rights issues on the international agenda. While including women's rights as human rights represents an important advancement, such advancement should not come at the cost of marginalizing women of the global South. As development theorist Naila Kabeer states: "In listening to the voices raised by women to protest against the unfairness of patriarchal structures as they have experienced them, we do not have to choose between an authentic local voice and an imported Western feminism. These are voices of protest grounded in local experience and articulated in local idioms in societies which are not hermetically sealed off from the rest of the world" (2012, 230–231).

I have discussed the problem with seeing culture as homogenous, static, and isolated from other cultures, as well as the issue with seeing Western culture as neutral and value-free. Thinking about culture in a more nuanced way helps us to think about cultural particularities as well overlaps and interactions. But I want to suggest that thinking about cultures in terms of social norms and practices may be helpful in moving away from a negative focus on non-Western cultural traditions while remaining oblivious to harmful practices and social norms in the West. Even the use of these nonparallel terms (cultures versus social norms) to describe women's oppression or violence against women reinforces the perceived distance between different societies.

We can recognize that in every society there are benign as well as harmful social norms. For instance, in the United States it is customary to look people in the eye when you greet them (benign), and it is a social norm for women and girls to be thin (harmful when leading to eating disorders). In India, it is a social norm to treat guests with generous hospitality (benign), and it is a social norm for marriages to be arranged (harmful if the parties to the marriage strongly object). We understand social norms as various and conflicting within different societies, as related to particular groups within societies, as class based, as gender specific, and so on. These norms vary both within and between different societies, and whether a particular norm is harmful or benign depends on multiple factors. Each society has gender norms, and as feminists have pointed out, many of these gender norms have disadvantaged women, but we do not hear calls from feminists to abolish all social norms, just those that are harmful. Painting cultural traditions with a broad brush and selecting out only those that are harmful to women and focusing only on non-Western countries combine to mistakenly single out harms to women mainly as a result of (non-Western) culture. Moreover, as Uma Narayan points out in her comparison between dowry murder in India and domestic violence in the United States, there are often cross-cultural parallels that elude the attention of feminists concerned with a global standard for women's rights (Narayan 1997). As we have seen, characterizing culture as harmful to women polarizes the debate about the relationship between gender equality and respecting cultural difference, resulting in a false choice between rejecting the significance of culture in the interest of gender equality or sacrificing gender equality in the interest of culture.

One of the "spectacular" examples that Western feminists use to show that cultural traditions harm women is the example of sati (widows committing suicide by burning on the funeral pyre of their deceased husband). As we saw in the opening example of chapter 1 with Asmita's story, widow suicide in India may have much less to do with cultural tradition than with the lack of economic resources and options for widows to meet their basic needs as well as economic motivations by the family: "Economic motivations for sati—in particular the widely shared desire to be rid of the financial obligation of supporting the widow, and the desire to foreclose the widow's claim to a share of the husband's property, a claim that existed in some communities—have been recognized since colonial times" (Narayan 1997, 69–70).

Although sati is very rare in contemporary India, and was outlawed in 1829, the sati of Roop Kanwar in 1987 brought international attention to the issue, and it is cited by many feminists as an example of a harmful cultural tradition in India that needs feminist intervention. I cannot do justice here to the complicated history of sati and its construction as an authentic cultural practice.[22] Here my aim is to provide a look at the response of SEWA to show the ways that women's empowerment through organizing around labor and work also provides a community of gender solidarity from which to challenge women's devaluation in general, and to take political action. An extended example from SEWA here is instructive:

In 1987 an incident of sati (a woman who immolates herself in "honour" of her dead husband) in Rajasthan focused national attention on Roop Kanwar, an 18-year-old woman who sacrificed herself on her husband's funeral pyre. Despite the illegality and gruesomeness of the act, thousands of spectators had gathered to witness the event and receive the blessings of the sati. Hundreds of thousands of rupees were collected to construct a temple in her honour even as press reports began to surface which suggested the young woman had been drugged, terrified, and forced into the fire by her in-laws. The events were unclear, but what became clear was that no one had backed her up in life. The sati brought her husband's family fame and prestige. To them, her continued life would have meant one more mouth to feed. To herself, it could have meant ostracism, poverty and the remainder of her life as a widow.

Shortly after the incident, at SEWA's General Body Meeting, the issue was brought up for discussion. SEWA's carpenters, smiths and cart pullers are largely of Rajasthani origin and orthodox in social practices. When Elabehn asked the members, "Who among you is ready to commit sati?" the Executive Committee member Mirabehn, raised her hand. Besides being an extremely skilled craftswoman, she is a gifted singer of religious epics.

The other women present got agitated and began chiding and condemning her. They spoke out about negative pressure on women to commit these kinds of acts. They argued that women do useful work in society whether their husbands are drunkards, or hardworking, or honest, or unemployed, or dead or alive. Women's status did not just depend on men, as much of society tries to imply. They argued that they were valuable just as they are, for all the work and life they contribute. By the end of this discussion, Mirabehn stood up and said to Elabehn, "I just raised my hand—but the sisters are right—I would not commit suicide."

What the members spoke at that meeting they formulated into a memorandum of protest condemning "the outdated and inhumane ideal which victimized a young woman at the hands of her community." A delegation went from SEWA to Jaipur and marched in silent protest with thousands of other women from all over the country, and presented their memorandum to the Chief Minister of Rajasthan. (Rose 1992, 110–111)

This description of sati characterizes it as both an act of sacrifice and as a result of coercive force by the in-laws. Leaving aside an analysis of the ways that this description involves two competing interpretations of this act of sati, I want to focus on the reaction of SEWA's members, who seem to recognize the act of sati and its endorsement by factions of the community as part of the larger social structural forces that devalue women, and can and should be resisted.[23] These women are also poor, and if widowed, may also face ostracism, economic deprivation, and increased social marginalization. They are from the state and community where Roop Kanwar's sati occurred, where thousands supported the act by witnessing it and by providing contributions for the temple.

In their discussion they do not argue for sati as a "cultural tradition," nor do they argue for women's and gender equality as a formal right; after all, sati is already illegal. Instead, they criticize the social norms that devalue women, and they articulate their resistance to them. A resistance not only evidenced by the fact that they themselves would not commit sati but by the fact that they joined in the protest of the sati with thousands of other Indian women and took further political action by presenting the Minister of Rajasthan with their memorandum condemning the ideal of sati. But condemning sati does not mean a wholesale rejection of their culture, only the social and cultural norms that harm and devalue women. Their commitment to resisting exploitation includes resisting social and cultural norms that devalue women, and also imperialism and colonialism that devalue their culture. This reflects a nuanced analysis of culture, social norms, and gender discrimination and harm to women, which shows that these stand in a complex relationship in every society. By contrast, opposing cultural tradition to gender equality often functions as an imperialist method, rather than a helpful and illuminating strategy for social justice for women globally. Women's devaluation cannot be changed through legislation alone but also must be confronted through transforming social practices. Practices that "reflect the fundamental devaluing of women" must be tackled through "consistent feminist politics" (Menon 2015, 6). Nivedita Menon notes that "Looking for 'solutions' through state policy is certainly an easier task than the hard consistent work required to hegemonise common sense, to seize the meanings of practices and to work towards a world in which women would value themselves" (Menon 2015, 6).

To sum up, all too often, liberal feminists who focus on rights and multicultural feminists who emphasize culture seem to come to an impasse. But some feminist philosophers, such as Uma Narayan, urge us to move beyond the juxtaposition of rights and culture; they question the concept of culture itself (Narayan 1997). She cautions against a reified and monolithic view of culture, urging us to recognize the variety of heterogeneous and often contradictory practices that make up a single culture. I agree with her view that cultures are heterogeneous and complex, and that feminists should employ a nuanced understanding of cultural difference with respect to gender equality. Moreover, I suggest that thinking about social norms and gender norms, alongside cultures, might help to disentangle the various strands of cultures and cultural traditions, and help us to think more about heterogeneity within cultures. Legal remedies have limits; they cannot "hegemonise common sense" or transform prevalent societal attitudes and social practices that devalue women.

Often those devalued, in this case, women, internalize this negative view of themselves, resulting in internalized oppression. Overcoming internalized oppression involves countering this devaluation, both through resistance to external social attitudes and transforming one's own view of oneself as capable, powerful, and worthy. Seeing oneself as worthy and also as capable empowers those who are marginalized and devalued. A feminist social justice approach includes a focus on women's empowerment, which combats internalized oppression and centers women as agents of change. As we shall see, empowerment has been utilized by women's organizations and NGOs, and it has figured centrally in development strategies:

> Because the process [of empowerment]—and its effects and impacts—was so shaped by the interests and contexts of those engaged in it, and hence less predictable in its outcomes, the empowerment approach is not sufficiently "results-oriented," an important priority in current development funding. *In such agencies, the "rights-based" approach* (as though empowerment is about anything but rights!) *finds greater favour, because rights-based* interventions—greater access to redress, achievements of the Millennium Development Goals, new legislation—*are more readily quantified.* But these approaches often shift agency into the hands of professional intermediaries (lawyers, NGO activists, policy specialists) and away from marginalised women and communities. *They also focus on formal structures and equality, rather than on the informal institutions and cultural systems that older empowerment processes attempted to transform* (though not always successfully). (Batliwala 2007, 563, emphasis added)

For feminists interested in abolishing gender discrimination against women globally, the rights framework can provide important structures of accountability at the state level and transnationally. But without corresponding attention to social and economic inequalities, women will remain in a vulnerable position. Moreover, as noted in the quote by Batliwala, the rights approach is targeted toward changing formal structures, such as laws. But even when the laws are implemented and enforced (which is not always the case), these legal changes do not address the informal institutions and cultural systems that hold social norms and gender norms in place.

While I have argued against a reductionist view of culture that takes Western culture as neutral and attributes gender violence in the rest of the world to culture, cultural and social influences on women and gender issues should not simply be set aside. The persistence of gender discrimination worldwide has a variety of elements: political, economic, legal, religious, and sociocultural. We need to recognize the interconnection of these various elements in order to effectively promote change.

In the next chapter I explore empowerment as a strategy for challenging gender discrimination. Specifically, I address the issue of women's economic empowerment and its importance, given that women's equality cannot be achieved through laws and politics alone. I continue to look at the ways that SEWA and MarketPlace India have addressed the issue of women's empowerment, and the relationship between economic empowerment and gender empowerment. I look at these issues in the context of globalization and its neoliberal economic policies, which have a differentially negative impact on women.

Conclusion

To summarize, in this chapter I have argued that although the "women's rights as human rights" approach made significant contributions to international women's issues, the rights framework has a number of limitations: neglect of cultural, religious, and ethnic communities and identities; a culturally and historically specific view of the self, as atomistic and abstracted from context; and a persistent focus on civil and political rights at the expense of social and economic rights. I have argued that rights are an important, but limited strategy for pursuing gender justice. Rights provide a minimal formal structure for equality, but they do not guarantee or provide support for substantive equality; substantive equality involves access to economic and social resources and opportunities. Even when economic and social resources are taken into account, rights often rely on a distributive justice framework that looks at fair distribution within the system but does not challenge the system itself. In other words, persistent and systemic inequalities of wealth and power can remain, even when rights are protected. Moreover, sometimes rights (such as the right to private property) serve to support these systemic inequalities. Without addressing these systemic inequalities, it is likely they will simply persist. The individualism of rights abstracts individuals from their social contexts and denies historical contexts of the global phenomena of resource extraction and labor exploitation.

And, although universal human rights is an ideal held as an international standard, rights rely on enforcement by nation-states whose power is eclipsed by transnational corporations and world financial institutions. In the context of globalization, people's day-to-day lives are affected by neoliberal economic policies at the global level. One may object that the control of people's lives by transnational corporations and global financial institutions could be a reason to renew and augment calls for human rights as a protection from economic and corporate policies that violate human rights. Often, however, states and the elite within them benefit from these neoliberal economic policies and so are reluctant to limit the power of transnational corporations. In spite of the limitations I have pointed out, human rights clearly have a role to play in promoting justice within and among states. But much more is needed. As I suggest, adopting a feminist social justice framework can further the project of justice for all. Recently, human rights theorists and practitioners are also adopting a social justice framework (Lettinga and Troost 2015). Human rights theorists and practitioners have recognized the limitations of rights without also having a social justice framework that addresses systemic oppression, cultural marginalization, and economic exploitation.

As I have argued, using a feminist social justice approach—which views rights as indivisible and within the framework of structural social and political inequality—provides a better framework for addressing so many of the pressing issues for feminists engaging in transnational activism and scholarship. And it offers an alternative that is grounded in local practices of resistance. This grounding can help us to avoid imposing ethnocentric and imperialist frameworks, so long as we keep in mind that this framework is fallible and revisable. The shift from the individualistic choice-based framework of traditional liberal theory and human rights theory to a feminist social justice framework involves relinquishing the certainty of approaches that abstract out from social context and material circumstances. The reproductive justice movement recognizes that approaches based in rights and individual choice do not account for oppression, material deprivation, and social and economic inequality, so they shift from a rights paradigm to a social justice paradigm. Likewise, I am suggesting that a social justice, rather than a rights, approach would better serve those interested in global gender justice. The social justice model recognizes all rights within the human rights framework—legal, political, economic, social, and cultural—but it goes beyond the rights framework. A social justice approach recognizes structural inequality, oppression, power differences, and issues of identity and recognition as central, whereas the rights framework does not lend itself easily to accommodating these issues. As we saw in our earlier discussion, it is difficult to address issues of cultural and religious diversity, colonialism, and differences in the power of social groups within the rights framework. Moreover, the social justice approach is compatible with contemporary feminist positions on oppression, intersectionality of identities, structural inequalities, power differences, and the importance of historical, social, and political context.

I have demonstrated the need for a new framework that takes these multiple criticisms of human rights seriously. The feminist social justice framework assumes the indivisibility of political, civil, economic, social, and cultural rights, and it is not susceptible to the critiques of rights discussed earlier. A feminist social justice framework includes community and social group membership, accounts for diverse identities and inequality; and acknowledges cultural, religious, and social differences. Furthermore, unlike the classic liberal model, which is at odds with theories of oppression and domination, the social justice framework is grounded on the fact of structural violence, and, correspondingly, oppression and exploitation. Finally, the feminist social justice framework allows for the reflective and culturally sensitive use of human rights discourse to protect and maintain life, bodily integrity, and basic freedoms. In other words, rights are a part of the toolkit of the feminist social justice framework, but they are not the entirety of it. Moreover, the feminist social justice framework is at odds with many of the assumptions of the rights framework, including abstract individualism, difference-blind justice, and the lack of a power analysis. Thus, the feminist social justice framework promotes more radical social transformation and social change.

Feminists concerned with empowering women to improve the quality of their lives can adopt a social justice framework without completely rejecting the need for a strategic employment of human rights cross-culturally. Reframing feminist issues around empowering women to improve the quality of women's and their families' lives rather than the issue of women's liberation or equality may ameliorate some of the negative effects of an uncritical cross-cultural application of human rights. Although the discourse of empowerment itself may have culturally and historically specific origins, it allows women to decide for themselves what they need to improve the quality of their lives. For example, land reform may be more important to poor, rural women than gender equality. Nivedita Menon discusses this complex issue of land reform: women's claim to property plays into the dominant capitalist framework of property as individual rather than communal, thus making individually held property easier to buy and develop, which may result in less land and food security for poor women (Menon 2015, 485–486). Deciding or ranking the priority of issues, such as property rights, from outside the sociocultural context, may risk repeating the mistake of a cultural-theoretical imperialism that assumes that defending women's right to property is the best route to gender equality in all contexts.

Finally, in our era of globalization the human rights approach has practical limitations as well. Generally, human rights are articulated, encoded, and enforced by states, or by international agreements and institutions. However, currently transnational corporations have more power than states, and they are more difficult to hold accountable. And it is not only privately held corporations that perpetuate global economic inequality but also international organizations that set trade and economic policy, such as the International Monetary Fund, the World Bank, and the World Trade Organization.

In the next chapter, I examine the ways that globalization has had a disproportionately negative impact on women, especially on poor women in the global South. While the rights framework can prohibit dangerous working conditions, such as being locked in a factory (there are many recent cases of fatalities during earthquakes and fires), it does not point to alternative ways of social organization. Because the feminist social justice approach looks at systemic inequality and exploitation, it can provide a more radical critique of existing social and economic systems, and the possibility of better alternatives, such as cooperatives and self-managed workplaces. In chapter 3, I discuss how cooperatives, a structure employed by both SEWA and MarketPlace, differ from standard business enterprises, particularly from large corporate factories and microfinance projects. And I provide examples of the ways that these specific grassroots organizations in India address gender discrimination, alongside economic and social marginalization. These organizations, I believe, provide a powerful model for women's empowerment.

CHAPTER 3 | Globalization and
Women's Empowerment

> There is an ongoing debate on how to deal with poverty in the
> area of liberalization and globalisation. Unfortunately, many of
> the solution[s] being proposed do not really correspond to existing
> situations, especially in developing countries. This has led to the
> exclusion of the majority of the poor who work in the informal
> economy from the solution being proposed, not because there is any
> intention to exclude them, but, just because they do not "fit in."
>
> —RENANA JHABVALA, SEWA researcher (quoted in Raval 2001)

IN CHAPTER 2, WE SAW how rights discourse could secure opportunities and access within existing systems but did little to challenge the reproduction of systemic inequality within those systems. Systemic inequality is reproduced within many institutions, significantly political, economic, social, and cultural institutions. Human rights can address legal and political inequalities through national laws and international covenants and agreements. The reproduction of economic and social inequality is more difficult to legislate, especially in light of the interdependence of the global economy. In this chapter, I briefly discuss the differential impact of economic globalization on women, focusing particularly on the ways that it affects women's employment opportunities and labor. I then turn to issues of women's empowerment, including the role of economic empowerment. Recently, feminists and postdevelopment theorists have taken issue with the economic paradigm of empowerment, arguing that it is reductive in the sense that it privileges material goods over other goods. Furthermore, critics argue that economic advantage does not simply translate into empowerment.

These criticisms clearly have purchase; however, access to material re-sources and a sustainable income play an important role in improving the material conditions of daily life for women and their families. The con-nection between this improved material status and women's empowerment depends, in part, on how empowerment is defined. Research in develop-ment links women's status to the improved quality of life not only for indi-vidual women but also for their families and communities. According to a Population and Development report from the United Nations, "promoting the status, education, and health of women is an essential human rights goal, and also holds the key to social development in all societies, improving lives and strengthening families and communities" (PCI 2004). But some feminists view development projects' focus on women's economic em-powerment in the global South with skepticism. These critics claim that nongovernmental organizations (NGOs) involved in development often serve to disempower rather than empower those they serve; I discuss these criticisms in the section on "Nongovernmental Organizations, Women, and Development."

After these first three sections on globalization and the feminization of poverty; women's empowerment; and NGOs, women, and development, in the fourth section I return to the issue of empowerment, this time fo-cusing on women's economic empowerment. Nongovernmental organi-zations promoting women's economic empowerment often do so through microfinance institutions. In subsequent sections, I discuss the aims of microfinance projects and some criticisms of microfinance as a vehicle for empowering women. While some believe that microfinance projects targeting women are a panacea for poverty, others criticize microfinance by claiming that it strains familial and community relationships and fosters neoliberal values such as competitiveness and individualism. I agree with critics that microfinance projects are grounded in a neoliberal economic system that stresses individualism and self-reliance. Critics also argue that in spite of microfinance projects' purported focus on empowering women, they can undermine women's agency rather than increase it.

Moreover, as I discuss in the section on "Women's Empowerment," talk of "empowering women" and "women's agency" fails to distinguish between the goals of increasing a woman's concern for her own welfare and her ability to challenge sexist gender norms. Furthermore, studies show that the outcome of microlending is not successful when it leads to increased vulnerability and debt. Many microfinance projects lack ad-equate training and support. But even when microfinance programs pro-duce successful outcomes for individual women, they fail to challenge the neoliberal economic policies of globalization, the emphasis on paid labor, or on market values.

I suggest that the model of supporting cooperatives and organized labor that Marketplace India and SEWA employs does not reproduce the neoliberalism of microfinance. Economic empowerment of women needs to be connected to social and political empowerment to engage in changing exploitative relationships, as well as to jobs and skills training and support. In the section "Cooperatives: Economic Empowerment and Social Equality," I discuss the history and values of cooperatives. I argue that cooperatives' commitment to social equality and democratic participation is a key aspect of the successful strategies that SEWA and MarketPlace India have pursued. An empowerment model based on social equality and democratic participatory engagement goes well beyond simply giving women access to credit or an income; it fosters poor women's ability to speak up and to change the conditions of their own lives.

I argue that economic neoliberalism is challenged on a micro-level by workers' cooperatives, and that these cooperatives form pockets of resistance to the neoliberal economic policies of globalization. Rather than merely reproducing neoliberalism at the micro-level through individual entrepreneurship and microfinance institutions (MFIs), workers' cooperatives are part of an alternative solidarity economy that prioritizes human needs over profits and values cooperation over competition. Recognizing that worker-owned and worker-managed enterprises can provide small-scale alternatives to exploitive work relations within a neoliberal framework certainly does not preclude social and political action against the national and international policies of neoliberal globalization. On the contrary, developing leadership skills and social and political engagement on the local level can promote, rather than inhibit, marginalized populations working for structural change (as I illustrate through the activist work of SEWA and MarketPlace India). And small-scale alternative economic institutions, such as cooperatives, connect to the transnational solidarity economy through engaging in Fair Trade.

Globalization and the Feminization of Poverty

Feminists have long been concerned with women and economic issues, from pay equity issues to the feminization of poverty. These issues must be addressed within national laws and policies, and also through international and global policies and decisions. Increasingly, the effect on the global South by the wealthier countries of the global North exacerbates poverty in the global South, especially for women and children. As we consider which frameworks best address justice and equity for women, we must consider economic issues and access to material resources to be among the primary concerns, as there are clear gender discrepancies in terms of inequalities of wealth and power. Obviously, material inequalities such as access to jobs, opportunities for education and training, income levels, and wealth are affected by multiple types of systemic oppression, including sexism, racism, ableism, heterosexism, and so on. In many countries race and ethnicity correlate with class because of the historical consequences of slavery, exploitation, and oppression.[1] For instance, in the United States there is a wealth gap as well as an income gap between African Americans and white Anglo Americans (Mills 1997). And, as we saw in the Introduction, the gender gap in wages breaks down along racial and ethnic lines.

My focus in this book is on the economic empowerment and resistance strategies of poor women in India, but, of course, poverty is a global phenomenon. Economist Amartya Sen notes that "deprived groups in the 'First World' live, in many ways, in the 'Third.' For example, African Americans in some of the most prosperous U. S. cities (such as New York, Washington or San Francisco) have a lower life expectancy at birth than do most people in immensely poorer China or even India" (Sen 2003, xii). While here Sen singles out race as a factor in material deprivation, gender also plays an important role; women and children make up the largest and fastest growing population living under poverty level all over the world. Because of this correlation between gender and poverty feminists must continue to struggle for economic and social rights as well as political and legal rights in order to improve women's status and quality of life worldwide.

The World Bank estimated that over 1 billion people were living in absolute poverty in 2011. Of these, about 400 million people in absolute poverty lived in South Asia. Of the 1.2 billion people in the world who are recognized as the "absolute poor" (living on less than $1.25 a day), over 900 million are women. These figures mean that 75 percent of the world's absolute poor are women. In the United States 1 in 3 American women (42 million women, plus 28 million children) either live in poverty or are right on the brink of it (Shriver Report, January 2015).[2] The feminization of poverty, where women rank among the poorest members of society, continues to increase in spite of the fact that the number of women entering the paid workforce has increased overall in the past ten years. As feminist scholars note, one effect of economic globalization is the global feminization of poverty (Pettman 2006, 438).[3] The neoliberal economic policies characteristic of contemporary globalization exacerbate the feminization of poverty in a number of ways. Later I provide a general definition of globalization before focusing in on economic globalization and its neoliberal policies. Then I discuss the differentially negative impact of globalization on women, particularly women in the global South. These sections provide background for the discussions of the development strategy of income-generating projects for women and women's empowerment.

Multifaceted and complex, globalization affects nearly every aspect of contemporary life.[4] Put simply, globalization is the "intensification of global interconnectedness" (Inda and Rosaldo 2003, 4). This interconnectedness is evident in myriad ways: through technology and communication, through the global circulation of cultures and ideologies, and through the global economic system. Scholars of globalization and global studies articulate both the positive and negative aspects of globalization in a large and growing literature.[5] Given the rapid changes in technology, communication, and transportation over the past fifty years that allow us to have almost instantaneous communication with someone around the world from us, the "intensification of global interconnectedness" seems inevitable. However, simply seeing globalization as the intensification of interconnectedness overlooks the fact that globalization has exacerbated economic inequality, as well as other types of inequalities, between the global South and the global North.[6]

Globalization results in economic changes because of the spread of neoliberal ideologies of capitalism, such as the requirements of privatization and trade liberalization foisted upon many countries as a result of the structural adjustment programs (SAPs) imposed by the International Monetary Fund (IMF) as a precondition for lending. Neoliberalism, like liberalism, purports to increase freedom and opportunities by deregulating, individualizing, and privatizing. Neoliberal economic policies benefit transnational corporations and the wealthy, while widening the gap between rich and poor and further disenfranchising the poor. In addition to policies imposed by the IMF, the World Bank, and the World Trade Organization, economic change also results from the creation of Free Trade Zones and Export Processing Zones, and the relocation of transnational corporations to the global South in search of cheap and outsourced labor. These economic changes have complex effects. For laborers in the global North, the outsourcing of jobs to the global South means fewer jobs and less money in local economies. But the increase of jobs in the global South, especially those in free trade and export processing zones, is not an unmitigated good. The new jobs are often low-paying factory jobs with long hours, no benefits, and little in the way of safety and health protection. The outsourcing of production from the global North often undermines local economies in the global South as well. Additionally, environmental degradation and increased immigration (both within and between countries) also result from globalization. Ela Bhatt notes, "The poor are also increasingly affected by globalization of markets and natural resource management concerns" (Bhatt 1995a, 1). Moreover, globalization's effects are gendered. Environmental degradation often affects women more negatively, as gathering water and fuel in rural areas for cooking is usually women's work.

Discussing the impact of SAPs on India's poor, SEWA researcher Renana Jhabvala notes that the liberalization of the economy that SAPs promote does not fulfill its promise of "trickle-down" economics touted to alleviate poverty; thus, it is an inadequate replacement for government welfare programs. Yet she believes that existing government programs are often inefficient and corrupt. Rejecting the false dichotomy of either a liberalized, free market economy devoid of social welfare programs or heavily centralized and highly bureaucratic government social welfare programs, she suggests that poverty alleviation is best achieved through local organizations of poor people self-organizing (Jhabvala 1995, 5–6). Some may object that expecting those living in poverty to be responsible for developing and participating in their own poverty alleviation absolves the state of responsibility for providing employment, social programs, access to free health care and education, and social security. But these local organizations can develop local and regional economic and social infrastructures while still challenging neoliberal economic policies at the state level and holding states accountable for delivering these services in a transparent and efficient manner.

Some grassroots poverty alleviation efforts put pressure on states to do just this, as we saw from the example discussed in chapter 1 of MarketPlace India joining with other organizations to protest the corruption in the distribution of rations of oil and rice to the poor. SEWA tobacco workers also held the state accountable for honoring its minimum wage and social security laws (SEWA Academy 2000, 4). But poverty alleviation needs to also address the need for decent work and a sustainable livelihood in local communities, and organizations like SEWA and MarketPlace India address this need as well as holding the state accountable for its role in social and economic programs to alleviate poverty and to provide adequate education, health care, and social security. In the context of globalization, we need a multilevel approach to combatting women's poverty and the exploitation of women's labor.

Women are differentially affected by economic globalization in a variety of ways: globalization has increased the number of women working in both the formal and the informal labor market, which was already dominated by women (Naples and Desai 2002). Engaging in paid labor, whether in the formal or informal sphere, often increases a woman's responsibilities as women still bear the greater burden of domestic and caregiving labor. Moreover, in terms of paid labor, the expansion of the formal economy may simultaneously undermine the informal economy by promoting policies and structures that do not recognize informal labor. Because women are overrepresented in informal labor (94 percent of women in India who are engaged in paid labor work in the informal labor sector), this has a more pronounced negative effect on women. In addition to women's overrepresentation in the informal sector, women still do the majority of unpaid care work worldwide, such as childcare, elder care, and caring for sick family members. The privatization required by the structural adjustment programs, including cuts in public support of education, health care, and other public services, increases women's burden of unpaid labor.

Economic globalization includes policies that lower trade barriers and tariffs, which make it easier for transnational corporations to relocate to countries where they can pay a lower wage. Consequently, more factories have opened up in the global South, and more jobs are available for women in the formal labor market. However, along with this increased number of jobs in the formal labor market, there has been a feminization of the global labor force in the formal sector. In other words, there are more women in the formal labor sector, but they continue being recruited into low-paying jobs in factories or in the service sector. Along with this increase in the formal sector of labor, globalization has retrenched and expanded the informal sector since the formal sector relies on it (Damodaran 2015).

As discussed in chapter 1, in the sphere of informal labor, there are no legal structures protecting workers such as minimum wage, benefits, or job security. In a report prepared for UNIFEM, SEWA's founder, Ela Bhatt, notes, "it would be pertinent to thwart the negative effects of structural adjustment programmes at the level of especially the poorer strata of households in rural as well as urban areas. More specifically, effects of such policies on the marginalized sections of the labour force must be avoided by incorporating household production with the mainstream economy and the market" (Bhatt and Das 1995, 5). Rather than eliminate the informal sector, SEWA's mission involves organizing and making visible women's work in the informal sector.

Viewing women's labor in the context of globalization allows us to see the connections among global economic policies and inequalities and the ways they differentially impact women, particularly in and from the global South. It is not surprising that globalization has a differential effect on women since gender stratification pervades most cultures and societies, although, of course, the specifics of gender stratification vary from society to society, and within societies. Currently, women are overrepresented in three spheres of precarious labor: informal labor, exploited factory labor, and care work. Paradoxically, globalization serves both to re-create and transform traditional gender roles. While entering the formal economy challenges the traditional role of women as wives and homemakers, often the type of work available reinforces traditional gender roles. This is most evident with care work but also applies to the recruiting of women for specific factory jobs. With the rise of multinational corporations and the switch to "light industries" of clothing and electronics manufacture as opposed to the "heavy industries" of construction and mining, women became the preferred employee. Multinational corporations prefer to employ women for a variety of reasons. Seen as supplementary workers rather than as main wage earners, they are paid less than men. Women are also viewed as more "docile" and better suited to tedious repetitive tasks. "Multinationals want a workforce that is docile, easily manipulated and willing to do boring, repetitive assembly work. Women, they claim, are the perfect employees, with their 'natural patience' and 'manual dexterity'" (Fuentes and Ehrenreich 1983, 12). Women are presumably sought after for their "natural feminine" qualities of patience and small hands with nimble fingers. But in actuality employers target women as employees because they can be paid less than men, and they are less likely to strike or organize unions.

As we saw from several examples in chapter 1, for many women, entering the paid workforce in and of itself stretches the boundaries of traditional gender roles, especially if they are the primary earners. SEWA promotes women's collective strength as workers by organizing unions or cooperatives. In the case of unions, this allows the women to bargain for better wages and better working conditions. In the case of cooperatives, it allows the women to organize to control their own labor.

Although some might argue that factory jobs in the export processing zones of the global South open up opportunities for paid labor for women, the negative effects on women workers in factories are well documented. In addition to the exploitative working conditions discussed earlier, the placement of large factories in urban areas results in women moving away from their homes and often living in substandard housing provided (at a high cost) by the employer. In this situation, female workers are exploited, displaced, and objectified. In contrast to this model of transnational corporations drawing women to urban centers to work in exploitative conditions, many development projects seek to empower women through access to a sustainable livelihood through employment or income-generating projects that they can do in their own village.

As I discuss in the following sections, neither MarketPlace India nor SEWA fits the profile of a typical development project, and although both are NGOs, they better fit the profile of grassroots "people's organizations," specifically "women's organizations." People's organizations and women's organizations might have origins in an NGO, and there are various relationships between these grassroots organizations and the parent NGO. The distinction between NGOs and these grassroots people's organizations "is particularly important if we are interested in women's empowerment (rather than simply in service delivery mechanisms) since, by definition, people owning and managing their own organization are more empowered than those who are the beneficiaries of someone else's organization" (Carr, Chen, and Jhabvala 1996, 6). Grassroots organizations are often not as constrained as NGOs in regard to donor funding, or conforming to the goals of large parent organizations (such as an international nongovernmental institution). Moreover, grassroots organizations that are "by and for the people" build both leadership skills and collective capacities.

Women's Empowerment

Much research on economic projects targeted toward women relies on the notion of "empowerment" to measure the success of the project. In this section, I look at the ways that women's empowerment has been articulated in the areas of gender and development and development ethics. Building upon this work, I provide a definition of women's empowerment that includes, but goes beyond, economic empowerment to include collective capacity. Later in this chapter, I conclude that because the democratic and participatory structure of cooperatives builds collective capacity, they are better suited than MFIs to supporting women's empowerment when empowerment is understood as including transforming the structures that reproduce inequality. Defined in this way, women's economic empowerment is neither reductive nor ignored; it is one piece in a larger project of social transformation.

As many have noted, empowerment has become a "buzzword" in development literature, most often used in connection with women (Kabeer 1999, 2005a; Batliwala 2007; Khader 2011). Disagreement about how to define empowerment and how to accurately measure it abound; these disagreements can have high stakes when future funding for an NGO depends on proven results. Critics of empowerment note that it has been coopted by neoliberal corporations, development agencies, and even the United Nations (Batliwala 2007; Koggel 2013). One line of criticism holds that empowerment is primarily psychological and individual, involving changes in individuals' beliefs and attitudes without changes in oppressive and unjust social relations. Let's call this "individualist empowerment." Much of the discussion of women's empowerment in development literature looks at women's empowerment in relation to her ability to make choices or increase her agency. Increasing women's agency is important, but empowerment goes beyond merely increasing agency.

As I shall argue, empowerment has a social and collective dimension that involves changes in social relationships and institutions. In this latter case, empowerment is inextricably linked to political issues (Kilby 2011, 33–34). Critics of the ideal of empowerment often target "individualist empowerment," claiming that changes in beliefs and attitudes do not necessarily lead to social and political change. But as we shall see, often these two aspects of empowerment go together: "Empowerment has both cognitive and political dimensions" (Kilby 2011, 34). When empowerment is understood within the feminist social justice framework, it includes not only changes in beliefs and attitudes, such as improved self-confidence or self-esteem, but also the capacity to challenge social, political, and structural barriers that lead to one's devaluation and limited opportunities. Including the capacity to challenge structural barriers and promote social change in the definition of women's empowerment moves the analysis of its effectiveness from an individual level to a social and political level.

Definitions of women's empowerment in development literature often do not specify what it entails. Theorists have worked to define and clarify empowerment, in part because of its frequent use in international documents, such as the UN Development Programme Report, World Bank publications, and the UN Millennium Goals (Kabeer 1999, 2001, 2005a, 2011; Koggel 2010, 2013; Khader 2011, 2014; Drydyk 2013). Gender and development theorist Naila Kabeer defines empowerment as including three interrelated dimensions: agency, resources, and achievements (Kabeer 1999, 2005a). Many accounts of women's empowerment in development literature only focus on agency and access to resources. Agency and access to resources are connected; in order for agency to be meaningfully exercised, it relies on the agent having a range of acceptable choices.

As I argue in chapter 2, just as political and legal rights cannot be exercised without economic and social rights, personal choice and agency are constrained by a lack of material economic and social resources. Providing or increasing access to resources, both economic and social, provides the conditions for exercising a wider range of choice, or even exercising choice in a meaningful way. As Kabeer notes: "There is a logical association between poverty and disempowerment because an insufficiency of the means for meeting one's basic needs often rules out the ability to exercise meaningful choice" (Kabeer 1999, 437). It is this link between poverty and disempowerment that Kabeer points out that leads to the assumption that poverty alleviation will empower its beneficiaries. But as we will see, empowerment not only involves an expanded range of choices; one must also choose in ways that make one's life better, and, as I shall argue, a feminist understanding of empowerment moves beyond the merely personal to the collective (McLaren 2007, 2011; Kabeer 2012).

Viewing empowerment merely as an expanded range of choices and an increase in individual agency without attention to social context and relationships ignores the background conditions that shape our choices, such as global capitalism and gender inequality. Simply assessing empowerment outcomes by people "living the lives they want" does not challenge social structures that perpetuate dominance and subordination. For instance, as Kabeer notes, for an Indian woman having many sons to bring in large dowry payments may be an individual measure of success, but it does little to challenge the structures that maintain gender discrimination and oppression (Kabeer 1999, 257). Development ethicists Jay Drydyk and Christine Koggel make a similar distinction. For example, Koggel notes that Drydyk distinguishes agency from empowerment, noting that agency is individualist and subjective, while "empowerment refers to a process of change that enables one to shape one's own (or a group's) life by one's own (or a group's) choices *for the better*" (Drydyk 2013; Koggel 2013, 267). Note that even the qualification "for the better" does little to mitigate the individualism implicit in this notion of empowerment; empowerment here can be individual or collective. On Drydyk's view, empowerment has three distinct but essential aspects: agency, well-being freedom, and power (Drydyk 2013, 260). Agency refers to one's ability to choose autonomously; well-being freedom can be thought of as choosing things that make one's life better. And power, on Drydyk's view, refers to asymmetries of agency, for instance, the asymmetry between politicians' ability to shape government policies and the power of ordinary citizens. Additionally, because power is fundamentally relational, so is empowerment (Drydyk 2013; Koggel 2013).

Naila Kabeer also recognizes the limitation of defining empowerment as people "living the lives they want" and adds that definitions of empowerment must go beyond the individual to challenge social structures and patterns of dominance and discrimination (1999). Moreover, she distinguishes between "effective agency," where one simply gets better at achieving the outcomes that she desires, and "transformative agency," which involves "greater ability on the part of poor women to question, analyze, and act on the structures of patriarchal constraint in their lives" (Kabeer 2005a, 15). This distinction between effective agency and transformative agency is critical for an adequate understanding of empowerment as changing social relationships and entrenched patterns of asymmetrical power; empowerment involves transformative agency, not merely effective agency. For feminists concerned with women's empowerment, this distinction is crucial. Serene Khader makes a related distinction. She points out that "welfare agency" (women's ability to pursue their own welfare and to value their own welfare) is not the same as "feminist agency" (challenging sexist norms), though the two are often conflated in development literature (Khader 2014). Khader rightly identifies a persistent problem in development literature and projects that conflate an increase in women's welfare with an increase in their (feminist) empowerment.

While this is often true in cases where microfinance projects focus on access to resources alone—assuming that empowerment will follow—some organizations are simultaneously attentive to both women's welfare and challenging their gender subordination, effectively enhancing both welfare agency and feminist agency. Both SEWA and MarketPlace India are simultaneously concerned with increasing women's welfare agency and with supporting women's feminist agency by challenging patriarchal gender norms. Moreover, although I agree with Khader that welfare agency and feminist agency are analytically distinct, I have observed that in practice they often go together; additionally, other empirical research supports this observation (Carr et al. 1996; Datta and Gailey 2012). When women work to improve their own welfare, for instance, by organizing a union to improve their working conditions and raise their wages, this often leads to a greater sense of efficacy to engage in other types of collective projects to transform other social relationships with unequal power such as patriarchal gender relationships.

Returning to Drydyk's three-pronged notion of empowerment as agency, well-being freedom, and power, it is clear that empowerment involves all three, as others have also noted (Kabeer 1999, 2012; Sen 1999; Khader 2011; Koggel 2013). I wish to expand on the third element, power. Whereas Drydyk sees power as asymmetry between groups, feminist analyses view power as having multiple dimensions, including interpersonal, structural, and collective, as well as asymmetry between groups. Among these multiple dimensions of power, feminists often distinguish three main forms: "power over," "power to," and "power with." "Power over" is the unilateral exercise of power to shape or limit someone's choices and opportunities. "Power to" refers to the ability to make choices and act on them. And "power with" is about our collective capacity for power—the type of power that emerges when a group works together to make change. This distinction is important because one effective route to changing asymmetrical group relations is collective power. Feminist discussions of power, empowerment, and solidarity provide a rich resource for understanding empowerment as transforming social relations through collective action (Allen 1999; Mohanty 2003; Ferguson 2009c). Feminists' multilevel, multidimensional understanding of power reveals how empowerment can work at multiple levels, and how individual empowerment can facilitate collective empowerment and social and political action.

Understanding empowerment as collective power to transform unjust social relations addresses the criticism that empowerment has been depoliticized (Batliwala 2007). In its earlier uses by social movements seeking equitable, participatory, democratic social change, empowerment entailed a shift in social and political power within and across social groups.[7] As I argue, cooperatives share this commitment to participatory processes, democratic structures, and social equality. Because these values are integral to cooperatives, they explicitly promote empowerment among their members; significantly, cooperatives build and develop collective capacities that enable women to engage in collective action to change political and social circumstances. Cooperatives' values of social equality and participatory democracy often challenge prevailing social norms; this, in turn, enables members of cooperatives to challenge social norms in the larger society, such as gender or caste inequality. I illustrate this through examples from the women's cooperatives of SEWA and MarketPlace

India; the self-confidence developed within these organizations is a catalyst for social and political activism, enabling the women to meet with political leaders, challenge authority, and make demands for fairer treatment.

In my view, empowerment includes both individual and social/collective dimensions that lead to an increased sense of self-confidence/self-esteem; an increased access to resources and opportunities; a broader range of choices; the capacity to act on those choices in both the personal and the public sphere; and the ability to analyze, question, challenge, and help to transform structural barriers that are oppressive and exploitative, including economic inequality, laws, and social attitudes and customs.

According to this definition, empowerment includes and often begins with the individual, but it never remains there. As Kabeer puts it: "The project of women's empowerment is dependent on collective solidarity in the public arena as well as individual assertiveness in the private" (Kabeer 1999, 457). Empowerment necessarily has a social, collective dimension and results in challenging the social structures that contributed to disempowerment and marginalization. For women specifically, this will include challenging patriarchal attitudes and gender discrimination. But because patterns of structural injustice interact and are mutually reinforcing, it will include challenging other structures as well—such as the global economic order; imperialism and neocolonialism; the policies and decisions of neoliberal states that perpetuate economic inequality both within and among nations; environmental degradation (which often has a greater direct impact on rural women in the global South); social attitudes about indigenous people and ethnic, racial, and religious minorities; agricultural policies; trade policies; labor policies; and so on. The recognition that power is pervasive, and that structural injustices are intersectional and affect people in multiple domains of their lives, means that empowerment involves challenging power relations at the interpersonal, institutional, and structural levels.

My definition of empowerment aligns with the definition developed by activists in South Asia who "defined empowerment as a process that shifts social power in three critical ways: by challenging the ideologies that justify social inequality (such as gender or caste), by changing prevailing patterns of access to and control over economic, natural, and intellectual resources, and by transforming the institutions and structures that reinforce and sustain existing power structures (such as the family, state, market, education, and media)" (Batliwala 2007, 560). Empowerment involves shifts of power in all three areas, not just one area, such as access to resources, in isolation. As we shall see, economic development projects that target women, such as microfinance, often focus on access to resources and its impact on individuals. By contrast, women's cooperatives are a collective enterprise that change patterns of access to economic resources and challenge the ideology of social inequality. Additionally, the democratic, participatory structure of cooperatives fosters involvement, leadership skills, and collective capacity that are useful for social and political activism to transform unjust institutions.

In the following sections I identify some significant criticisms of NGOs and MFIs as vehicles for women's empowerment. Using the examples of MarketPlace India and SEWA, I demonstrate that some NGOs have developed approaches and models for women's empowerment that simultaneously address issues of poverty and social inequality, while building women's capacity to engage in social and political change. Their approaches are comprehensive, participatory, member directed, and democratic. Moreover, these organizations recognize and embrace diversity and have developed and worked within the cultural and social context of their members, which I discuss further in chapter 4. We can learn from the successes of these organizations to develop best practices and praxis-informed theories.

Nongovernmental Organizations, Women, and Development

Politicians and policymakers alike acknowledge the centrality of a woman's status and well-being to the overall quality of life for her, her children, and her family. An enhanced quality of life for families contributes, in turn, to a better of quality of life for communities. Consequently, the United Nations as well as NGOs, target women as the focus for development projects. There are both historical and instrumental justifications for the centrality and importance of women in international development projects. Historically, women were excluded from international development projects, reflecting the widespread gender inequality in both the global South and the global North at the dawn of women's liberation movements in the late 1960s and early 1970s. Challenging this in the early 1970s, Esther Boserup argued that women's work, both paid and unpaid, made important contributions to national economies, and thus gender plays a significant role in economic and social development (Boserup 1970).

More recently, many United Nations documents couch women's empowerment and gender equality as an instrumental goal that generally helps economic development and quality of life. For instance, the 2006 United Nations Development Report notes that: "Women's empowerment helps raise economic productivity and reduce infant mortality. It contributes to improved health and nutrition. It increases the chances of education for the next generation" (UNDP Report 2006, 20). In this UN document, women's improved status and well-being is instrumental to improving the overall quality of life for her children and her family, rather than a good in and of itself. However, feminists have questioned this instrumental justification for improving the status of women, arguing that improving women's status should be a goal in itself, and not just a means to further goals (Jaggar 2014a).

In response to these feminist criticisms, the 2012 World Development Report claims that gender equality is a goal in itself, and not just a means to poverty alleviation, improving economic productivity, or improving access to basic resources for families (Jaggar 2014a). Instrumentalist approaches assume that gender equality and improving women's material status are concomitant goals. However, the project of improving women's material status has a more complicated relationship to achieving gender equality, and at times these two goals may even be at odds (Khader 2014). Development NGOs often assume that an increase in women's welfare or material circumstances will result in an increase in her status or improve gender equality. In this section, I look at some general criticisms of NGOs; in the next section I return to the issue of women's economic empowerment and improved material welfare and its relationship to feminist empowerment defined as the ability to challenge unjust social and political structures.

Critics of NGOs claim that they operate as a "shadow state" by providing benefits that were once provided by the state. This creates two problems. First, it alleviates the state of its responsibility to provide, for instance, basic health care, welfare, and food benefits. And second, NGOs lack accountability both to the people they serve and to the government; they are primarily accountable to their funders/donors (Gilmore 2007; Karim 2008, 2011; Kilby 2011). This accountability to funding agencies and donors constrains the range of goals and activities that NGOs can engage in; for instance, often they are required to act as service providers rather than activist or political organizations. Moreover, the hierarchy and bureaucracy of NGOs result in more resources going toward administration and reports than is the case with grassroots organizations without an overarching international organizational structure. This criticism of NGOs as shadow states is especially salient in the light of neoliberal economic globalization because, as mentioned, the SAPs imposed on nations by the IMF and World Bank include the cutting and privatization of public services, such as health care, education, childcare, welfare benefits, and food rations—public goods and services over which the state had primary responsibility.

In addition to operating as a shadow state, further criticisms of NGOs include the following: paternalism or imperialism; ineffective strategies; unsuccessful outcomes; providing small-scale solutions to issues that are large scale and structural; and relatedly, offering short-term solutions for long-term systemic problems. In this section, I address the criticisms that NGOs function paternalistically, or promote cultural imperialism, and the related worry that NGOs treat the population they work with as clients, resulting in a passive provider–client relationship that fosters dependency and passivity. I also address the concern that NGOs provide small-scale solutions to structural problems, thereby inhibiting the potential space for real, structurally transformative political action. I return to the criticism that NGOs function as shadow states in a later section on criticisms of microfinance institutions.

NGOs function paternalistically when they treat their clients like children and have a "top-down" model of power and of operating that does not respect the intelligence or autonomy of the people with whom they are working. This occurs when NGOs subscribe to the "helping model" that views NGO staff as experts who are positioned to help a "poor and underserved, oppressed, minority group." For instance, Ann Ferguson notes that women from the global South "are subject to paternalism (or more appropriately 'maternalism') . . . by projects designed to benefit women seen as Other, as objects of relief rather than subjects who could take place in the planning process themselves" (Ferguson 1998, 100). Donors in the global North often fund NGOs in the global South; this compounds the unequal model of power relations because usually the donors have control over the budget and decide which programs to fund. This imbalance of power between funders and staff from the global North, and "recipients" or "clients" from the global South adds cultural imperialism to paternalism.

On the ground, cultural imperialism can take many forms, but in general NGOs impose ideas, norms, values, and practices from the funding nations (usually the wealthier nations of the global North) onto the populations served by the NGO. In extreme cases, this cultural imperialism may be explicit, with programs intentionally designed to undermine not only the cultural integrity but also the health and well-being of the target groups. Such was the case with some reproductive policies which promoted involuntary sterilization targeted at poor women in India that were initially funded by international agencies and countries from the global North (Brown 1984; Buckingham 2006; Hogberg 2008; Singh et al. 2012). Less drastic than direct policy intervention aimed at controlling women's reproduction, but still significant, is the framing of development from a particular perspective. Discussing the importance of women's sustainable livelihood, Ela Bhatt emphasizes: "There is an urgent need to shift from the development paradigm of 'Northern' nations that defines employment mainly within the macro context of market and industrial growth" (Bhatt and Bishwaroop 1995, 6–7). She is not alone in this criticism of the paradigm of development, which uncritically replicates "Northern" systems, structures, and values (Escobar 1995).

Paternalism and cultural imperialism may operate separately or together, and may be explicit, but more often they are perpetrated through unconscious biases or practices and strategies uninformed by a power analysis and the harm caused by these approaches. Moreover, paternalist and imperialist attitudes and practices are not confined only to relationships between those from the global North and those from the global South but may also arise within organizations comprised of staff and members solely from the global South (or global North) because of other types of power differences, such as class, educational background, caste, race, and ethnicity. Awareness of these power dynamics, and a commitment to working in partnership, rather than replicating the asymmetrical power dynamics, social inequalities, and hierarchies in the larger society within the NGO, effectively counters these paternalistic relationships and provides a model of social equality within the organization.

As I discussed in chapter 1, both MarketPlace India and SEWA have a collaborative, participatory structure. The organizations are designed around their members' needs, and leadership of the organizations is developed from within.

SEWA's vision as an organization explicitly rejects a paternalistic, imperialistic model. The organization sees its role as supporting its members: "Our role is defined around our members' needs. We provide need-based training, marketing support, designing and on-the-job-services. . . . Training ceases to be a top down flow of education but an internalized partner relationship of development" (Krishnaswamy 2002, 12). Likewise, MarketPlace India responds to the needs of its members and develops leadership from within the organization. Both organizations build capacity for individual women to become leaders and for each member of the organization to recognize the power of acting collectively.

The activist orientation of SEWA and Marketplace India challenges the criticism that NGOs limit the potential space for real, structurally transformative political action, as well as the related criticisms that NGOs provide small-scale solutions to issues that are large scale and structural, offering short-term solutions for long-term systemic problems. As mentioned in chapter 1, in a recent and comprehensive study of NGOs in India, Patrick Kilby distinguishes between two main types of NGOs: those that are action oriented and those that are welfare oriented. Welfare-oriented NGOs see themselves as apolitical and provide services to the poor, whereas action-oriented NGOs seek to empower their constituencies to challenge the very structures that disenfranchise them (Kilby 2011, 17–18). The criticisms that NGOs provide small-scale solutions to large-scale structural problems, and that they inhibit transformative political action, apply much more readily to welfare-oriented NGOs than to action-oriented NGOs. Whereas welfare-oriented NGOs are merely service providers, action-oriented NGOs recognize the structural inequalities that necessitate providing basic services to the poor and disenfranchised and explicitly work to transform those structural inequalities. Reproducing those structural inequalities within their own organization, for instance through paternalism, runs counter to their aim of transforming unjust social relations. Action-oriented NGOs aim not to simply transform the unjust social relations within their organizations but also to develop the capacities of the oppressed and disenfranchised to challenge the unjust social structures that disadvantage them.

These unjust social structures include economic exploitation and social marginalization that result in material deprivation. If NGOs merely provide access to basic resources without changing the unjust structures that cause poverty, then they merely alleviate a symptom of the problem without addressing the root cause of economic inequality. As discussed in the Introduction, I advocate a dual-track approach to challenge social injustice: an approach that focuses on long-term systemic solutions to situations of economic inequality and social injustice, and that also recognizes the importance of meeting basic needs. Ideally, organizations adopt this dual-track approach to rectifying injustices, as SEWA and MarketPlace India do. The Self-Employed Women's Association provides a paradigmatic example of such an approach, but it is not unique. My research with MarketPlace India reveals an intentional and explicit focus on political and social engagement by their members to change unjust social circumstances and structures, alongside the goal of providing sustainable and dignified employment. These organizations not only directly challenge unjust social structures but also nurture and support the involvement of their constituencies in social and political action aimed toward long-term, systemic change.

Some feminist criticisms of NGOs focus specifically on development projects that target women and focus on income generation. In the next section I address these criticisms.

Economic Empowerment

During the past four decades, development projects that target women have focused on income generation. There are a number of related assumptions that underlie this focus: if women have access to an income, they will be empowered in other areas of their lives; women's economic independence is important as a route to gender equality; and income alone is sufficient to improve the quality of women's lives. These assumptions dovetail with the pragmatic reasons that women become the target of development projects; most important, that women are much more likely to spend money on basic necessities for themselves and their families than men are. Additionally, women's income correlates positively with her educational level and that of her daughters. Women with higher levels of education have fewer children; this, in turn, is related to both their and their family's quality of life; scarce resources divided among fewer people go further. Moreover, when loans are involved in the income-generating projects, women reliably repay them.

Postdevelopment theorists and feminists raise some important issues about the focus on women and economic issues in development. For instance, this focus on women's access to economic resources may reduce the concept of human flourishing to access to material goods, and thus elide other significant sources for human flourishing, such as a connection to nature, spiritual devotion, or familial and social affiliations (Khader 2011). In a 2006 study, Patrick Kilby asked women to rank their own indicators of empowerment, and economic change was ranked lower than education for children (Kilby 2011, 41). Kilby seconds Khader's concern about the economic paradigm for women's empowerment: "The economic paradigm is dependent on a rather narrow social construct that describes women as economic beings, rather than social and political beings" (Kilby 2011, 41). Related to this worry about reductionism is the concern that simply equating access to income and material goods to women's empowerment ignores social and political barriers, including gender discrimination. And it also denies women's role in empowerment by ignoring the role of consciousness, agency, and collective action.

A solely economic approach to women's empowerment may improve her material welfare without addressing social and gender inequality, or increasing her capacity to advocate for structural, political changes. NGOs that have a dual focus on poverty alleviation and transforming unjust social and political structures, like MarketPlace and SEWA, address inequality and injustice on multiple levels and understand that there are connections among them. SEWA's founder, Ela Bhatt, questions the separation of economics from social reality stating, "laws of economics operate in social reality, [that] society cannot be reduced to the market, [that] social capital is the basis on which economic capital can have a stable and sustained growth" (Bhatt 2000, 10).

Recognizing the interconnections of the social and the economic underscores that material resources and income are an important aspect of improving the quality of poor women's lives, but not the only aspect. The participatory, collaborative structure of cooperatives combines meeting economic needs with developing the confidence and skills to challenge oppressive social structures: "The poor women must also be equipped to shed the sense of inferiority because of gender, caste, illiteracy, poverty, by building their organised strength through self managed, self owned, viable economic organisations. It is the organised economic strength that helps them exercise their political rights, resist oppressive forces" (Bhatt 2000, 10). While having a psychological sense of empowerment does not always result in the capacity to change social relations, it is often a prerequisite to do so. I have illustrated this connection among various senses of empowerment—psychological, economic, and sociopolitical—through many examples in chapter 1. Women in MarketPlace India and SEWA often attribute their ability to meet with political leaders, challenge authority, and make demands for fairer treatment to an increase in their self-confidence and self-esteem.

Conversely, economic empowerment may lead to a feeling of personal empowerment. For some women, such as SEWA member Karuna, there is a direct connection between economic empowerment and feeling empowered. Karuna lived in an urban area in a hut with no door. She made items out of bamboo to support herself and her two daughters, but after working all day, she was unable to sleep at night for fear that someone would come into her home. After working for several years, she took a loan from the SEWA Bank to install a door on her hut. She said she was finally able to sleep in peace after years of sleepless and anxious nights. When asked at the SEWA Bank meeting what this felt like, she replied: "I felt full of power—as if a thousand light bulbs lit up my body" (Nanavaty 2000, 1). For a woman who has been fearful for her safety, vulnerable, and lacking the basic conditions for a decent life (adequate shelter), economic empowerment, or welfare agency is, in and of itself, a good. Therefore, one could say that economic empowerment is a necessary, but not sufficient condition for the empowerment of poor women. The reason is simple: if empowerment includes the ability to choose among reasonable options, then having reasonable options—such as access to adequate nutrition for one's family or the financial ability to send your children to school—often depends upon having financial resources. As discussed earlier, empowerment is not just an attitude (individual psychological) or the ability to choose (agency), although it does include these dimensions. It also includes the ability to challenge oppressive and discriminatory social relations (in this case gender and caste) and the possibility of transforming them to more equal and just social relations. As already discussed, this aspect of empowerment is necessarily collective; we do not transform social relations by ourselves or in a vacuum.

In the following two sections, I discuss MFIs as a type of development project that aims to empower women; first, I provide some background on microfinance institutions; then I explore a number of criticisms of MFIs. I demonstrate that while these criticisms are valid when applied to MFIs, they cannot be legitimately extended to women's cooperatives because the empowerment model of women's cooperatives lies in large part in their democratic and participatory structure, not solely in income generation. The democratic and participatory structure of cooperatives helps to foster collective capacity in their members; this collective capacity involves the women working together to speak up and take action to challenge structural injustice within the larger society. Moreover, cooperatives and unions are collective entities that can specifically exercise economic and political power to improve the income and working conditions of members, and to influence laws and policies. SEWA and MarketPlace India embrace a multifaceted and comprehensive approach to women's empowerment that includes economic issues, but it does not stop with economic issues nor reduce all aspects of empowerment to access to income and material goods. Critics have rightly pointed out the reductive nature of the assumption that women's empowerment will be achieved through income generation alone. In the next section, I take a closer look at the claims of MFIs to illuminate the differences between MFIs and grassroots member-based organizations.

Microfinance and Economic Empowerment

Perhaps the best known type of development projects that rely on the economic paradigm of women's empowerment are the types of microfinance projects which gained popular recognition after Mohammad Yunus won the Nobel Peace Prize in 2006 for founding the Grameen Bank in Bangladesh. The Grameen Bank is one among a great number of different kinds of MFIs. The common denominator among MFIs is that they provide loans to poor people who do not generally have access to loans or credit.[8] Microfinance first emerged as part of a broader development strategy that was implemented primarily through NGOs. As a development strategy, the goal of MFIs seems prima facie unobjectionable: to offer credit in the form of loans to the poor who do not have access to loans because they lack material collateral or have no permanent address. These loans are most often targeted toward women in the global South to enable them to finance small businesses. However, since 2000, MFIs have also been backed by private capital, which is increasing this strategy as it proves to be profitable (MacFarquhar 2010). Subsequently, there are two broad approaches to microfinance: (1) the financial services approach, whose primary goal is to provide banking and financial services to the (previously underserved) poor (this approach is often connected with international financial systems); and (2) the poverty lending approach, which aims to provide not only financial services to the poor but also training and support to prepare borrowers to become successful entrepreneurs (Johnson and Rogaly 1997; Gulli 1998).

The Grameen Bank, following the poverty lending approach, extended its loans to improve the lives of poor people. Coincidentally, their approach also proved that the poor are bankable because the repayment rate of the loans offered to the very poor was over 95 percent. This repayment rate rivals that of Citibank; consequently, an entire segment of the world's population previously thought to be not worthy of credit because of their lack of collateral and limited opportunities for income was now targeted by commercial financial services as preferred clients. With this proven profitability, private financial institutions entered the microfinance market, which has become increasingly commercialized. Critics of this commercial and for-profit microfinance contend that profit ought not be made off the backs of the poor. Understandably, they argue that these commercial microfinance institutions simply further the exploitation of the poor by facilitating debt and then charging high interest, which then contributes to the profit of large corporate financial institutions. In their analysis of microcredit as a form of accumulation by dispossession, Christine Keating, Claire Rasmussen, and Pooja Rishi call these "wealth extracting forms of microcredit" (Keating et al. 2010, 159). Assuming that exploiting poor people is not consistent with either a rights approach or an empowerment approach, we can exclude these commercial and profit-based MFIs from further discussion here. More interesting, however, are criticisms that apply to microfinance at its best: that is, with an eye toward positive social outcomes rather than profit.

The poverty lending approach aims toward positive social outcomes, such as alleviating poverty and increasing women's social status. As noted, these two goals are often assumed to be concomitant: improving a woman's welfare will, in turn, improve her gender status. These two claims are entangled with debates about the effectiveness of MFIs in alleviating poverty and the wisdom of women entrepreneurs bearing the burden of economic development. From the beginning, MFIs favored women as loan recipients for two main reasons: women are more impoverished than men, and they are more likely to pay back the loans. Some earlier development studies had also found that women were more likely to use money to pay for household expenses, such as food for the family, whereas men often spent money on alcohol and gambling (Kabeer 1998; Bales 2003; Krenz et al. 2014). As already mentioned, improved material status does not simply translate into gender equality; economic empowerment may not change women's status. In fact, critics argue that this focus on women to bear the burden of economic responsibility actually increases their labor and overall responsibility (Chant 2016).

I suggest that organizations like SEWA and Marketplace India that take a dual approach—improving women's welfare and economic opportunities through creating collective institutions, as well as explicitly and simultaneously challenging social inequality, including gender inequality address critics' concerns. Examining common criticisms of MFIs will help to highlight the contrast between their approach to economic empowerment and an approach that engages women in building collective economic institutions, such as cooperatives and unions. The experience of building a collective institution, combined with the democratic and participatory structure of cooperatives, develops women's capacities for collective action, which can then be used in the social and political arena.

While the financial services approach simply offers loans and credit to poor people, MFIs that take a poverty lending approach include explicit social objectives, which go far beyond providing credit. For example, the Grameen Bank supports the following social objectives:

> It promotes credit as a human right; it is aimed towards the poor, particularly poor women; it is based on trust, not on legal procedures and systems. Moreover, the aim of providing loans is to create self-employment, income-generating activities and housing for the poor, as opposed to using the loans for consumption. It was started to challenge the assumption held by the traditional banking industry that the poor are not "credit-worthy." It provides financial services in the rural villages, so that poor villagers do not need to travel to the city to get loans. And it gives high priority to building social capital.[9]

These social objectives have been widely adopted as the Grameen Bank model proliferated. By 2009, the Grameen Bank had spread to thirty countries on five continents. In the United States alone, thirty of the fifty states have group-lending programs similar to the Grameen model (Armendariz and Morduch 2010, 13).

What features of the Grameen Bank make it so successful? One of the primary features, in addition to targeting women, is the group-lending model. Loans are made to individuals, but the entire group is responsible for the repayment in the following sense: if anyone fails to repay her loan installment on time, this harms the ability of everyone in the group to procure future loans. This classic Grameen model of group lending is often cited as one of its most innovative features, and it is credited with the success of the high repayment rate. This group-lending model relies on the networks of family and friends in the community and is referred to as group responsibility or joint liability.[10] Because of this, if one member cannot repay her loan, others in the group may pay it for her, or lend her money to repay. There is considerable social pressure to pay the loan installments on time or to risk the censure and disapproval of friends and community members (Brett 2006; Karim 2008, 2011; Krenz et al. 2014). In this way, microcredit relies on kinship and social ties to secure the loans in lieu of material collateral.

The Grameen Bank has often been the target of criticisms directed at MFIs because of its visibility, prominence, and reputed success. Indeed, its spread to five continents and the fact that the model has been replicated the world over indicate the importance of evaluating the criticisms raised against Grameen in particular and MFIs in general.

Criticisms of Microfinance Institutions as a Vehicle for Empowerment

Anthropologists, feminists, and development theorists, including development ethicists, critically appraise microfinance as a vehicle for women's empowerment. First, as already mentioned, if MFIs have a high interest rate, this may serve to increase rather than decrease debt, exploiting the women they are ostensibly helping (Strangio 2011; Wichterich 2012). Second, anthropologists worry that MFIs violate local norms of cohesion and community (Brett 2006; Karim 2008, 2011; Moodie 2008). Third, some see MFIs as part of the neoliberal project of development, both contributing to powerful development myths and creating neoliberal subjects (McMichael 2005; Karim 2008, 2011; Lindio-McGovern 2009). Fourth, MFIs are often administered by NGOs; and as discussed earlier, some believe that NGOs operate as a shadow state because they provide services previously provided by the state, but unlike states, NGOs are not accountable to citizens (Gilmore 2007). Relatedly, NGOs that administer MFIs often view themselves in provider–client relationships to the women to whom they provide loans. But this individual services approach does not aptly address the structural injustices that caused the women's poverty. In fact, critics argue, this individualist approach limits the potential space for real, structurally transformative political action (Keating et al. 2010; Karim 2011). Additionally, an unintended consequence of promoting women's entrepreneurship is the "double-shift" created for women who still do all the housework *and* are expected to run a business (Poster and Salime 2002; Churchill 2004; Brett 2006; Chant 2014, 2016).

MFIs have come under fire for the inordinate pressure they put on borrowers to repay loans. In extreme cases, borrowers have committed suicide; in Andhra Pradesh, India, there was a rash of over eighty suicides by MFI loan recipients in 2010 (Biswas 2010). This epidemic of suicides caused MFIs to come under critical scrutiny. In India, over 30 million households have accessed microloans, and many microloans programs target women. Thus, it is important for feminists to explore the issues surrounding MFIs and women's empowerment. Of the many criticisms of MFIs, here I shall focus on three. First, are family and community relationships strained during the implementation of group-lending MFIs? Second, does the introduction of MFIs reproduce values of neoliberalism, including the ways that women internalize those values? And third, do MFIs limit the space for transformative political action? I then compare the approach of MFIs to women's cooperatives, arguing that they, in contrast, foster relationships, challenge neoliberal values, and promote structural change.

Anthropologists have found that the much-lauded group-lending model of the Grameen Bank exploits existing kinship structures and cultural norms (Brett 2006; Karim 2008, 2011; Moodie 2008). In order to illustrate some of the issues with MFIs that anthropologists revealed through ethnographic studies, I draw on some specific examples from Lamia Karim's fieldwork in Bangladesh and support these ethnographic narratives with other research studies (Karim 2008, 2011). Operating within what Karim calls the economy of shame, rural Bangladeshi women are the traditional custodians of family honor. Often protecting women's honor means limiting their access to public places and their contact with males who are not relatives. However, because women are the sole recipients of the loans offered by the NGOs, maintaining their honor shifts from staying out of the public sphere to their proper behavior in the public sphere. When women are unable to repay their loans, they are often thrown in jail. These women are not only criminalized, but an overnight stay in a jail results in a loss of virtue, according to cultural norms. This disgrace to the family has even resulted in several of the women being divorced by their husbands (Karim 2008, 19).[11]

Moreover, making all the members of the group responsible for the debt of each group member sometimes has unwelcome consequences. When an individual member of the group is unable to repay her loan, thus jeopardizing future loans for the entire group, the other women in the group feel justified in "repossessing" any material items the woman and her family have. This has resulted in some groups descending on the defaulting member's house and taking whatever is valuable to sell in order to repay the loan, including personal jewelry, cows, chickens, trees, and the rice and grain for the family's meals. In extreme cases, the group will engage in housebreaking, selling off all the family's possessions, including their house.

This economy of shame, and its resulting violence, is systematically ignored by the NGOs who provide the loans; their main concern is a high loan repayment rate. Keep in mind that group lending works because of the close bonds of family and community in rural areas. Moreover, contrary to the claim that MFIs offer independence and empowerment to women, women's status decreases if they must borrow money from family to repay the loans from the MFI. This, as well as the strictures of group lending, may strain relationships among family, friends, and community members (Brett 2006). Repayment of the loans is often made more difficult if the borrower is not in control of the loan, or if she does not have decision-making power about the money from the loan once it is dispersed (Goetz and Sen Gupta 1996; Poster and Salime 2002). These examples clearly demonstrate that some forms of microcredit not only strain family, friend, and community relations but also exploit bonds of friendship and community to serve their own interest.

Additional criticisms of MFIs fall into three main categories: they reproduce suspect values and practices endorsed by neoliberalism; they focus on individual and small-scale solutions when structural change is needed; and they are ineffective because they do not produce successful outcomes. An example from Karim's fieldwork illustrates well the criticism that microfinance reinforces neoliberal values, including individualism, competition, and self-interest. In Bangladesh the most profitable and widespread business from microcredit is moneylending.[12] Microcredit allows women to borrow money at 50–60 percent interest, well below the 120 percent interest rate that moneylenders charge, and then loan it to other women at the higher (120 percent) rate. This creates cycles of dependency and debt within the community among the most vulnerable members, those who are unable to get or pay back a microloan from an NGO. Thus, far from reducing moneylending, microcredit by NGOs creates a whole new class of female moneylenders.

Even without this secondary usurious form of moneylending, microcredit still promulgates neoliberal values simply by prioritizing entrepreneurship, and all that it entails, over other activities. For instance, women are encouraged to start their own businesses, rather than to engage in collective projects. Microfinance emphasizes the importance of money and self-reliance, and this may lead to defining one's self in terms of one's success or wealth, rather than community and kinship relations. Furthermore, the encroachment of a cash economy in areas where barter and subsistence farming still exist needs to be examined critically. Imposing practices such as lending, credit, debt, and entrepreneurship upon rural women as the route to success surely disrupts and displaces former practices, such as growing one's own food and relying on extended family to share food during hard times. Moreover, as women enter into new relationships as clients (of the MFIs) and consumers in a cash economy, they are positioned as neoliberal subjects under the disciplinary regime that prioritizes compliance to debt repayment and consumer culture. This financialization of everyday life in Indian villages results in a feminization of debt (Wichterich 2012). This simply reinforces the intertwining of feminism and women's empowerment with the aims of neoliberal capitalism (Keating et al. 2010).

Often MFIs further the agenda of neoliberal globalization, rather than offering an alternative to it. "We run the risk of allowing the value of empowerment to be appropriated by the political rationality of neoliberalism if we do not challenge both the legitimating structure of neoliberalism and the practices that it produces" (Keating 2010, 171). As demonstrated, microfinance posing as a solution to poverty remains firmly within the neoliberal logic of the globalization of capital.

To the extent that MFIs remain within a neoliberal logic, they limit the possibilities for social and political change. Avenues for transformational politics are closed down, critics claim, by the hierarchal, disciplinary relationship between the MFI and the member (Mayoux 1999; Isserles 2003; Karim 2008, 2011). The MFI distributes loans only if their protocol is followed, treating the women as passive clients subject to control and discipline. Moreover, the individualized solution of entrepreneurship to ameliorate poverty forestalls the urgency of structural change. Thus, critics claim that the individualized solution to poverty that MFIs provide upholds neoliberalism and discourages activism for structural change (Mayoux 1999; Isserles 2003; Keating et al. 2010).

Finally, in terms of outcome the successes of MFIs are mixed. Naila Kabeer provides a comprehensive literature review of the impact of microfinance projects on women's empowerment; the studies have contradictory results (Kabeer 1998, 2001, 2005b, 2012). Some studies claim that microfinance fails to empower women because women do not control the loans or make the financial decisions with regard to them; domestic violence increases in households where women receive the loans; and intrahousehold gender inequality persists (Goetz and Sen Gupta 1996; Schuler et al. 1996). However, other studies demonstrate that women often control the money for the loans, including making decisions about how to spend or invest the money; domestic violence decreases in households where women receive MFI loans; and women receiving loans share more equally in household decisions (Hashemi et al. 1996; Zaman 1999; Kabeer 2001).

In spite of these mixed results of the effectiveness of microfinance projects in empowering women, Kabeer concludes, "microfinance offers an important and effective means to achieving change on a number of different fronts, economic, social and perhaps also political" (2005b, 4718). Yet she exercises caution about seeing microfinance as a broad strategy for social change and women's empowerment: "However effective the role of microfinance organisations in providing financial services to the poor, they cannot substitute for broader policies to promote pro-poor economic growth, *equitable social development and democratic participation in collective forums of decision-making.* In the absence of such policies, microfinance may at most provide a safety net for the poor rather than a ladder out of poverty" (Kabeer 2005b, 4718, emphasis mine). In what follows, I suggest that women's cooperatives are more effective than MFIs in increasing women's empowerment because of their commitment to democratic participation, collective forums for decision making, and social equality.

In the next section, I look at the possibilities for cooperatives to improve the quality of life for women and their families in the global South and to empower women to challenge structural injustice. Cooperatives do more than provide a sustainable income for women; their structure is collective, and their goals are not simply economic but also social.

Cooperatives: Economic Empowerment and Social Equality

Cooperatives have a much longer history than microfinance institutions. Unlike MFIs, they did not emerge out of international development projects; they emerged in the mid-1800s as a form of resistance to the emergence of industrialization and global capitalism. Significantly, cooperatives are member owned and engage in democratic decision making. According to the International Cooperative Association website: "Co-operatives are businesses owned and run by and for their members. Whether the members are the customers, employees, or residents, they have an equal say in what the business does and a share in the profits" (International Cooperative Alliance 2014). Betsy Bowman and Bob Stone offer a broader definition: "A cooperative . . . is an autonomous, non-governmental association formed to meet its members' economic, social, and/or cultural needs through a jointly-owned, democratically-controlled enterprise" (2007, 1).[13] The common thread in these definitions is that cooperatives are member owned and democratically controlled organizations. By definition, cooperatives have a higher goal than simply making profits—that is, to have a collective, sustainable enterprise that provides employment while meeting the needs of the community. Moreover, when a cooperative is for-profit (as many are), the profits are shared equally among the members, or in a way that all members have agreed to or voted on. Cooperatives are distinguished from other business enterprises by their egalitarian structure, goals, and values. The explicitly held values of cooperatives include *self-help, self-responsibility, democracy, equality, equity, and solidarity*

(International Cooperative Alliance 2014). As I will argue, these values—especially democracy, equality, equity, and solidarity—mark an important difference between microenterprise supported by microfinance institutions and cooperatives.

Cooperatives have a long tradition, beginning with the Rochdale Society of Equitable Pioneers, established in England in 1844. Historically, cooperative communities and their projects have been based on an alternative vision of society premised on cooperation, rather than on the pursuit of individual self-interest. The Rochdale Society was founded by a group of twenty-eight weavers who opened their own store in December 1844 to provide basic foodstuffs to workers who could no longer afford them. Mechanization had forced skilled workers, such as the weavers, into poverty through the wide availability of cheap, mass-produced goods. As such, they banded together to create a business based on equity and democracy, rather than profit alone. The seven principles of "cooperativism," as initiated by the Rochdale community, are still accepted globally as guidelines for cooperatives: voluntary and open membership, democratic member control, member economic participation, autonomy and independence, education and training, cooperation among cooperatives, and concern for community (Bowman and Stone 2007, 3).[14] In addition to these principles, most cooperatives also practice environmentalism, emphasizing ecological sustainability and a low impact on the environment. The seventh principle, concern for community, links the internal structure and values of cooperatives to the larger society.

The principles underlying cooperatives and the alternative vision for society that they represent are exemplified by the cooperatives of SEWA and Marketplace India: "Cooperation is a way of life, a philosophy, an approach to human problems, based on the principle of equity and justice. All human beings are equal in their right to live and to develop, and can be free only if they are not exploited by others but are independently productive and creative members of society" (Bhatt 1995b, 11). Bhatt expresses a fuller vision of human equality and freedom than a minimalist view of human rights. Her vision of freedom includes a structural analysis—freedom from exploitation, as well as a more robust idea of what a full human life entails, including creativity. Here we can see that the on-the-ground analysis, as well as the practices of SEWA, do not fall prey to the criticisms leveled against the paradigm of economic empowerment for women used by MFIs.

Economic issues, such as sustainable income and independent productivity, are an important component of feminist social justice, but equally important is social equality. From the beginning, cooperatives aimed to improve social and economic conditions of the socially and economically oppressed (Bhowmik and Sarkar 2002). Perhaps less well known than the origins of cooperatives in the history of the Rochdale Pioneers is that cooperatives and "rural development schemes" have a significant place in India's history. As early as 1902, "the concept of cooperative institutions was introduced in India as instruments of social reforms" (Krishnaswamy 2002, 4). Mohandas K. Gandhi writes about cooperatives as the route to the economic self-sufficiency that he saw as important for national sovereignty, and also as a practical solution for providing a sustainable living for people in a country that was rich in human resources.[15]

Cooperatives are unique in that they are economic institutions with overriding social goals (not purely economic goals). The principles articulated by the Rochdale community and adopted by the International Cooperative Association serve as both practical guidelines for cooperatives and as a moral compass. The International Cooperative Association claims: "In the tradition of their founders, co-operative members believe in the ethical values of honesty, openness, social responsibility and caring for others" (International Cooperative Alliance 2014).

Cooperatives are not targeted toward women, unlike microloan and income-generating development projects. But they also do not exclude women; cooperatives open up economic opportunities to the previously disenfranchised. The first principle of cooperatives can be expressed as follows: membership must be voluntary and without discrimination with regard to race, sex, religion, caste, or social and political affiliation. This anti-discrimination requirement was extraordinarily forward thinking in the mid-1800s, and it remains important today. This is especially true in situations where women, or any minority group, are routinely barred from paid employment, as is still often the case in rural India. The second principle, sometimes paraphrased as "One member, one vote," serves as the basic core of the democratic nature of cooperatives (International Cooperative Alliance 2014). As we shall see, this is especially important in cases where the members of the cooperative have previously had little or no voice in their community. Recognizing all members of the cooperative as valuable and equal, and encouraging everyone to speak up, promotes habits of engagement and democratic political participation. The fifth principle, education and training, remains key to successful cooperative enterprises; most successful cooperatives have ongoing skills training, as well as educational opportunities, for cooperative members and their families.

I argue that the values endorsed by cooperatives, especially democracy, equality, equity, and solidarity, mark an important difference between MFIs and cooperatives. Because of their democratic structure, cooperatives provide more than just a job for their members; they also bolster self-confidence and foster solidarity. Furthermore, cooperatives have "social objectives over and above business objectives. They need to be inherently sensitive to social, community and environmental needs" (Krishnaswamy 2002, 4). The positive benefits of collective economic empowerment for women through cooperatives go well beyond simply providing a sustainable income. Rather than falling prey to the criticisms of microfinance raised earlier, women's cooperatives provide a collective solution for economic empowerment and foster economic and political solidarity. This focus on shared and collective capacities to engage in sustainable work, and to shape the future builds women's collective capacities. Because of these collective capacities cooperatives, contrary to the criticisms leveled against MFIs, strengthen relationships, mitigate against the values and structures of neoliberalism, and foster social and political agency leading to structural transformation. I illustrate these theoretical claims with specific examples from SEWA and MarketPlace India.

Developing Women's Empowerment, Building Feminist Solidarity

The cooperative structure of MarketPlace India incorporates the core values of participatory decision making, social equality, cooperation among cooperatives, and concern for the (larger) community. A recent study suggests that the success of women's cooperatives in India be measured by elements of empowerment embedded in the organizational structure itself and members' perceptions of their own empowerment (Datta and Gailey 2012). I have already discussed several reasons why the participatory, collaborative structure of cooperatives is well suited to women's empowerment, both economic empowerment and social and political empowerment, to challenge gender inequality and structural injustice. I have also addressed some criticisms of women's empowerment through economic empowerment. While I maintain that access to decent work and a sustainable livelihood are important aspects of empowering women, I have also pointed out that political and social empowerment are fostered through leadership development programs, providing education such as literacy training, and developing skills such as speaking out.

I return to some of these examples in what follows and share some of the members' perceptions of their own empowerment. Women in MarketPlace and SEWA develop the confidence to speak up, make changes in their own lives, and challenge oppressive social norms.

SEWA's cooperative bank provides an informative contrast to MFIs. One of the earliest cooperatives formed by SEWA was its cooperative bank founded in 1974, prior to Yunnus's Grameen Bank. Although on the surface these institutions may seem similar—after all, both lend money to poor women previously unable to secure credit or loans—there are fundamental differences between the institutions. As a cooperative bank, the SEWA Bank is owned and run by its members. The idea for the bank came from one of SEWA's members; one of the obstacles the women faced as they organized themselves into unions and cooperatives was their lack of capital to buy raw materials or items to sell in bulk. This had kept them vulnerable to moneylenders who charged extremely high interest rates. At a meeting of four thousand SEWA members, a woman spoke up: "We may be poor, but we are so many, why not a bank of our own?" (Krishnaswamy 2002, 36). The SEWA Bank began by each woman saving small amounts of money and pooling her resources; four thousand women deposited 10 Rupees each. So the first significant difference is that the SEWA Bank is based on a savings model, not a debt model. The second difference is that the bank is owned and controlled by SEWA members, who are also its clients. Cooperatives not only provide an alternative economic model; they exemplify an alternative social vision of cooperation, not exploitation. In both loan circles and cooperatives, women's fates are linked. But microfinance institutions that promote loan circles do so to ensure repayment, not to foster relationships. Because cooperatives are jointly owned and managed by the women themselves, they must work together to be successful. Additionally, in the SEWA Bank, there is no third-party relationship to an NGO, and members are not responsible for each other's debts. So, rather than harming relationships, cooperatives build relationships of goodwill and mutuality, not only among family members and friends but also among coworkers.

These mutual and supportive relationships developed within the cooperatives provide the support that some women need to make changes in their lives. In one MarketPlace cooperative a coworker provided shelter for a woman and her daughters after they were kicked out of the house: "[The cooperative] is like a mother to us. It shelters us and cares for us. One of the women's husbands used to go out drinking. He never used to work and he threw her and her daughters out of the house, so they were living at my house. We all came together in a meeting about this and went to her husband and talked to him and got him to realize what he had done and he went into treatment and got better" (Littrell and Dickson 2010, 145). Unlike the situation of MFIs in Bangladesh, these women are not repossessing one another's property and forcibly evicting friends and relatives from their homes. Moreover, these mutual and supportive relationships developed within the cooperatives contribute to the women's ability to act collectively for structural change; they can be thought as what Serene Khader calls "enabling relationships" (2015).

Three members of MarketPlace India express this relationship between empowerment and working for social and political change very well: Asha comments, "I have learned to struggle with life, like I have some power; I don't feel so powerless. There is inspiration that I can change some things in my life." Meenakshi observes, "I was unaware of how to speak in front of people and even how to have conversations because I had always lived in a village. Now I know how to meet and talk with other people." And Jayashree chimes in: "I used to not attend meetings or even have contact with other people. Now I will join protest groups!" (Littrell and Dickson 2010, 144).[16] In these three statements we can see that members of MarketPlace India connect feeling empowered with the ability to change things. Moreover, working in groups in a democratic, participatory organization imparts skills like communicating, public speaking, teamwork, and the knowledge that collective strength is a powerful force for social and political change. In other words, MarketPlace India and SEWA build the women's collective capacity.

This collective capacity challenges neoliberal values and frameworks. While MFIs encourage individual businesses, competition, and material gain, cooperatives are collective enterprises based on cooperation and sustainability. Because the women are worker-owners and members of the cooperative, and the structure is egalitarian, one person does not profit from another's loss, as in the example of the female moneylender who maximized her profits at her neighbor's expense. Describing the structure of SEWA's cooperatives, Lalita Krishnaswami says: "The co-operative consists of a group of workers who have contributed share capital to become members of the co-operative. They are the collective owners of the co-operative. They elect a Managing Committee to manage the day-to-day affairs of the co-operative. A member of the Managing Committee is elected chairperson. The members work in their own co-operative and are worker-owners" (Krishnaswami 2002, 9). Cooperatives rely on a group working together for the common good; interdependence is prized instead of individualism.

MarketPlace India uses the method of cross training; each member of the cooperative learns all aspects of the process of production. As discussed in chapter 1, this involvement in the overall production process allows artisans to understand the entire production process, fosters a sense of empowerment, and leads to a sense of shared responsibility for the welfare of the whole organization. Additionally, working in a cooperative encourages cooperation, not competition with one another. For example, a member of one of the MarketPlace cooperatives is HIV positive and very weak; the other women in her cooperative save work for her to ensure that she has enough work to earn an adequate income (Littrell and Dickson 2010, 108). If neoliberalism is defined in part by the values and norms of a competitive, capitalist ethos that fosters individualism and competitiveness, then cooperatives actually work against this dominant paradigm by instead recognizing the power and value of collective action and enterprises, and promoting cooperation.

I turn now to the third criticism of NGOs and microfinance discussed earlier: that they limit the space for real, transformative political action. When MFIs have a "services approach," the women involved are treated like clients; these NGOs often utilize the client-consumer mentality perpetuated by the framework of neoliberalism. Critics claim NGOs also replace the state in providing services and benefits, thus weakening even traditional routes of political action by remaking citizens with rights into clients who must act compliantly to access previously public services.

My experience with cooperatives shows, on the other hand, that they can increase individuals' capacities to engage in social and political transformation. For example, MarketPlace India includes education and training components such as a global dialogue program and a social action program. As discussed in chapter 1, for the social action program, each individual cooperative chooses an issue important to them and their local community and develops a strategy for change. In 2000, several cooperatives took up the issues of community and preventive health, and the Pushpanjali cooperative was successful in their campaign to get the city to cover the sewage ditches in their neighborhood.

While Pushpanjali worked to change their local community through activism and political organization, the Marketplace India cooperatives have also engaged in activism and political organization at the national level. As described in chapter 1, several of the cooperatives worked together with other organizations to call attention to, and ultimately to stop, corruption in the public food distribution program. Moreover, as detailed in chapter 1, MarketPlace India not only provides each individual with knowledge, skills, and a fair wage but also fosters a sense of solidarity and collective empowerment. Making the state accountable for fairness in its welfare and benefit programs directly challenges the view that NGOs contribute to the privatization of social and political problems by acting as a shadow state providing goods and services previously provided by the state.

SEWA has made a significant impact on national laws and policies by winning the first Supreme Court judgment in favor of women vendors, playing a pivotal role in establishing the National Commission on Self-Employed Women, which gathered data and included eight hundred public hearings nationwide, and Ela Bhatt's appointment as the first woman on the national Planning Commission, a powerful long-term planning committee which sets India's agendas and priorities for the future (Rose 1992, 31). Internationally, SEWA successfully lobbied the World Labor Congress to include home-based work in its definition of work, and consequently, to accord home-based workers some of the rights and protections granted to other workers. As mentioned in chapter 1, SEWA also initiated the founding of two international organizations, HOMENET, an international network of home-based workers; and WEIGO, women in informal employment. SEWA also participates in the global coalitions STREETNET, a worldwide network of street vendors; GRASSNET, an international network of grassroots handicraft workers; and the Global Trading Network of Grassroots Entrepreneurs. Far from limiting the space for social and political transformation, cooperatives can build individuals' capacities to be change agents, and they can also highlight the importance of collective action and structural change.

Women's cooperatives can address the everyday practical needs of poor women, provide opportunities for new types of social relationships, including solidarity, and lead to collective social and political action. It is not women's access to resources alone that enables them to challenge gender norms as well as other forms of injustice, but their capacities as leaders and social activists. Because of their structure, history, and explicitly held values, cooperatives are very different than microfinance institutions, and they are not subject to the major criticisms of microfinance. First, because cooperatives are not based on loans, but instead provide jobs, they are not subject to criticisms about the feminization of debt. Second, because they have a collective structure that is based on equal participation rather than group responsibility for debt, working in a group builds relationships rather than undermines them. Third, when a cooperative such as MarketPlace India emphasizes collaborative and sustainable work with dignity, the income earned increases women's welfare without exploitive relations of unjust labor or unfair moneylending practices. Fourth, some women's cooperatives, such as MarketPlace India and SEWA, focus on the dual goals of challenging gender inequality and improving women's welfare. Both are explicit, with organizational and programmatic aspects targeted toward improving women's welfare and challenging gender inequality; ongoing education, training, and support are significant factors in achieving these goals successfully. As demonstrated, this is built in to the very structure of cooperatives, and therefore cooperatives are more likely to be successful at empowering women than microfinance projects that do not endorse social equality as a primary objective.

Conclusion

Women's empowerment must be seen within, and occur within, projects that are part of a broader movement for social justice, including economic justice. Moreover, economic justice involves structural transformation, as does gender justice. Just as organizations that seek to improve the lives of poor women through economic empowerment must address immediate needs such as adequate food and shelter, while at the same time changing the structural conditions that produce poverty and social exclusions, they must also have a multilevel approach (immediate as well as institutional) to challenging gender oppression: "[E]mpowerment takes the consciousness and capabilities of individual women as its starting point, gender justice is concerned with the quality of the institutional arrangements that govern social relationships" (Kabeer 2012, 220). Organizations, such as cooperatives, that address the day-to-day needs of poor women and build capacities such as leadership skills, democratic participation, and social and political involvement are a promising route to comprehensive and sustained social justice movements, including gender justice, because of their focus on empowering their members to be agents of social and political change.

Moreover, because of their structure, history, and explicitly held values, cooperatives are very different than microfinance programs and are not subject to the same criticisms. Cooperatives distinguish themselves by being member owned and controlled, and egalitarian. From their earliest vision, cooperatives have been based on fundamentally different ideals and principles than unfettered capitalism. Cooperatives put people before profits; they are environmentally responsible; and they do not exploit the labor of some to benefit others. Unlike MFIs, which mirror neoliberal economics on a smaller scale, cooperatives actively challenge individualism, hierarchy, and capitalist exploitation. Cooperatives, like unions, empower their workers.

As we have seen through the work of SEWA and MarketPlace India, part of this empowerment involves challenging the structures and policies that create systemic inequality. In this case, addressing systemic inequality means challenging not only current state and government policies but also international policies. Although no one organization or group can undermine pernicious policies of globalization alone, it is important to work at both the local and global levels to create alternative structures and policies. Alternative institutions such as cooperatives are part of a larger social movement toward a solidarity economy. Solidarity economies reject exploitative economic and social relationships in favor of cooperation and mutuality. I discuss solidarity economies further in chapter 5.

The work of SEWA and MarketPlace India demonstrates the connection between the personal and the political and the local and the global. We have seen how individual empowerment in terms of increased confidence and leadership development can lead to engagement in the public, political arena. Members of the cooperatives acted together to change national laws and policies. We have also seen how access to the resources provided by the SEWA Bank allowed Karuna to sleep at night and feel empowered as a result of her increased economic resources, which directly led to increased physical security for her and her daughters. Both SEWA and MarketPlace keep the needs of their members central; this means that poverty alleviation cannot be sidelined in favor of only political work. Yet both these activist grassroots organizations foster leadership and political engagement among their members to transform the conditions that continue to produce structural inequality. Finally, SEWA has been very successful in establishing international connections and influencing policy at the international level. Addressing the increased poverty for poor women as a result of some of the economic policies of globalization involves protecting their livelihoods, namely by supporting a sustainable income; and challenging aspects of globalization that undermine this possibility, for instance, by the privatization of water and the placement of dams that flood family farms and ancestral homes. As globalization renders nation-state boundaries more permeable and less powerful, theorists and activists seek global solutions for problems, such as poverty, economic exploitation, and environmental issues. Taking a global perspective on these issues therefore requires a global framework for justice. In the next chapter I evaluate and discuss cosmopolitanism approaches to global justice.

CHAPTER 4 | Toward a Relational Cosmopolitanism

Neither the colourless vagueness of cosmopolitanism, nor the fierce self-idolatry of nation-worship, is the goal of human history.

—RABINDRANATH TAGORE (1918, 6)

Putting the problem simply, it seems that cosmopolitan accounts of morality and justice, including many liberal accounts of justice, are often fellow-travellers with old and ugly forms of imperialism, and sometimes rely on exaggerated, indeed false, assumptions about human rationality, independence, and self-sufficiency. On the other hand, anti-cosmopolitan (e.g. communitarian) accounts of morality and justice fail the distant poor and vulnerable in even sharper ways, because they have nothing much to say about action toward those who are distant or different, since they exclude "outsiders" from the domain of justice.

—ONORA O'NEILL (1995, 140)

COMING FROM TWO DIFFERENT philosophical frameworks, two different nations, and two different historical periods, Rabindranath Tagore and Onora O'Neill both identify problematic features of a cosmopolitan approach: it is colorless and vague (lacks particularity, specificity, and richness of detail); it is often allied with imperialism; and it relies on false and exaggerated claims regarding human rationality, independence, and self-sufficiency. Their criticisms of cosmopolitanism capture well the limitations of certain moral cosmopolitan approaches, namely those that are universalist and rely on an atomistic individualist notion of the self abstracted from all social identities and circumstances.[1] Yet cosmopolitanism is the prevailing approach to questions of global justice, and questions of global justice are more important than ever with increased migration, the mobility of global capital across national borders, and the gaps in wealth and opportunities both within and between nations. As I have argued in chapter 3, issues of global gender justice require attention to economic inequality because women are overrepresented among the poor, and processes of globalization impact women more negatively, exacerbating their poverty. This gendered impact of globalization requires gender-specific remedies for poverty alleviation, including projects that focus on the economic empowerment of women as well as on women's social and political empowerment.

In chapter 2, I examined the adequacy of the universal human rights framework to address questions of justice, including gender justice, across national borders, concluding that the human rights approach provides a powerful, but limited, strategy for addressing issues of social justice. Cosmopolitanism provides a different approach to addressing questions of global justice. Yet as we shall see, mainstream cosmopolitan approaches share basic assumptions with the human rights approach, including assumptions about hyperindividualism and the moral irrelevance of social identities. I introduce a "relational cosmopolitanism" based on the work of Rabindranath Tagore that informs the more comprehensive approach that I am proposing to issues of social justice globally.[2] And I show how this relational global justice approach can work for feminist aims, and how the Self-Employed Women's Association (SEWA) and MarketPlace India employ this relational cosmopolitan approach in their work.

In this chapter, I discuss two mainstream moral cosmopolitan positions: individualist cosmopolitanism and institutional cosmopolitanism, arguing that both positions fall short in terms of providing a framework that is adequate to address the systemic character of global inequality, especially the features of the positive recognition of social identities, group oppression, and historical colonialisms and their contemporary legacies. In contrast to these mainstream accounts, relational cosmopolitanism begins with the fundamental fact of our interdependence and the diversity of people and societies, and it includes strong critiques of colonialism and of nationalism. Tagore's cosmopolitanism is fundamentally relational and views our differences as resources for mutual learning. This relational cosmopolitanism fits well with a feminist social justice perspective because both acknowledge our specific and diverse identities, provide an analysis of (asymmetrical) power relations, including economic exploitation and social and political marginalization, and begin with a recognition of our interdependence.

First, I provide some historical background on cosmopolitanism and discuss the variety of ways it has been taken up by contemporary theorists. I focus on moral cosmopolitanism, rather than on political or economic cosmopolitanism. Next, I explicate an influential contemporary account of moral cosmopolitanism advocated by Martha Nussbaum, which I call individualist cosmopolitanism. I argue that this version of cosmopolitanism fails to deliver on its promise to address issues of global justice; it falls short by not incorporating a robust notion of identity as morally relevant and also by failing to acknowledge systemic power differences, both of which are central to feminist analyses and to projects of global justice. I show that Nussbaum's ethical universalist approach to cosmopolitanism falls prey to many of the same criticisms feminists raise about the framework of liberal political theory and deontological ethics, specifically that it is hyperindividualist and abstracted from context.[3] And I argue that her individualist cosmopolitanism neglects power relations and systemic asymmetries of power among individuals, groups, and countries and that these must be accounted for to pursue global justice.[4]

Institutional cosmopolitans, such as Thomas Pogge, address systemic economic inequality and include an analysis of structural injustice that is missing from Nussbaum's individualist cosmopolitanism. However, it still does not address social group or cultural differences, including systemic inequality, such as sexism and racism. Poverty is a highly gendered and racialized issue both within and among nations, so cosmopolitan approaches to global justice and poverty alleviation must include analyses that account for the gendered and racialized structure of the economic system. Pogge's account of institutional cosmopolitanism focuses on our responsibility for poverty, but it lacks an analysis of gender and race. Cosmopolitanism must recognize differences as well as commonalities among people, and this includes differences of power and privilege as well as cultural, ethnic, and religious differences.

I argue that cosmopolitan positions that are unable to account for differences, both in terms of asymmetries of power and in terms of human diversity, are ill equipped to fully address global justice, especially from a feminist perspective. One of the limitations of individualist cosmopolitanism and institutional cosmopolitanism is their grounding in a European philosophical tradition that views difference as anathema to equality and justice. Nussbaum's individualist cosmopolitanism has its historical roots in the Stoics and the Cynics, as well as in Immanuel Kant's political and ethical writings, while Pogge's institutional cosmopolitanism is heavily influenced by John Rawls's political liberal theory of justice.[5] Shifting the theoretical framework of cosmopolitanism away from this philosophical framework of justice may allow us to ask different questions regarding issues that are global in scope, such as how to meet basic needs and how to value difference as a source of connection.[6]

I propose beginning from different historical roots to develop a new conception of cosmopolitanism: one that accounts for the moral significance of robust individual and social group differences, that recognizes structural inequality, and that offers a vision of human relationships and social bonds as central to the human condition. Rabindranath Tagore, a nineteenth-century Indian novelist, poet, painter, and essayist, is well known for embracing cosmopolitanism. Like all cosmopolitan positions, Tagore's cosmopolitanism eschews nationalism; but he goes further in his criticism of nationalism than either Nussbaum or Pogge. Tagore views nations as a destructive force organized around self-interest and greed. He also criticizes nations for colonialism and exploitation of other peoples. He sees this expansionist agenda of nations as contrary to our highest human ideals: harmonious development and disinterested love. While Tagore sees systemic power differences as destructive, he views human differences as integral to our lives. His cosmopolitanism centers differences, not commonality, as the basis on which to connect with and learn from others, and more important, to be affected and transformed by others. Tagore's version of cosmopolitanism, which values differences and sees them as a resource not just for learning about others, but for transforming our selves, our practices, and our traditions, fits well with aims of an anti-imperialist approach to cross-border feminist solidarity.

In the conclusion to this chapter, I connect Tagore's relational cosmopolitanism to Maria Lugones's "world traveling" and Audre Lorde's idea that our differences can serve as the basis for creative change. Rather than denying the moral relevance of difference to forge connection as justice-based moral cosmopolitan approaches do, relational cosmopolitanism begins from the fact of our interdependence and our diversity, and sees social harmony as a normative ideal. This shifts the emphasis in cosmopolitanism from an attempt to build relationships based on our similarities to the acknowledgment that we are in relationships already, and we must learn from our differences. Both SEWA and MarketPlace value diversity while recognizing interdependence, and both organizations have developed practices that foster engagement with people across caste, religious, and national differences. Specifically, MarketPlace has developed the

Global Dialogue program, as well as letters to and from their members to women in the global North, and SEWA has been instrumental in repairing relationships between Hindus and Muslims in Ahmedabad postriots, and it also has been a leader in developing global policy from local knowledge. Within each organization members of different ethnicities, castes, classes, and religions work together toward common goals. Working across, and learning from, differences is central to developing compassion and expanding moral imagination.

Cosmopolitanism: Introduction and Historical Background

The issue of cosmopolitanism currently enjoys a renaissance in philosophical discussion.[7] Cosmopolitanism has a long philosophical history beginning with the Cynics and the Stoics, and continuing through the unlikely trajectory of Immanuel Kant, Rabindranath Tagore, Jane Addams, Jacques Derrida, Martha Nussbaum, Kwame Anthony Appiah, Thomas Pogge, and Seyla Benhabib, as well as others.[8] Cosmopolitanism holds that our moral obligations transcend national boundaries; it is an approach to global justice. One of the primary problems it intends to solve is: what are our obligations to strangers (distant others)? Contemporary philosophers have revived cosmopolitanism as an ethical and political framework appropriate for addressing issues of global justice such as poverty, immigration, cultural diversity, and our ethical and moral obligations to strangers.[9] Cosmopolitanism, as a theory of justice developed by philosophers and political theorists, holds that the scope of justice transcends national boundaries and fellow citizens. The cosmopolitan scope of justice includes not only our compatriots but all humans. One of the fascinating things about contemporary accounts of cosmopolitanism is the breadth of approaches and positions it covers. Broad distinctions can be made among political, legal, moral, economic, and cultural cosmopolitanism, but even within, for instance, moral cosmopolitanism, there are a variety of positions. As Eduardo Mendieta notes: "By now, so much has been written about cosmopolitanism that when we try to survey this work what we encounter are the veritable ruins of a tower of Babel" (2009, 241). He illustrates his point by listing the forms of cosmopolitanism he has encountered in his reading: "imperial; post-modern; patriotic; discrepant; multicultural; rooted; elite; non-elite; left; consumerist; soft; attenuated; comparative; and actually existing" (Mendieta 2009, 241). To his list I would add: vernacular, banal, dialogic, interactional, institutional, equalitarian, sufficientarian, reflexive, and theological. As one surveys the contemporary scholarship on cosmopolitanism, a striking contrast emerges: those approaching cosmopolitanism from a literary, cultural, historical, anthropological, or theological perspective emphasize the multiplicity of cultures, cultural differences and interaction, and hybridity. By contrast, most of those approaching cosmopolitanism from a philosophical or political theory perspective appeal to similarity across cultures and a universal application of standards of justice.[10] Often this universal application of standards of justice prioritizes Western values and ideals, as we saw in chapter 2; this type of universalism is ethnocentric. Anthony Appiah sums up these opposing approaches nicely: cosmopolitanism embodies two ideals—the ideal of universal moral concern and the respect for legitimate difference (Appiah 2006). Unfortunately, these ideals are often contradictory; the ideal of respect for legitimate difference involves the task of understanding and appreciating cultural diversity, whereas proponents of the ideal of universal moral concern argue that cultural and social identities are morally irrelevant.

In the next two sections, I discuss two influential approaches to moral cosmopolitanism: the individualist approach and the institutional approach. I show that the fundamental assumptions of these types of moral cosmopolitanism inhibit rich understandings of interdependence, human diversity and cultural differences, and asymmetries of power. Moral cosmopolitan positions share three features: individualism, impartiality, and universality (Pogge 1992; Kang 2014). Individualism means that the ultimate units of moral concern are individuals, not states, communities, families, or ethnic, racial, or religious groups. Impartiality entails that each person is treated equally as the ultimate unit of moral concern; no one person or group is granted special consideration. Universality enjoins everyone everywhere to treat others as the ultimate unit of moral concern. In other words, everyone adopts the moral stance that all humans are equally the objects of moral concern. One further distinction within moral cosmopolitanism may be helpful; interactional cosmopolitanism applies to the conduct of persons and groups, and assigns direct moral responsibility for the fulfillment of human rights to persons and groups. Nussbaum's individualist cosmopolitanism falls under this category. Institutional cosmopolitanism assigns the responsibility for fulfilling human rights to institutions, and thus the responsibility of persons is indirect. As we shall see, according to institutional cosmopolitans, the responsibility of persons is to work for and maintain just institutions. Indeed, working for just institutions is central to global justice. But this alone will not address systemic inequalities or the background conditions in which those injustices arise. Cosmopolitanism rooted in Western philosophical approaches often rests on particular assumptions associated with Enlightenment philosophy, such as rationality as the defining feature of humanness, and an exaggerated sense of the independence and self-sufficiency of persons.

Some cosmopolitan approaches reject the problematic assumptions implicit in the ethical universalism that Nussbaum and Pogge endorse, namely, an excessive emphasis on rationality, hyperindependence, and self-sufficiency. For instance, "care cosmopolitans" such as Sarah Clark Miller explicitly reject these assumptions in favor of "the primary moral significance of human relationships" and acknowledgment of our dependence, vulnerability, and finitude (Miller 2011, 396).[11] Other cosmopolitan approaches argue that universalist cosmopolitanism, with its roots in Modernity and the Enlightenment, arose in the context of colonial conquest and imperialism. For instance, Walter Mignolo develops a critical cosmopolitanism that centers diversity rather than universality.[12] He demonstrates the way that colonialism is implicated in cosmopolitanism because of the way in which Modernity depends on the process of colonization as a process of expansion and "civilization." He claims that cosmopolitanism must account for "colonial difference" rather than "cultural differences" because colonial difference builds in recognition of the process of domination and exploitation that characterizes the colonial process. Mignolo offers a revised model of cosmopolitanism where the project of diversity, rather than universality, is central (which he terms "diversality"). This centering of diversity, rather than universality, accounts for structural power differences by recognizing that both cultural differences and claims to similarity emerge within unequal power relationships and historical contexts.

Both care cosmopolitans and Mignolo's diversality cosmopolitanism depart from the justice-based, individualist framework predominant in mainstream theories of moral cosmopolitanism. The emphasis on interdependence and vulnerability by care cosmopolitans and Mignolo's reframing cultural difference as colonial difference both add valuable dimensions to moral cosmopolitanism. As I have argued, the recognition of our interdependence, an analysis of structural power differences, and valuing diversity are important for any theory of social justice, in this case global social justice.

In the remainder of this chapter, I explore how the elements of what I have termed "feminist social justice"—acknowledgment of interdependence, recognition of diversity, challenges to asymmetries of power (social, economic, legal, political, and cultural), acknowledgment and criticism of colonialism—can be used for a relational cosmopolitan approach. In the conclusion to this chapter, I develop a feminist cosmopolitanism that acknowledges structural power differences, centers diversity, and sees mutual transformation as key to achieving global social justice.[13] This feminist cosmopolitanism, informed by Tagore's ideas, as well as those of contemporary feminist thinkers, recognizes the importance of both diversity and differential power relationships and offers a promising new approach to questions of moral and political obligation in the context of global interdependence, contested borders and authority of nation-states, and globalization.

Ethical Individualist Cosmopolitanism

In her essay "Patriotism and Cosmopolitanism," Martha Nussbaum examines the limits of patriotism and advocates a cosmopolitan education.[14] She argues that patriotism may serve to undermine the moral ideals of justice and equality, the very ideals that it aims to support.[15] Many features of Nussbaum's argument for cosmopolitanism are attractive, including the criticism of an exaggerated and uncritical American patriotism, the need for more knowledge of other countries, the recognition that many problems cannot be solved nationally but require international cooperation, and the extension of moral obligations outside of national boundaries.

However, in thinking about how cosmopolitanism can be useful for transnational feminist solidarity projects, I believe that there are limitations to Nussbaum's view. Many feminists have challenged the notion of the self at the heart of liberal moral theory, specifically, the emphasis on the rationality and hyperindependence of the self. Having such a view of the self as the lynchpin for global moral concern, I will argue, overemphasizes some aspects of our moral relationships to others, while downplaying other aspects. For instance, Nussbaum sees reason as the primary feature upon which human connection is based; she also sets aside the notion that individual identity, including in terms of social group membership, may be relevant to issues of justice, and her position prizes individualism over interdependence. Approaching moral cosmopolitanism from the framework of the feminist social justice framework that I am proposing reveals certain limitations of a justice-based and individualist cosmopolitanism.

As we shall see, in many ways the ethical individualist cosmopolitan position that Nussbaum advocates mirrors the same assumptions underlying the universal human rights position: hyperindividualism, abstraction from context, and the absence of an explicit power analysis.[16] In contrast to justice-based approaches to ideal moral theory, nonideal moral theory begins from actual situations of injustice and so must take into account considerations of unequal power, historical domination and colonialism, and systemic injustice. As articulated in the Introduction, a feminist social justice framework recognizes these asymmetries of power and advocates a normative framework based on nonexploitation, anti-oppression, and anti-domination. In this section, I discuss and evaluate Nussbaum's cosmopolitan position with respect to this normative framework and in the context of globalization. I think that cosmopolitan theories would do well to start from the position that we are interconnected and interdependent. As Chandra Talpade Mohanty points out: "globalization is an economic, political, and ideological phenomenon that actively brings together the world and its various communities under connected and interdependent discursive and material regimes" (2003, 241).

As I discussed in chapter 3, the effects of globalization disproportionately disadvantage women, resulting in a racialized feminization of poverty. Given this background situation of injustice as unevenly distributed not only over individuals but also over groups whose members share social situations of disadvantage, accounts of global justice would do well to recognize that justice claims rely on recognizing that one's group membership positions people differently in a system of burdens and benefits. As Hye-Ryoung Kang points out, "cosmopolitanism's concern with individual well-being is better addressed by employing the concept of collectivities" (2014, 52). She goes on to argue that collectivities provide a space for vulnerable individuals to discuss and make their claims for justice visible. The organizing work of SEWA and MarketPlace India, which brings poor and lower caste women together to make claims for political and economic justice, is an example of how collectivities can empower vulnerable individuals. Kang suggests that a cosmopolitanism that takes women's collectivities as agents of justice, rather than individuals or nations, is better suited to the task of understanding that "significant injustice has been systematically created among collectivities who are differently situated in the transnationalized social and economic spheres by global factors" (2014, 50). Kang's approach is consistent with a feminist social justice approach that begins from actual situations of injustice; this nonideal approach to justice differs from a moral cosmopolitanism that addresses questions of moral obligation in the abstract.

Many of the criticisms that care ethicists direct toward theories of justice also apply to cosmopolitan theories of justice. In her development of care cosmopolitanism, Sarah Clark Miller criticizes justice-based moral cosmopolitanism for its assumptions of hyperindividualism, abstraction, idealization, and acontextuality. Hyperindividualism is the view of the self as isolated and independent; this atomistic view of the self stands in contrast to the notion of care ethicists' view of the significance of relationships to the self, which holds that the self is best understood as relational. Idealization refers to a particular view of human beings, most often associated with the Kantian tradition, as defined by their rationality, rather than, for instance, their vulnerability or ability to suffer. As we shall see, Nussbaum adopts this view of what is valuable about humans, namely our reason and moral capacity.[17] Abstraction involves abstracting from the particular and specific aspects of our identity to arrive at a shared humanity that is the basis of moral obligation, resulting in an abstract notion of the self. And acontextuality asks us to ignore the context of a situation in our moral deliberations. In contrast to this, the feminist social justice framework recognizes the significance of both identity and context for understanding our moral obligations, as well as the significance of relationships of interdependence, and of power relations, which situate us differently in social and political contexts.

As we shall see, Nussbaum views all specific features of our identities, communities, and social locations as irrelevant to questions of justice. For instance, she insists on viewing particularity as "merely an accident of birth," subordinating particular group affiliations to a recognition of one's common universal humanity. In response to Nussbaum's view of cosmopolitanism relying on this abstract notion of self, Gertrude Himmelfarb notes: "We do not come into the world as free-floating autonomous individuals. We come into it complete with all the particular, defining characteristics that go into a fully formed human being, a being with an identity" (2002, 77). In a different context Seyla Benhabib develops a notion of a "concrete other," that is, an other with a rich particular identity, that complements the view of the "abstract other," which is the self abstracted from all particularities. Benhabib argues that we need both understandings of the self to develop an adequate account of morality and justice (Benhabib 1987). Abstracting the self out of social circumstances, relationships, emotional ties, and power relations, as Nussbaum does in her essay on cosmopolitanism, impoverishes our view of both the self and moral life.

Extending these criticisms from care cosmopolitanism, I argue that justice-based cosmopolitanism because of its commitment to hyperindividualism, abstraction, idealization, and acontextuality overemphasizes certain features of humans and limits itself to addressing moral obligations outside of actual circumstances of inequality and power differences. In other words, this type of cosmopolitan position does not account for asymmetries of power among groups that often result from our particular social locations and group affiliations. These asymmetries of power are often morally relevant because they shape opportunities and life chances. Moreover, because we are already situated in economic and social relationships that position us differently vis-à-vis burdens and benefits, we already have moral obligations to one another based on our different positions in economic and social systems. Finally, the commitment to abstraction in individualist cosmopolitanism asks us to transcend and ignore differences to embrace commonality.

By contrast, I advocate a moral cosmopolitanism that asks us to embrace particularity and specificity. Rather than privileging an abstract rationality as the basis of our commonality, this position is grounded in recognizing our common vulnerability, our interdependence, our particular identities based on culture and social group membership, and our different positions in social and economic systems. A rich understanding of our differences based on our particular identities would, I argue, make possible a mutually transformative interaction of persons or cultures that would result in hybridity and new possibilities.

In examining the view of cosmopolitanism that Nussbaum puts forth in "Patriotism and Cosmopolitanism," we can see how the features of hyperindividualism, abstraction, idealization, and acontextuality are articulated. Nussbaum develops her cosmopolitan position out of the philosophical context of ancient Greek philosophers (Stoics and Cynics) and Immanuel Kant, as well as referring to Rabindranath Tagore's novel *Home and World*. These multiple sources could result in a rich vision for cosmopolitanism; the Stoic model of interdependence could balance Kant's strong commitment to independence. Tagore's deep appreciation of cultural difference and his astute criticisms of colonialism could temper the Kantian reliance on similarity grounded in our rationality and the assumption of equality abstracted from historical and political power relations. But ultimately Nussbaum's cosmopolitanism has more in common with the Kantian tradition than with Tagore or the ancient Greeks.[18]

For example, although Nussbaum draws upon sources that value both interdependence and independence, she ultimately privileges independence. As care cosmopolitans note, a strong view of independence (hyperindividualism) overlooks the fact that we live our lives in relations of dependency and views the self as atomistic rather than as relational. According to Nussbaum, the Stoic model of cosmopolitanism sees the self at the center of concentric circles, which expand outward from smaller, closer group affiliations to all of humanity, for example, family, community, humanity. Relatedly, Stoics hold an organic, interdependent view of humanity. In order to stretch our understanding beyond ourselves and our own circumstances, Nussbaum urges us to engage in a Stoic thought experiment of "world thinking," which involves conceiving "the entire world of human beings as a single body, its many people as so many limbs" (Nussbaum 2002, 10). This organic model stresses human interdependence, but Nussbaum cautions that this interdependence must be tempered by "the fundamental importance of the separateness of people and of fundamental personal liberties" (Nussbaum 2002, 10). In terms of the balance between interdependence and independence, she ultimately emphasizes independence over interdependence.

Not only does she explicitly state the importance of independence, but her approach underscores this. She views our global moral obligations as what each of us owes to others as an individual. While this is an important task for cosmopolitanism, it does not explicitly address the issue that we may have different moral obligations to groups of people based on their situatedness in transnational economic and social structures. By contrast, my feminist social justice approach recognizes interdependence as a primary feature of our lives, and it acknowledges that each of us exists in a web of power relations. While she recognizes that the Stoic model emphasizes interdependence, Nussbaum endorses a commitment to individualism and independence associated with the Kantian view. As we shall see in my analysis of Tagore's cosmopolitanism, taking our interdependence as central to our moral experience may yield a richer view of human relationships and what we owe to one another.

Taking interdependence of humans seriously and acknowledging our vulnerabilities offers a different starting point for human connection and moral obligation than rationality. For instance, Sarah Clark Miller argues that the duty to care arises out of the recognition that human beings have fundamental needs that must be met in order for human flourishing to be realized. This recognition of connection based on vulnerability and needs provides a different starting point from viewing human connection primarily based on reason or rationality, which represents an idealized view of humans.

Both the Stoic notion of cosmopolitanism and Kant's universal moral theory hold that our shared features of reason and moral capacity allow us to identify with the larger human community; Nussbaum agrees with this privileging of reason and rationality. As Nussbaum puts it, "We should recognize humanity wherever it occurs, and give its fundamental ingredients, reason and moral capacity, our first allegiance and respect" (Nussbaum 2002, 7).[19] She finds in the Stoics support for believing that what is most important about humans is our capacity for moral reasoning: "what is especially fundamental about them [people], most worthy of respect and acknowledgement: their aspirations to justice and goodness and their capacities for reasoning in this connection" (Nussbaum 2002, 8). She notes that this Stoic idea is the source of Kant's kingdom of ends, stating: "One should always behave so as to treat with equal respect the dignity of reason and moral choice in every human being," and like Kant, she appeals to universal moral norms. She emphasizes that it is capacity for reason, especially moral reason, that is the grounding for human connection: "the basis for human community is the worth of reason in each and every human being" (Nussbaum 1997, 7).

Might there be other grounds on which human connection could be based, for instance, the capacity to suffer? Feminist philosophers, disability theorists, and postcolonial thinkers have criticized privileging the capacity for reason as the most important human quality, and especially the quality on which moral inclusion depends.[20] In the history of philosophy, often rationality has been used to exclude some groups of people, such as women, foreigners, and slaves, from being fully human. Nussbaum herself recognizes this limitation in *Frontiers of Justice* when she tries to rework justice theory to include people with disabilities, inhabitants of poor countries, and animals as worthy of inclusion in the moral community.[21]

Focusing on reason and moral capacity as the quintessential human features fails to account for the historical tendencies of colonialism to use reason and moral capacity to exclude white women, non-Europeans, and people of color from the human community. Postcolonial and decolonial theorists warn against the conflation of Western norms and values with universal norms (Mignolo 2011). Historically, colonizers associated rationality and reason with Western cultures and lauded Western ideas of abstract reason and rationality as the teleological endpoint of human civilization. Nussbaum defines what is worthy of respect and valuable in humans on the very features that have been used to historically exclude groups of people. A cosmopolitanism that hopes to be truly inclusive of humanity should be attentive to assumptions about what constitutes or is most valuable about "the human."

Her cosmopolitan approach, which centers reason and moral capacity, differs from other approaches that emphasize human vulnerability and interdependence or diversity, such as that of care cosmopolitans, or Mignolo's diversality cosmopolitanism. Nussbaum uses Indian writer Rabindranath Tagore to reinforce her argument that cosmopolitanism should hold sway over nationalism and patriotism. Relying on Tagore's novel, *Home and World*, an intense narrative about love, loyalty, and the independence movement in India, Nussbaum claims that the message of the novel where the nationalist is the anti-hero supports "world" over "home," making the case for cosmopolitanism. A prolific essayist, artist, and fiction writer, Tagore's ideas about cosmopolitanism can be found in multiple sources of his written work, as well as his ideas about education and culture that have been instantiated in the school he founded.[22] Later in this chapter, I explore his ideas on cosmopolitanism in more detail, suggesting that his model of cosmopolitanism offers a non-Eurocentric, mutually influential, dynamic interaction among people and cultures.

Cosmopolitanism offers the possibility of a robust view of social and cultural differences, such as the view in Kwame Anthony Appiah's rooted cosmopolitanism, "a world in which everyone is a rooted cosmopolitanism, attached to a home of his or her own, with its own cultural particularities, but taking pleasure from the presence of other, different places, that are home to other, different people" (Appiah 2002, 22). While Nussbaum acknowledges the importance of our concrete circumstances and affiliations, she views them as arbitrary and morally irrelevant. Ultimately, she holds that identities and affiliations always give way to our shared humanity. She argues that nationality is an "accident of birth" and so should hold no moral weight, likewise with our ethnic, racial, and gender identities (2002, 7). Abstracting out from all the particular features of our identities leaves us with only an abstract notion of the self. This abstract notion of the self cannot account for our different positions in social relations and networks of power.

Nussbaum argues that because gender, race, ethnicity, and nationality are merely "accidents of birth," they ought not matter. But they do. Her denial of the moral relevance of identity categories makes it difficult to see that many social identity categories are shaped by structural oppression, and thus put members of certain groups in specific situations in relation to their group identity; for example, women are more vulnerable to sexual harassment and rape, African Americans are more vulnerable to police violence because of racism, and so on. Because members of ethnic, racial, and gender groups are positioned differently in society, this impacts on how they are affected by sexual violence or police violence. Although our gender, race, ethnicity, nationality, and social status can rightly be called "accidents of birth," it does not follow that in societies in which opportunities and costs are distributed with respect to these identities that they remain morally irrelevant.

However, Nussbaum agrees with the Cynics that "Class, rank, status, national origin and location, and even gender are treated by the Cynics as secondary and *morally irrelevant* attributes. The first form of moral affiliation for the citizen should be her affiliation with rational humanity; and, this, above all, should define the purposes of her conduct" (Nussbaum 1997, 5, emphasis mine). She supports not giving moral weight to our particular affiliations in favor of a moral universalism based on human similarity. As I have argued, viewing our identities and social group memberships as morally irrelevant fails to recognize the ways that our identities position us in unequal relationships of power.

But then, in what seems like a departure from the view that identities are of no consequence for cosmopolitanism, Nussbaum agrees with the Stoics that we do not have to give up our "special affections and identifications, whether ethnic or gender-based or religious," and indeed, we may even "think of our identity as partly constituted by them" (2002, 9). Nussbaum's acknowledging of the importance of identities and that our identities are partly constituted by our "ethnic, gender-based or religious" affiliations reveals that she allows that identities are existentially important, although morally irrelevant.[23] Yet identities are morally relevant in two ways: first, as I have argued, in societies structured by asymmetrical power relations among members of different classes, races, genders, and sexualities, identities do have moral relevance. And, second, as I discuss in my Introduction, our identities are partly shaped by recognition, and the misrecognition of identity can inflict harm by viewing others in a distorted manner, particularly if the misrecognition denies aspects of their identity that they feel are constitutive of themselves. Recognizing someone in his or her particularity is an aspect of overcoming social oppression. In my discussion of Tagore's cosmopolitanism, I demonstrate that embracing a robust notion of identity, including cultural identity, highlights the ways that we can learn to connect across our differences, and not only on the basis of our similarities.

An idealized view of humans emphasizes rationality as the basis of our similarity. This privileging of similarity over difference extends not only to this idealized view of the self but to the goals of moral reasoning as well. Nussbaum repeatedly refers to the presumed outcome of moral reasoning as "substantive universal values of justice and right," "the world community of justice and reason," and "the right of other human beings to life, liberty, and the pursuit of happiness" (Nussbaum 2002, 5, 8, 13–14). Here she moves from the privileging of the shared capacity of moral reason as quintessentially human to an endorsement of substantive values. Each of these passages appeals to a rights-based model of justice centered on liberty (negative freedom), individual choice, and justice abstracted from the history of material and social inequality. Nussbaum claims that cosmopolitanism is "in grave jeopardy . . . when we find that the very values of equality, personhood and human rights that Kant defended, and indeed the Enlightenment itself, are derided in some quarters as mere ethnocentric vestiges of Western imperialism" (Nussbaum 1997, 24).[24]

But as we saw in chapter 2, there is not universal agreement on values. Lila Abu-Lughod's caution bears repeating here: "We may want justice for women, but can we accept that there might be different ideas about justice and that different women might want, or choose, different futures from what we envision as best? We must consider that they might be called to personhood, so to speak, in a different language" (Abu-Lughod 2002, 787–788). Respect for diversity and plurality must extend to the critical examination of our own principles and cherished ideals. If cosmopolitan calls for learning about others, as Nussbaum claims, then self-reflection about the historical context of the Enlightenment and its values is an important task. By acknowledging the pluralism of evaluative standards, we open ourselves up to the transformative potential of human diversity.

Applying Western liberal values and frameworks in every situation may inhibit new ways of thinking about how those values themselves may obscure new ways of negotiating moral conflict. For example, Indian feminist Nivedita Menon criticizes Nussbaum for imposing a Western liberal framework on dowry and religious (personal) law. Menon argues that Nussbaum's "strong universalism" wrongly sees specific Western values as universal. Because of this, Menon believes that Nussbaum's solution—seeing disagreements over dowry as a conflict among liberal values that can be resolved through rational debate—fails to take into account the political, historical, and cultural context. Menon notes that the persistence of the practice of dowry has to do with a variety of factors; agreement about its legality is not one of them. She notes "the Central Dowry Prohibition Act was passed in 1961, amended under pressure from the women's movement in 1984. The problems have had to do with implementation, loopholes in the law, the overwhelming pressure of patriarchal family ideology—all factors that have to do with power and politics, rather than lack of reasoned debate, a lack which Nussbaum is so eager to make good" (Menon 2002, 163).

Menon, I suggest, takes a nonideal approach to moral issues, viewing them in their social, political, and historical context. Taking a nonideal approach means that issues of power and politics, as well as cultural understandings, must be taken into account when we seek to resolve moral issues. This implies that the strong universalism, which as Menon points out is ethnocentric by assuming Western values are universal, must be replaced by a weaker version of universalism that arises from the interaction of cultural and moral paradigms, rather than the imposition of Western liberalism.

All justice claims rely on a normative framework, including feminist social justice. How can we employ a normative framework without assuming and imposing particular universal values? Here Carol Gould's distinction between abstract universality and concrete universality may be useful. She states that abstract universality often results in imposing "Western liberal conceptions of norms of development and rights under the guise of the universally human" (Gould 2004, 51). By contrast, in "concrete universality" norms develop out of conversation and consensus.[25] Gould is not alone in advocating for developing cross-cultural understandings and agreements through dialogue; many transnational feminists also advocate this strategy. Employing "concrete universality," where norms emerge from dialogue and consensus, can accommodate the reality of cultural and social differences, and also our different positions in economic and social systems.

Recognizing that we are differently situated reveals that we stand in varying and unequal obligations of responsibility to one another, in part based on the unearned advantages we derive from these unequal social and political structures. For instance, while the humanitarian impulse of individualist cosmopolitanism is obviously better than indifference or apathy to the plight of others, its "helping model" obscures the ways in which peoples and nations are connected through institutions and transnational structures, and the ways that these connections already implicate us in our responsibility for the consequences of these tragedies, including natural disasters. For instance, the differences in the infrastructures of wealthy and nonwealthy nations are, in part, a consequence of the unjust global economic order, which is discussed further in the next section. But, of course, unjust economic orders occur within nations as well. The devastation wrought by Hurricane Katrina in the United States in 2005 provides a vivid example of the ways that although all humans are vulnerable to natural disasters, we are not all vulnerable in the same ways, or to the same degrees. Any account of humanitarian aid as disaster relief should recognize that some groups of people might be more affected by the disaster because of social and economic marginalization. Recognizing the real differences of social locations and histories of both individuals and groups means that our similarities should not be the sole basis of our ethical concern.

Instead, social justice often requires the recognition of difference and the addressing of past harms. For instance, in postapartheid South Africa, the Truth and Reconciliation Commission was set up to "enable South Africans to come to terms with their past on a morally accepted basis and to advance the cause of reconciliation" (Truth and Reconciliation Commission 2018). One of the subcommittees, the Reparation and Rehabilitation subcommittee, was charged with ensuring that the Truth Commission process restored victims' dignity and to formulate policy proposals and recommendations on rehabilitation and healing of the survivors, their families, and communities (Truth and Reconciliation Commission 2018).

Recognizing the harm done to a group on the basis of their racial identity can be an important part of the healing process, and even considered as part of the necessary reparations. In another example, in 1994 the Florida legislature awarded $2.1 million to the descendants of those killed in the Rosewood massacre to "grant equity, justice, fairness and healing" to the survivors. As Rosewood descendant Arnett Doctor said: "History has taught us that unless we address the inequities of the past, they are due to repeat themselves" (Fallstrom 1994). Significantly, both the South African and the US reparations cases mention dignity and healing; moreover, recognition that groups were targeted because of race was an important part of the process of reconciliation and healing.

As I have argued, the feminist social justice framework respects differences as significant to one's lived experience, acknowledges these differences as morally relevant, and includes acknowledgment of differences of privilege and power. I have shown that Nussbaum's model for cosmopolitanism acknowledges the importance of identity, but not its moral relevance, and does not discuss our moral obligations in the context of our asymmetrical power relations and social positions. I believe that, because of this, the individualist approach to cosmopolitanism only partially addresses our global obligations to one another. Significantly, it separates the moral realm from the political and economic realm, and relies on individuals to adopt a cosmopolitan attitude, rather than promoting institutional change to rectify inequalities.

Near the end of her essay, Nussbaum offers four arguments in support of cosmopolitan citizenship: we learn more about ourselves; we make progress solving problems that require international cooperation; we recognize our moral obligations to others; and consistency—if we appeal to commonality to overcome racial and ethnic differences within nations, then why not appeal to shared humanity across national borders? Examining each of these claims more closely allows us to see some of the implications of the individualist cosmopolitan view.

At first, the argument that we learn more about ourselves seems anti-cosmopolitanism. After all, isn't the point of cosmopolitanism to go beyond our individual selves, and our "citizen-of-a-nation" selves as well? By embracing cosmopolitanism, we are, in some sense, downplaying the importance of ourselves in favor of humanity. But Nussbaum argues that learning about other cultures—for instance, family structure, gender, sexuality, treatment of the elderly—exposes the particularity and contingency of our own cultural practices. This, in turn, undermines the idea that our way is the only way, or the best way to do things. Questioning one's own cultural practices and rejecting ethnocentrism align with cosmopolitanism's goals of respecting diversity. Yet the individualist cosmopolitan approach misses the dimension of power relations, which is central to a feminist social justice approach.

Many feminists also argue that cross-cultural studies denaturalize and destabilize the taken-for-grantedness of our own cultural practices. In this way, the study of other cultures is intimately tied to knowledge about our own culture, especially the limitedness of the assumptions underlying our practices and institutions. However, simply valuing other cultures for what we can learn about ourselves falls short of a real feminist engagement that would value studying the history and practices of other cultures to learn about the other culture, not simply one's own. Moreover, in addition to simply undermining our own assumptions about social and cultural norms, a feminist cosmopolitanism would account for systemic power differences and structural oppression. In other words, it is not only that my own cultural practices are particular and contingent (and by implication, I assume, no better than yours), but that the "practices of my culture" such as unbridled militarism, or disproportionate consumption of energy and food resources, directly shape the "practices of your culture." The global scope of cosmopolitanism should make us recognize that differences of power and privilege do not magically disappear when moral obligations extend across national borders but are, in many ways, exacerbated.

Nussbaum cites food supply, population, and environmental issues as three examples of problems that require international cooperation. Feminist activists have been engaging in global dialogue about these issues, as well as many others. Transnational feminist networks and alliances have contributed to the visibility and steps toward solutions of these issues. For example, Vandana Shiva successfully spearheaded an education campaign and boycott against multinational food conglomerate Monsanto. In the wake of structural adjustment policies and the resulting liberalization of trade, Monsanto bought up Indian seed companies, sold hybrid seeds that required fertilizer, and priced both the seeds and the fertilizer out of the range of most independent Indian farmers, resulting in massive suicides among farmers in India. Shiva links food supply and environmental issues to globalization, the neoliberal global economy, militarization, and the US war on terror. Shiva's approach to solving global problems reveals the connections among the various problems as well as exposes the inequalities among nations that contribute to the problems in the first place. Calling simply for international cooperation obscures the different interests and power that are often at play in international concerns such as environmental crises. Moreover, as Shiva points out, issues of food supply, population, and environmental crisis are interconnected. These complex problems need to be addressed in a variety of ways, including transnational networks of activists working simultaneously within the national and international arenas.[26]

The model of international cooperation that Nussbaum proposes assumes a voluntary coming together of nations to solve problems that they share because the problems cross borders, such as climate change or natural disasters. This idea of voluntary international cooperation fails to recognize that nations are already deeply intertwined, not only to solve common problems but in the ways that wealthy nations play a causal role in environmental degradation of poorer nations, through resource extraction, the outsourcing of waste, or laws that privilege transnational corporations, in the first place.

Individualist cosmopolitanism urges individuals to recognize that our moral obligations are global, rather than local or national. But it does not articulate the many ways that we are already in relation to one another through our various unequal positions within our nations and among nations. In her third argument, Nussbaum suggests that an appeal to Kantian universality would make Americans realize that our high standard of living cannot be universalized, and thus should prompt us to recognize the injustice of maintaining such a high standard of living while others struggle to get their basic needs met. While Nussbaum suggests that such recognition of injustice would have large-scale economic and political consequences, she does not explicitly discuss that our high standard of living literally comes at the cost of others. Surely, she knows that the history of imperialism and colonialism, the current inequalities in global resources, the biases of global economic policies toward wealthy countries, and the exploitation of labor all make it possible for some individuals to maintain a high standard of living at the expense of others. In addition to an abstract appeal to Kantian universality, an analysis of how we are already connected through economic and social relationships may serve to better explain our cross-border moral obligations and motivate us to act. I explicate just such an approach, Iris Marion Young's social connection model of responsibility, in chapter 5. Of course, there are situations of global injustice that fall outside of our economic and social relationships to one another, and for these an appeal to Kantian universality may suffice.

Nussbaum's fourth argument for cosmopolitan citizenship, consistency—if we overlook difference to forge national identities, then we should overlook difference to forge a global human identity—again overlooks the moral relevance of difference. Feminist, critical race, postcolonial and decolonial theorists have all argued for the moral relevance of difference. Feminists such as Audre Lorde, Maria Lugones, and Chandra Talpade Mohanty argue that difference provides a resource for connection rather than an impediment to it (Lorde 1984; Lugones 1987; Mohanty 2003). Likewise, recognizing one's social location, or postionality, allows one to understand oneself as involved in a matrix of power relations that structure society and unequally confer power and privilege (Hill-Collins 1990; Crenshaw 1991). Color-blindness works against those with nondominant racial identities in a racist society. As Carol Pateman and Charles Mills have demonstrated convincingly, citizenship is, in fact, constituted on sexual and racial difference (Pateman 1988; Mills 1997; Pateman and Mills 2007). To extend this "difference-blind" strategy from nation to globe simply enlarges the scope of the error. Ignoring the moral relevance of difference in societies structured by difference makes it difficult to perceive and change systemic patterns of oppression and exploitation.

To sum up, I have questioned the assumptions of a self that is abstracted from social context and identity and the idealized view of rationality as the quintessential human quality that underlies individualist cosmopolitanism. I have offered critiques of this view that point to the importance of a robust notion of cultural and social difference and the importance of acknowledging that these differences may be morally relevant in societies that structure opportunities and life chances around such differences. A robust notion of difference can allow us to learn from those with different social group identities and those from different cultures. Nussbaum offers two resources for bridging these differences, cultivating our emotion of compassion and expanding our moral imaginations. In the conclusion to this book, I expand on moral imagination as a resource for social and political change.

Individualist cosmopolitanism does not explicitly articulate the role of structural injustice and economic inequality, and our interconnections through these relationships in its analysis of our global moral obligations. Additionally, its staunch commitment to individualism makes individual actions, rather than institutional change, bear the weight of global justice. In the next section, I turn to an analysis of institutional cosmopolitanism to assess it as a framework for global justice.

Institutional Cosmopolitanism

Like individualist cosmopolitans, institutional cosmopolitans maintain that justice ought to have a global scope. Both approaches base their argument on an acceptance of universal human rights, but individualist cosmopolitanism (also referred to as interactional cosmopolitanism) focuses on individuals, while institutional cosmopolitanism focuses on institutions.[27] Both types of cosmopolitans argue that those in wealthy countries bear moral responsibility for poverty and poverty-related deaths in poor countries, but individualist cosmopolitans assign direct responsibility to persons and groups for these preventable deaths, whereas institutional cosmopolitans assign indirect responsibility. In other words, while individualist cosmopolitans advocate charitable giving and humanitarian aid, institutional cosmopolitans believe we have a shared responsibility to change institutions by supporting just practices and institutions. Moreover, "one ought not to participate in an unjust institutional scheme (one that violates human rights) without making reasonable efforts to aid its victims and to promote institutional reform" (Pogge 1992, 50).

In this section, I discuss Thomas Pogge's influential account of institutional cosmopolitanism, which goes beyond individualist cosmopolitanism, by arguing that if justice has a global scope, then the moral responsibility for preventable deaths from hunger or easily eradicable disease lies with those who benefit from keeping unjust global systems in place. Institutional cosmopolitanism relies on a rights framework, but shifts from an individual understanding to an institutional understanding. Pogge redefines a right as a claim that someone makes on an unjust social system. This move switches rights from an individual remedy to claim goods or services, to an issue of access and opportunity. The responsibility for ensuring that systems are just is one that is shared by all; hence, the rights claim made against the unjust social system simultaneously confers an obligation on everyone in society to actively work for a system that does not disadvantage individuals or members of groups. This shift provides a way to criticize systemic injustice: when institutions violate individual rights, the institutions need to be changed, and those benefiting the most from the unjust institutions have greater responsibility to change them.

In *World Poverty and Human Rights: Cosmopolitan Responsibilities and Reforms*, Thomas Pogge sets out a cosmopolitan approach that bases our moral responsibility for others, not on their similarity to us, but because we are responsible for upholding unjust global institutions that lead to their impoverishment and, often, death. Like Nussbaum, he questions the relevance of nation-state boundaries as the limit of our moral obligations to one another. But he argues that global moral obligations hold because we all participate in, and are connected through, a global economic and institutional order. Where other philosophers see cosmopolitan justice as a matter of positive duty, helping others when we can, he sees it as a negative duty, not to unduly harm others. He formulates human duties in the standard way; negative duties are those duties that enjoin us not to harm others, and positive duties are those duties that prescribe helping others. Generally, moral philosophers hold that negative duties trump positive duties. In terms of positive duties, many moral philosophers acknowledge that we may prioritize helping those we know or those closest to us, including family, friends, community members, and compatriots (Pogge 2002). Pogge argues that we share a moral responsibility for global poverty because we support a global economic, institutional order that impoverishes. Because we share a responsibility for an unjust and harmful global economic and institutional order, our negative duty not to harm others by supporting a system that impoverishes them is invoked. This reverses the usual order of moral priority: it is more important to protect a stranger (or distant other, as philosophers like to call them) than it is to positively benefit one's kin or compatriots (2002, 132). He argues that because "all human beings are now participants in a single, global institutional scheme—involving such institutions as the territorial state and a system of international law and diplomacy as well as a world market for capital, goods, and services—that all human rights violations have come to be, at least potentially, everyone's concern" (Pogge 1992, 51).

Contrast this way of viewing our global moral obligations with an individualist cosmopolitanism. The individualist cosmopolitan grounds our global moral obligation on commonality and a shared humanity. On both views, alleviating poverty of those in other nations is seen as morally right. But the individualist cosmopolitan position views this as helping others, whereas the institutional cosmopolitan position views this as not harming others, which is a more fundamental moral duty. Viewing our global moral obligations in this way also changes what is required to fulfill them. On the individualist cosmopolitan view, we can give money to charity to discharge our positive duty of helping those in poor countries; on the institutional cosmopolitan view, we must change institutions so that they do not continue to disadvantage poor people in poor countries.

As we saw in our discussion of individualist cosmopolitanism, grounding our global moral obligations in a common humanity overlooks differences of identity, of social location, and of power. Differences of identity need to be addressed for social justice to include elements of social recognition that help to counter social marginalization; and differences of social location and of power are important in accounts of global justice in order to address material and economic inequities, and structural injustice. The institutional cosmopolitan account, unlike the individualist cosmopolitan position, addresses issues of structural and institutional injustice. However, it fails to address the issue of social recognition as an aspect of social justice.

Institutional cosmopolitans, such Charles Bietz and Thomas Pogge, hold that our global moral responsibility is to promote just institutions that do not result in global systems that impoverish millions of people. As Pogge notes, "Poverty so extensive and severe as to cause 18 million deaths a year requires a reflective moral response from each and every one of us" (2002, 145). The institutional cosmopolitan position makes significant claims on us in terms of our moral responsibility, including that we should work to change the unjust global economic and institutional order. Through a series of arguments in *World Poverty and Human Rights*, Pogge establishes that those from wealthy countries, because they benefit from the unjust global economic order, are responsible for deaths from poverty because these deaths are avoidable. Moreover, he claims these deaths are avoidable without even great sacrifice on the part of wealthy individuals or wealthy countries. He shores up his argument with specific details about international economic institutions such as the World Bank and the International Monetary Fund, but his argument also includes a rebuttal to those who blame poverty on corruption and mismanagement of the nation, rather than the injustice of the global economic and political order. Pogge calls the blaming of poverty on local and national factors "explanatory nationalism." In contrast to this, he argues that we share moral responsibility for global poverty because we support (and benefit from) a global economic and institutional order that impoverishes. He claims that "As ordinary citizens of the rich countries, we are deeply implicated in these harms" (Pogge 2002, 142). Our participation in these unjust economic and institutional orders means that we are also responsible for the ways that they impact other countries.

Here is a brief sketch of his main argument: International bodies such as the United Nations, as well as the governments of countries, recognize whoever is in power regardless of how they came to power. This recognition confers international borrowing privilege (the ability to borrow money from the International Monetary Fund [IMF] and World Bank) and international resource privilege (the ability to extract, possess, and sell resources). These privileges help to prop up despotic and unjust governments, as well as providing an attractive incentive for those in resource-rich countries to take power by military coup. This means that corrupt and despotic state governments are, at least in part, the product of an unjust global economic and institutional order for which those in wealthy countries (who have the most power in the system and have the most to gain) are responsible. Because citizens in wealthy countries are responsible for corrupt and despotic governments elsewhere, we cannot fall back on explanatory nationalism as though global economic and political institutions do not have a role in how and when these governments are recognized as legitimate.

Given the global economy and the power of wealthy nations to set the agenda for global economic policy, to determine political recognition in international organizations such as the United Nations, and to control international trade agreements, this analysis of structural injustice at the global level seems correct. As citizens, our passive participation in these global systems of injustice weakens a more robust democracy where citizens would actively work to change the unjust economic and institutional order, which is dominated and controlled by wealthy countries.

Democracy involves the fulfillment not only of important rights, but also of important responsibilities of citizens. To the extent that citizens abandon the responsibility that is exercised in their name, their country is less than fully democratic. Most citizens of the affluent states are abandoning this responsibility insofar as they choose to understand very little about how vast quantities of imported resources they consume are acquired and about the impact that the terms of such acquisitions have in the countries where these resources originate. (Pogge 2002, 166)

This lack of understanding of, and attention to, where our consumables originate and under what circumstances they are produced and imported makes us culpable in participating in and perpetuating the unjust global economic and institutional order. Pogge urges us to challenge and change the institutions that perpetuate international resource privilege; he even suggests a "global levy on the use of natural resources to support economic development in the poorest areas" (Pogge 1992, 62). Another way that the global economic order is skewed in favor of wealthy countries and the wealthy within them is through international speculative and commodity markets: "a change in Japanese interest rates or a speculative frenzy of short-selling on the Chicago Futures Exchange, can literally make the difference between life and death for large numbers of people half a world away—in Africa, for example, where many countries depend upon foreign borrowing and cash crop exports" (Pogge 1992, 66).

In addition to trade, import and export laws and policies, and international resource privilege, the conditions under which products are made directly affect the lives of the producers, especially the working poor in the global South, as I have discussed in chapter 3. As consumers, we have a moral obligation to learn about the origins and conditions under which the products that we purchase are made and traded. As we shall see, this part of Pogge's argument has similarities with Iris Marion Young's social connection model of political responsibility. Her social connection model sees persons as connected through institutions and structures, and holds that our relationships as producers and consumers connect us across national borders. Because of this, we have a political responsibility to ensure that the conditions under which products are made are fair and just.

In chapter 5, I extend Young's argument by showing that we have an obligation to support alternative trade, now known as Fair Trade. Pogge and Young both discuss relations of production and consumption as sites where global justice can be enacted by challenging the prevailing unjust global economic institutions. Even if people in wealthy countries are "too selfish" to give up their national resource privilege, Pogge claims that, by thinking about the ways that their consumption impacts on those in

poor countries, "they will at least better understand how they are caus-
ally connected to poverty and oppression in the developing world. They
will better understand that they and their countries face here not merely
opportunities for occasional charitable contributions, but severe harms to
which their economic practices and policies are substantially contributing
and which they therefore have a weighty duty to mitigate" (2002, 166). He
also notes: "Their [the poor's] very survival often crucially depends on our
consumption choices, which may determine the price of their foodstuffs
and their opportunities to find work" (Pogge 2002, 199). In chapter 3, I have
made some connections between the lives and livelihoods of women in the
global South and their reliance on the consumption choices of those in the
global North, as well structural and institutional conditions. MarketPlace
India, whose entire production is done by poor women in India, and who
markets the goods primarily to women in the United States, is a prime
example of the connections between producers in the global South and
consumers in the global North.

Institutional cosmopolitanism offers a theory of global justice that accounts for structural and systemic injustice. As I have discussed in chapter 3,
recognizing the unequal effects of neoliberal economic globalization is an
important aspect of global justice, and to do so, we must recognize the
ways that unjust global economic institutions are responsible for ongoing
deprivation and misery of the world's poorest people. Institutional cosmopolitanism also enjoins us to change those unjust institutions because
we (those in wealthy countries) bear moral responsibility for them and
also benefit from them. So, in short, institutional cosmopolitanism calls
upon us to work for a just global economic and institutional order not because by doing so we go beyond our moral duty, but because by failing to
do so we do not fulfill our moral duty. We are responsible for the effects
of the unjust systems that we support, even if our support is passive and
unintentional. When 18–20 million people a year are dying from hunger
and treatable diseases, we need to work for a fair and just global system
that does not result in these preventable deaths: "In such a case of avoidable deprivations, we are confronted not by persons who are merely poor
and starving but also by *victims of an institutional scheme—impoverished
and starved*" (Pogge 1992, 56, emphasis mine). As I discuss in chapter 5,
Iris Marion Young's theory of political responsibility also calls upon us to
work for a just economic and institutional global order.

Institutional cosmopolitanism provides an important analysis.
Significantly, it accounts for the structural injustice of an unfair global
economic order and calls upon us to work to change the institutions

that perpetuate it. However, Pogge pays scant attention to other types of structural injustice, such as sexism and racism. Sexism and racism are intertwined with economic structural analyses because systems of labor are in part organized by sex and race. Not only is an analysis of racism, sexism, and gender issues absent from his account, his treatment of these issues trivializes them. His singular focus on economic injustice obscures the interconnections between economic injustice and other types of systemic injustice.

When gender arises as an issue in the context of violence against women, it is treated as a "special interest" issue. In his discussion of human rights violations, Pogge claims that human rights can only be violated by a government, or an agent or representative of the government, not by individuals: "Human rights can be violated by governments, certainly, and by government agencies and officials, by the general staff of an army at war, and probably also by the leaders of a guerilla movement or of a large corporation—but not by a petty criminal or by a violent husband" (2002, 57–58). Using the example of a violent husband as not violating human rights fails to recognize the structural and systemic patterns of violence against women. Moreover, his view that domestic violence is not a human rights violation illustrates once again that human rights has a limited purview in terms of countering structural injustice.

Excluding issues of violence against women as human rights violations goes against the United Nations 1993 Vienna Declaration and Programme of Action that recognizes gender-based violence as a violation of human rights. No account of justice, including global justice, can be complete if it fails to analyze systemic injustice based on social identity and location, such as gender and race. We live in a world in which these features make a difference to our life chances and opportunities, and in order to work toward a world in which they no longer condition our life chances and opportunities, we need to recognize that social and economic marginalization often go hand in hand and that patriarchy and white supremacy are forms of systemic injustice. As I have discussed in chapter 3, any account of globalization and economic justice must include a gender analysis because women are among the poorest in every country and are differentially impacted by the economic policies of neoliberal globalization.

Recent feminist work points out the lack of gender analysis in Pogge's work with respect to his discussion of resource privilege. As is the case for other economic goods, women are more negatively affected by the distribution and control of resources. Resource-rich countries suffer in specific ways from the systems of global injustice that confer resource privilege on corrupt or despotic leaders. From the perspective of those producing goods and laboring to extract resources, the resource privilege turns into a resource curse. This resource curse has three aspects: it exacerbates conflict, it enshrines rulers who use force instead of the rule of law, and it appropriates the profit from the labor of the population. In each of these areas, women are affected differently and more negatively than men (Wiser 2014). One of the ways that women are affected differently is that they are more likely to suffer gender-based violence such as rape in conflict-ridden countries and countries ruled by force. Recognizing gender-based violence as a consequence of the unjust global institutional and economic order reinforces the importance of a gender analysis. Institutional cosmopolitanism must thereby attend to gender in two ways: by recognizing that the impact of the unjust global economic and institutional order is gendered in its effects, for example, the differential impact of economic neoliberalization on women; and by extending its analysis to include gender oppression as a form of systemic and institutional injustice, for example, sexual and gender-based violence.

Both individualist cosmopolitanism and institutional cosmopolitanism enlarge the scope of justice beyond family, community, and nation to the globe and also provide an account of our moral responsibility to others beyond these familiar relationships. Nussbaum's approach seeks to justify our moral responsibility on the basis of our shared humanity, whereas Pogge shows that we owe moral concern because we bear the moral responsibility for the harm in the first place. His account of global structural injustice is, as he states, compatible with any number of political positions and relies on a very thin moral universalism. However, his analysis ignores the gendered dimension of poverty and globalization, which are integral to any structural analysis, especially one that views preventable death from poverty as the key moral issue.

Moreover, the moral cosmopolitanism of both Nussbaum and Pogge adheres to a staunch individualism, which makes human commonality bear the explanatory weight in a cosmopolitan theory. Assuming that people are independent, rather than interdependent, means that we must justify why we have moral obligations to people we do not know. Usually that justification is based on our similarity to one another. Both the individualist and the institutional cosmopolitan positions begin from assumptions that individuals are independent from one another, and that our identities and social group affiliations are irrelevant to considerations of justice. For these approaches, which base our moral obligations to others on our similarity to them, considerations of identity, tradition, and cultural differences serve as obstacles to our global moral responsibility to others. In the next section, I introduce a cosmopolitan position that I call relational cosmopolitanism, which explicitly values differences of social identities and cultural traditions, and begins from the idea that humans are interdependent.

Relational Cosmopolitanism

Instead of emptying out the "richness and color" of everyday lived experience into a kind of abstract rationality, cosmopolitanism can instead highlight what can be gained from multiple and diverse experiences, perspectives, and traditions. Relational cosmopolitans value tradition and begin from particularity rather than an abstract universal conception of reason; they emphasize that diversity is at the heart of the cosmopolitan project.[28] Focusing on diversity not as something to be overlooked, but as a resource for learning and understanding provides a fundamentally different starting point for cosmopolitanism. For this perspective, I think Rabindranath Tagore is particularly instructive. As mentioned, Nussbaum also draws upon Tagore when she discusses cosmopolitanism. She interprets Tagore's cosmopolitanism as similar to her own view; for instance, she claims that he prioritizes a type of abstract identity associated with being human over particular identities. And she associates Tagore's cosmopolitanism with a type of free-floating secular humanism that seeks to transcend local attachments. Contra Nussbaum, I elucidate the ways that Tagore's cosmopolitanism is a mediation between the local and the global, rather than a repudiation of the local for the global. I argue that Tagore offers a form of cosmopolitanism not easily assimilated into neo-Enlightenment versions (such as Nussbaum's which relies heavily on Kant). Instead, Tagore provides a model of a cosmopolitanism rooted in India, cognizant of the importance of cultural differences, and well aware of power relations. His cosmopolitanism criticizes values associated with modernity and the West, and provides a source of resistance to imperialism.

I draw out elements of his writings that show that he recognized and opposed systemic power differences while valuing cultural differences. His anti-nationalist cosmopolitanism retains the value of differences in societies, civilizations, and ways of life. His cosmopolitanism is specifically anti-nationalist and anti-colonialist (as well as anti-capitalist and anti-racist). As I illustrate later, he sees nations as historical formations intended to serve economic, military, and expansionist goals. He offers a unique perspective on nationalism because he was writing about it in preindependence India. Drawing on Tagore's work provides a non-Western perspective in contrast to locating the origins of cosmopolitanism in the Stoics and Immanuel Kant. Tagore's cosmopolitanism offers a model that recognizes human differences as well as our ethical obligations to one another. He also provides a critique of power differences, especially with regard to colonizing nations and the colonized. His cosmopolitan approach values diversity and does not assume commonality or similarity at the base. Instead, Tagore's relational cosmopolitanism sees our relationality, human sociality, and social harmony as the source of our connection.

Rabindranath Tagore offers a cosmopolitanism that does not begin from universalism or sameness, but from particularity. The motto he chose for the university he founded in Shantiniketan, Visva-Bharati, "Where the whole world meets in a single nest" nicely condenses the idea of coming together as an achievement or a project, and creating something new from cultural interaction. In his essays on nationalism, Tagore provides a trenchant criticism of nations as cold machines of economic efficiency geared toward maximizing profit at the expense of human relationships. Thus, his concerns about nationalism are accompanied by concerns about capitalism, modernity, colonialism, and ethnocentrism. Living in India during British rule, and having been educated in England, Tagore was no stranger to cross-cultural interaction, education, and travel.

His view of cosmopolitanism differs from the one advocated by contemporary theorists such as Martha Nussbaum who endorses cosmopolitanism as a version of ethical universalism based on similarity. Tagore was interested in the interaction of cultures and their ability to influence and transform one another. He did not see cultural influence as unidirectional, and he focused on cultural interactions in Asia, the relationship between Japan and India, for example. The interaction of cultures and their mutual ability to transform one another is central to Tagore's idea of cosmopolitanism. In this way, his view of cosmopolitanism is closer to the idea of cultural hybridity than it is to an abstract ethical universalism. The idea of hybridity, championed by several postcolonial thinkers, is also evident in many contemporary anthropological analyses of globalization that look at the ways in which ideas and practices travel across borders and are then taken up in a different way and transformed within new cultural contexts.

I propose that Tagore's cosmopolitanism offers a model of cosmopolitanism that provides a power analysis through his critique of nationalism, colonialism, racism, and capitalism; I find his power analysis to be more comprehensive than institutional cosmopolitanism because he addresses colonialism and racism. However, he does not include a gender analysis, so his account must be supplemented to include a critique of sexism. Second, in addition to having a power analysis that can account for systemic injustice, Tagore has a rich understanding of cultural and social differences as resources for mutual learning, rather than impediments to global moral obligation. His cosmopolitanism also has a different starting point than individualist and institutional cosmopolitan positions; he begins with the understanding that we are interdependent rather than independent.

Tagore's notion of cosmopolitanism could be summed up as a social unity that respects differences. This differs from Nussbaum's view that Tagore ascribes to a cosmopolitanism grounded in an abstract view of human commonality. As Poulomi Saha notes:

> Martha Nussbaum and others have argued for reading Tagore as a model of cosmopolitan ethics and pedagogy, suggesting that his 1916 novel *The Home and the World* (*Ghare-Baire*) in particular demonstrates a humanist ideal of citizenship. Therein, the character Nikhil in the novel stands in for Tagore, and his "cosmopolitan stance" makes possible his primary "allegiance to what is morally good" (Nussbaum 2). However, the notion cosmopolitanism, in Nussbaum's account, that distanced Tagore from baser and more chauvinistic loyalties to nation and creed appears incongruous with Tagore's own explicit repudiation of both nationalism and cosmopolitanism as inadequate affective and communitarian ideals. Instead, in his writing and in his own relationships, he sought to negotiate local attachment with global engagement. (Saha 2013, 3)

Saha does not consider Tagore a cosmopolitan, but calls Tagore's position a "locally rooted globalism" (Saha 2013, 1). This has resonances with Anthony Appiah's rooted cosmopolitanism, which acknowledges the importance of place and particular identities and communities. I follow the practice of referring to Tagore's position as cosmopolitanism for reasons explained further later.

Tagore founded Visva-Bharati, a university in Shantiniketan, India, based on a vision of cosmopolitanism where people from all over the world would come to India to learn from one another. In Tagore's words: "Visva-Bharati represents India where she has her wealth of mind which is for all. Visva-Bharati acknowledges India's obligation to offer to others the hospitality of her best culture and India's right to accept from others their best" (Visva-Bharati 2015).[29] Nussbaum describes Tagore's attempt to found a world university as a failure saying: "If one goes today to . . . Vishvabharati (which means all the world)—one feels the tragedy once more. For all-the-world university has not achieved the anticipated influence or distinction within India" (2002, 16). When I visited Visva-Bharati in February 2014, I found a vibrant learning community with international students from over thirteen different countries and a group of artists from the Netherlands visiting for a study tour. I also enjoyed several cultural performances, including Indian classic dance and music, and another performance that was a fusion of American jazz music with traditional Indian music. This latter performance especially exemplifies Tagore's vision of cosmopolitanism, which is the interaction and mutual influence of cultures. This vision of cosmopolitanism as the interaction of cultures is affirmed on Visva-Bharati's website: "Santiniketan became a world university, Visva-Bharati, a centre for Indian Culture, a seminary for Eastern Studies and a meeting-place of the East and West." The university's name, Visva-Bharati, comes from a longer Sanskrit phrase: "The poet selected for its motto an ancient Sanskrit verse, *Yatra visvam bhavatieka nidam*, which means, "Where the whole world meets in a single nest" (Visva-Bharati 2015). As noted in the opening paragraphs in this section, this phrase carries a sense of coming together not in spite of differences, but to learn from one another's differences.

Tagore draws upon and honors the specificity of identity and the particularity of tradition as sources of moral ideals, not as their antithesis: "Tagore's liberal humanism, unlike the secularity of Western humanist discourse, was steeped in the Brahmo tradition central to his worldview. For him, humanism and spiritualism were not antithetical but rather productively synthetic" (Saha 2013, 19). As I argued earlier, Nussbaum's individualist cosmopolitanism fails to account for power differences, especially those relevant to issues of nationalism and world citizenship, such as colonialism. In the context of discussing Tagore's status as a cosmopolitan colonial subject, Poulomi Saha also questions an account of cosmopolitanism that lacks an analysis of differential power relationships: "Nussbaum's idyllic notion of cosmopolitanism is blind to the deeply vexed relationship between cosmopolitanism, imperialism, and citizenship rights" (Saha 2013, 14). As we shall see, Tagore himself was deeply aware of these vexed relationships and of the importance of analyzing exploitative and oppressive power relationships.

One of Tagore's most explicit and extended discussions of cosmopolitanism is in his essays on nationalism. These essays, first given as a series of four lectures in the United States and subsequently published in 1917 as *Nationalism*, provide a trenchant critique of nationalism. Tagore himself did not identify as a cosmopolitan (Saha 2013). The only time he mentions the word *cosmopolitanism* in *Nationalism* is in the quotation used as an epigraph at the beginning of this chapter: "Neither the colourless vagueness of cosmopolitanism, nor the fierce self-idolatry of nation-worship, is the goal of human history" (6). But because of his anti-nationalist stance, his interest in and openness to other cultures, his founding of an explicitly cosmopolitan university, and his embrace of globalism, he is widely viewed as a cosmopolitan. Also, considering him a cosmopolitan provides a new model of cosmopolitanism that respects diversity, values interdependence, and criticizes systemic power differentials, including processes of colonialism.

Characterizing his cosmopolitanism as similar to a Kantian ethical universalist position, as Nussbaum does, overlooks the unique contribution that Tagore makes to enlarging and redefining cosmopolitanism. A closer look at his critique of nationalism, and what he contrasts it to, can provide us with a fuller understanding of his idea of cosmopolitanism. Tagore defines nation as "the political and economic union of a people . . . organized for a mechanical purpose" (Tagore 1918, 7). He contrasts nation with society, which he says is "a spontaneous self-expression of man as a social being . . . a natural regulation of human relationships so that men can develop ideals of life in cooperation with one another" (Tagore 1918, 7). For Tagore, as for the Stoics, human society is organically connected through living bonds that naturally occur. He says: "Society is an organism, of which we as parts have our individual wishes. . . . But there is that other wish in us which does its work in the depths of the social being. It is the wish for the welfare of society" (Tagore 2011, 152). On his view, when we see ourselves as separate, we fail to realize that in truth, we are connected: "Those who can see know that men are so closely knit that when you strike others the blow comes back to yourself" (Tagore 1918, 30). This idea of human interdependence as the ground of our moral obligations resonates with the social justice view that our liberation is tied together, echoing Martin Luther King Jr.'s belief that: "Injustice anywhere is a threat to justice everywhere" (West 2015, 244). Tagore believes that when I harm others, I harm myself. King believes that when justice is threatened anywhere, it undermines justice everywhere. Both of these views rely on a strong view of interconnection and interdependence; this interdependence grounds our moral obligations to one another.

Tagore's view of our interdependence also has implications for his view of the self; for him, the individual self is illusory and we cannot thrive if we view ourselves as independent from others. He uses the analogy of an oil lamp to illustrate this. He relates: "The lamp contains its oil, which it holds securely in its close grasp and guards from the least loss. Thus it is separate from all other objects around it and is miserly. But when lighted it finds its meaning at once; its relation with all things far and near is established, and it freely sacrifices its fund of oil to feed the flame" (Tagore 2011, 149). The lamp becomes a lamp only in relation. So long as it is separate, it does not have any meaning or purpose; it only has meaning and purpose in relation to others. And so it is with the self, he argues. For Tagore, sympathy, mutual help, harmonious social relations, and social cooperation are the starting point for humanity, not some abstract ideal that depends on overcoming differences. For him, society is primary; individuals cannot flourish alone. As he says poetically: "But the individual is like the geometrical line; it is length without breadth . . . [it] will ever go on missing the ideal of completeness in its thinness of isolation" (1918, 42). Valuing human connection and the bonds of social relationships contrasts to the spirit of conflict and competition that Tagore says characterizes Western nations.

Western nationalism, exemplified for him par excellence by Europe, is soulless; it is organized around efficiency, greed, and competition for the purpose of material and monetary gain. It lacks a moral and spiritual dimension and destroys the harmony of social life (Tagore 1918). Nation is "the organized self-interest of a whole people" (1918, 9). Tagore finds this problematic because it pits groups of people against one another in the name of nationalism and, significantly, justifies not only nation building but also colonialism. In Tagore's essay on nationalism in Japan, addressed to a Japanese audience, he is explicit about the virulence of nationalism, especially the expansionist version at the turn of the twentieth century: "The political civilization which has sprung up from the soil of Europe and is overrunning the whole world, like some prolific weed, is based on exclusiveness. It is always watchful to keep the aliens at bay or exterminate them. It is carnivorous and cannibalistic in its tendencies, it feeds upon the resources of other peoples and tries to swallow their whole future" (1918, 24). Seen in the historical context in which it was written, Tagore's anti-nationalism is a type of anti-colonialism; he criticizes the expansionism of Europe and its colonizing tendencies. Contrast his view to Nussbaum's model of cosmopolitanism that calls for connection on the basis of an abstract rationality divorced from social and historical context.

Tagore believes that "All particular civilization is the interpretation of particular human experience" (1918, 28). And he thinks that the East has much to teach the West.[30] He urges those in Japan to recognize and appreciate their civilization built upon human relationships, relationships of the heart, harmony, and beauty (1918, 28). Tagore sees and values the connection between different ways of social life and civilizations, and the possibility that these differences will enhance, rather than inhibit, solutions to the collective welfare of humanity:

> For generations you have felt and thought and worked, have enjoyed and worshipped in your own special manner; and this cannot be cast off like old clothes. It is in your blood, in the marrow of your bones, in the texture of your flesh, in the tissue of your brains; it must modify everything you lay your hands upon, without your knowing, even against your wishes. Once you did solve the problems of man to your own satisfaction, you had your own philosophy of life and evolved your own art of living. All this you must apply to your present situation and out of it will arise a new creation and not a mere repetition, a creation which the soul of your people will own for itself and proudly offer to the world as its tribute to the welfare of man (sic). (1918, 23)

In this quote Tagore acknowledges the particularity of cultures and societies, and the ways that they shape individuals in myriad ways, even at the level of the body. This particularity is not an obstacle to working for the common good (welfare of man [*sic*]). On the contrary, the particularity of societies, cultures, and the ways that members of those societies and cultures carry their imprint serve as a resource for creative solutions for the common good globally.

For Tagore, it is the individualism, competition, greed, mechanistic abstraction, and exploitation of the organization of society-as-nations that needs to be explained and contested, not the sympathy, mutual help, fellowship, and cooperation that he sees as natural to human society. Needless to say, he would not accept the model that underlies much of contemporary economics and some philosophy: rational choice theory—man as the maximizer of his own self-interest.

Tagore poses a series of contrasts in his *Nationalism* essays: the nation of the West versus the spirit of the West; efficiency versus hospitability; abstract man versus personal man; things versus the heart; systems and policies versus the flow of living human relationships; appropriation versus assimilation; usefulness versus beauty; the universal distrust of humanity versus bonds of human relationship; and competition versus cooperation (1918, 12–42). In each of these oppositions, he advocates the latter of the pair: cooperation, the bonds of human relationship, beauty, assimilation, the flow of living relationships, the heart, personal man, hospitality, and the spirit of the West. These, he claims, are natural to humans; as discussed earlier, we do not thrive in isolation, and when we recognize our interdependence, we value social relationships and cooperation.

As I discuss in this book's conclusion, beginning from interdependence fundamentally shifts our ethical perspective. He attributes the former of each pair: competition, the universal distrust of humanity, usefulness, appropriation, systems and policies, things, abstract man, and efficiency to nationalism. And he sees nationalism as a Western project. But his contrasts are not between East and West; rather, they are between humanity as it is and humanity as it has become under nationalism. For Tagore, nationalism destroys the fabric of human society, by replacing social and human values with self-interest and materialism. He stresses the interdependence of humanity and argues that the West is committing [moral] suicide "in order to keep themselves in power and hold others in subjection" (1918, 30).

He sees the solution not in nationalism or in the denying of differences among social groups, but in a shared commitment to the ideals of humanity; these ideals are moral and spiritual, not political (1918, 36). These higher human ideals are sympathy and mutual help, and the spirit of cooperation (1918, 36). Each people, civilization, and nation has its own history, its own way of life, and its own way of doing things, but our common project is towards "harmonious development and disinterested love" (1918, 43).[31]

Tagore's cosmopolitan vision appreciates and values differences among peoples, but it does not view those differences as divisive or as obstacles to be overcome. Yet he does not reify difference or worship tradition. He criticizes the caste system and questions relying uncritically on the authority of traditions. His valuing of differences among peoples results neither in relativism, nor the uncritical acceptance of all social customs and traditions. He criticizes pernicious Indian social customs and traditions, those "which have generated a want of self-respect and a complete dependence," as well as nationalism and colonialism based on exploitation and dominance (1918, 18, 41). Tagore's cosmopolitanism weaves a path between recognizing the significance of culture and tradition and seeing them as a source of resistance to colonialism, while still criticizing specific cultural traditions.

He explores some parallels between (preindependence) India and America; he notes that both need to figure out how to unify the various races of which they are composed. Tagore is critical of the caste system in India. But he responds to American critics of the Indian caste system by saying that America has treated Native Americans and African Americans violently. He thereby challenges the implied moral superiority of the

American critics and reflects their critical lens back at their own practices. He makes visible their "colonialist stance" without defending the caste system. Rather than looking to "the West" for solutions of the issue of forging unity from difference, Tagore believes that India is a model of toleration: "For India has all along been experiments in evolving a social unity within which all the different peoples could be held together, while fully enjoying the freedom of maintaining their own differences" (1918, 41).

Tagore is fully aware of the tendency to slide from recognizing differences to reifying them, an issue that still persists today (e.g., in the essentialism/difference argument in feminist philosophy). His idea of human difference, however, allows for flexibility and change: "in human beings differences are not like the physical barriers of the mountains, fixed forever—they are fluid with life's flow, they are changing their courses and their shapes and volume" (1918, 41). Thus, differences make a difference but do not remain static. Moreover, this realization and celebration of humanity's diversity does not leave us in the impasse of contemporary philosophy between a conception of human nature that is essentialist contrasted to a diversity of individuals with nothing in common, or, worse yet, balkanized into warring factions. The recognition of the importance of difference and its fluidity yields a conception of human nature that is nonprescriptive: "human nature is not what it seems, but what it is in truth; which is in its infinite possibilities" (1918, 42). For Tagore human nature does not exist in a vacuum, and it is not predetermined. His conception of human nature is, paradoxically, a nonessentialist account. But this does not lead to the philosophical quagmire of relativism. Tagore believes we need certain conditions to thrive, including cooperative social relationships.

Tagore's cosmopolitanism values human connection and the bonds of social relationships, and he argues that when we recognize our interdependence, our lives will be guided by the higher social ideals of sympathy and mutual help. These higher social ideals should regulate economic ideals, reigning in greed and unbridled passion for unfettered economic growth. Comparing the United States to India, Tagore observes that the wealth, power, competition, and greed driving the expanding economy in the United States disrupt social harmony. By contrast, "In India the production of commodities was brought under the law of social adjustments. Its basis was cooperation, having for its object the perfect satisfaction of social needs" (Tagore 1918, 42). As discussed earlier, just economic systems are central to global justice. As I demonstrate in chapter 5, these social ideals are embodied in cooperatives and the contemporary Fair Trade movement; I discuss the importance of just economic systems further in chapter 5. If global human society had incorporated the value of subordinating economic ideals to social ideals, we would not have our current unjust global economic order.

To sum up, Tagore's essays in *Nationalism* include a strong anti-colonial critique of Western European nations; he takes them to task for their treatment of "aliens and immigrants" (1918, 27). He even points out the irony that a nation composed of immigrants would secure national borders, express xenophobia, and exploit immigrants and minority races, seeming to anticipate a century ago the current situation in the United States (1918, 27, 33). Because Tagore sees national boundaries as imaginary, national difference is also fictive. And because it impedes our ability to connect with one another by replacing social, moral, and spiritual values with efficiency, greed, and competition, national difference is contingent in a way that lived differences of "bone, skin, heart" are not. For Tagore, differences among humans, cultures, and civilizations are not only an inevitable part of the human condition; they are resources for learning and for formulating collective solutions to our shared problems, such as injustice and exploitation. Tagore's cosmopolitanism acknowledges and values cultural and human difference, but without seeing it as static and without uncritically embracing traditions or social customs that undermine self-respect or create dependence. In other words, our connection as humans is based on acknowledging our interdependence and valuing our difference, a clear departure from individualist and institutional approaches to cosmopolitanism that advocate ignoring our differences and valuing our independence.

Rather than proposing a universal standard of judgment for all, Tagore reminds us that "You have to judge progress according to its aim. . . . The mistake we make is in thinking that man's channel of greatness is only one" (1918, 25, 39). Valuing diversity implies a pluralism of evaluative frameworks. Canadian philosopher Charles Taylor offers one contemporary philosophical approach to this type of pluralistic evaluative framework. As Taylor puts it, the presumption of equal worth of other cultures requires a "willingness to be open to comparative cultural study of the kind that must displace our horizons in the resulting fusions" (1992, 73). Taylor employs a hermeneutic approach, that is, an attempt at understanding that may change our perceptions, values, and standards. This hermeneutic approach—understanding from one's own position while being open to transformation and change in ideas and identity—captures something significant that is also evident in Tagore's cosmopolitanism. As scholar

Saranindranath Tagore notes: "[C]osmopolitan identity, for Tagore, is not established as a consequence of an argument; rather such an identity is a discovery of hermeneutic reason as it negotiates the boundaries between my culture and their culture, myself and the selves of others" (2008, 1082). A cosmopolitanism that employs hermeneutic reason recognizes that not only do we learn from our interactions with different cultures and people, but also that we may be transformed through those interactions. This ability to be transformed through dialogue and interaction is central to relational cosmopolitanism. In my Conclusion, I draw parallels between this relational cosmopolitanism and the ideas of some contemporary feminist theorists. I also illustrate the ways that SEWA and MarketPlace India engage in relational cosmopolitanism through their global engagements. We have already seen in previous chapters the ways that women in these organizations demonstrate a sophisticated understanding of diversity, tradition, and power through their practices of valuing diversity and some traditions, while still criticizing oppressive traditions and structural injustice.

Conclusion

Relational cosmopolitanism recognizes human interdependence and differences as valuable aspects of our ethical lives. Recognizing interdependence and that we are selves-in-relation posits a social ontology at the heart of relational cosmopolitanism. Recognizing the moral relevance of difference allows us to both validate the significance of human diversity and criticize systemic patterns of asymmetrical power relations based on social identities.

Both individualist and institutional cosmopolitanism fall short of achieving a comprehensive framework for global justice because they cannot account for the broad range of injustices that people experience. Indeed, I have argued that in so far as cosmopolitanism may itself impose ethnocentric values such as secular humanism, or Enlightenment views of reason, it may perpetuate injustice in the form of imperialism.

As I have argued, we need a feminist social justice approach to global justice. The rise and persistence of social movements around the globe illustrate that justice requires that social identity be recognized as morally relevant, particularly in cases of systemic injustice, such as institutional racism, or sexism. Social justice is multilayered and multidimensional, requiring changes in political and legal systems but also in economic systems, cultural and social norms, and international institutions. As we have

seen, institutional cosmopolitanism provides an account of moral obligation across national borders that makes it incumbent on those in wealthy
countries to actively undermine the unjust and exploitative international
institutions and policies that perpetuate structural injustice and cause poverty. However, this economic and political account of structural injustice
needs to be informed by racial and gender analyses and an examination
of the role of colonialism in global injustice. Moreover, cosmopolitan
approaches should also include an account of human variety and difference beyond power differences and exploitation.

I offered an account of what I have called "relational cosmopolitanism,"
drawing from Rabindranath Tagore. Tagore's relational cosmopolitanism
includes a critique of power differences that underlie structural injustice,
yet also sees cultural and social differences as a rich source of mutual
learning. This mutual learning often means we are transformed through
our interactions with others; this transformation happens when we remain
open to a plurality of values, ideals, and evaluative standards. Relational
cosmopolitanism acknowledges power differences, recognizes human connection rather than similarity as the basis for our ethical obligations to one
another, values cultural differences, and views our specificity as both significant and subject to transformation. I suggest that relational cosmopolitanism could be further developed by drawing on feminist concepts such
as difference as a resource, world traveling, and transnational solidarity.

Feminists have struggled to reconcile the dual imperatives of
acknowledging the vast diversity of women and finding common ground
for feminist struggles on behalf of women. Early attempts at basing feminist
political struggle around a common identity as "women" were criticized
for minimizing the real differences in women's identities, situations, and
problems. These challenges within feminism have served to underscore
the importance of acknowledging structural inequalities, power and privilege, and the differences in identities and experiences among women. This
internal critique and struggle have led to a more robust, contested and
plural conception of feminism(s). In her Introduction to *Cosmopolitanism*,
Carol Breckenridge notes: [because] "feminisms have had to struggle with
their own universalisms" this struggle can provide a model for cosmopolitanism (Breckenridge et al. 2002, 7). In contrast to overlooking difference to forge global connection, feminists of color and transnational
feminists have advocated feminist politics as "an engagement in struggle
rather than transcendence of a man-made history" (Weir 2013, 74)). Note
that struggle is one of the twin pillars of SEWA's strategy (i.e., struggle
and development). Their struggle is against the many injustices that poor

women face—economic deprivation, police harassment, social stigma, caste prejudice, and gender oppression. Here we can see a type of solidarity that is achieved rather than assumed; it addresses both differences and similarities. Significantly, it is collective and oriented toward a larger shared goal of challenging structural injustice, and achieving social justice.

A cosmopolitanism informed by feminism's struggle with its "own universalisms" can benefit from insights in feminist theory. My reading of Tagore highlights his respect for differences and the ways we can be transformed through our interactions with others. I expand on those features here by drawing on contemporary feminist theory; two ideas are especially significant for developing relational cosmopolitanism into a feminist relational cosmopolitanism: Audre Lorde's insights on difference and Maria Lugones's concept of world traveling.

Audre Lorde believed that rather than viewing our differences as sources of division or conflict, we can understand them as rich resources for connection and creativity. Lorde presents a powerful picture of human difference as a positive source of connection, energy, and transformation: "Certainly there are very real differences between us of race, age, and sex. But it is not those differences between us that are separating us. It is rather our refusal to recognize those differences, and to examine the distortions which result from our misnaming them and their effects upon human behavior and expectation. . . . Too often, we pour the energy needed for recognizing and exploring difference into pretending those differences are insurmountable barriers, or that they do not exist at all. This results in a voluntary isolation, or false and treacherous connections. Either way, we do not develop tools for using human difference as a springboard for creative change within our lives" (Lorde 1984, 115–116).

For Lorde, we cannot hope to work together toward justice and against the systemic forces of racism, sexism, classism, and heterosexism without acknowledging our differences. Significantly, Lorde recognizes that in order for difference to be the basis for connection, rather than division, we must change how difference itself is perceived and constructed. She observes that Western European history constructs differences as simplistic oppositions and as hierarchical. In an interesting parallel to Tagore's focus on human needs and social values over profit, Lorde states, "in a society where the good is defined in terms of profit rather than in terms of human need, there must always be some group of people who, through systematized oppression, can be made to feel surplus, to occupy the place of the dehumanized inferior" (1984, 114). Lorde underscores the importance of valuing human differences, rather than attempting to ignore them.

Simultaneously, she criticizes systemic injustice based on the systematic oppression of people in relation to their social group identity. Her embrace of differences as resources for learning and her challenge to structural injustice bring important dimensions to cosmopolitanism.

Sometimes differences of culture, social group, ethnicity, national origin, and sexual identity can create different understandings that may be (at least partially) shared among the group. In an article about cross-cultural and cross-racial loving, Maria Lugones recommends the technique of playful world traveling as a way to "understand and affirm the plurality in and among women" (1987, 3). World traveling is a way to understand difference, diversity, and plurality. For her, world traveling is not necessarily about going to a new geographical place, but occurs when one individual enters into another's framework of meaning. According to Lugones, world traveling allows us to, "understand what it is to be them and what it is to be ourselves in their eyes" (1987, 17). To world-travel in this sense, one must employ loving perception, which opens up the possibility to understand across differences. Although Lugones uses examples of individual relationships across cultural difference, her idea can be broadened to include multiple differences across, as well as within, national borders. Ideally, the type of deep understanding across difference that comes of world traveling may displace our assumptions and settled notions, and transform us in the process.

It is this openness to transformation of our own framework and worldview that holds the promise for a shared vision for humanity not based on an assumed commonality, but achieved through struggle and dialogue. A feminist cosmopolitanism should advocate openness to difference, promote knowledge of others in their particularity, and recognize systemic power imbalances. A feminist cosmopolitan ideal would encourage global dialogue about international problems not in spite of differences, but with full awareness of the ways in which our multiple memberships position us differently in the world.

I have discussed the ways that both SEWA and MarketPlace India acknowledge and respect diversity, analyze and critique systemic injustices, and connect their local activism to global issues in the section entitled "Respect for Diversity and Global Connections" in chapter 1. But I would like to highlight again here the specific ways that each of these organizations enacts a type of feminist cosmopolitanism.

MarketPlace's Global Dialogue program brings the women workers together to discuss issues relevant to women in countries other than India. For instance, in response to a woman political leader being elected, the discussion may focus on the issue of what it means for women to be strong leaders, and what difference the political leadership of women might make in the world. Sometimes the topic for a Global Dialogue can be explored with reference to the women's own experiences, and the larger world, such as discussions about the meaning of beauty, redefining community, the power of identity, and living in harmony with nature. Sometimes discussions focus on a specific event or issue relevant to women, but outside of India, such as the Taliban forcing the women in Afghanistan to wear the burka. Yet other times discussion topics directly address some contested issues for women within India, such as the practice of dowry. Engaging in these discussions enlarges MarketPlace members' worldviews. One of the women attributes her increased curiosity about the world to her work with MarketPlace and these dialogues: "I get information about the outside world now. I used to just be at home and now I am more curious about the world, what is going on around me and in other countries, other parts of India. It has increased my curiosity. I understand more about people, why they are like they are" (Littrell and Dickson 2010, 146). Through the Global Dialogue program, MarketPlace encourages the feminist cosmopolitan ideals of global dialogue about international problems and of promoting knowledge of others in their particularity and difference.

Sometimes Global Dialogues are used to generate a theme for the next MarketPlace catalogue, for instance on topics such as tradition, identity, or beauty. MarketPlace artisans contribute stories from their own lives about these topics to be featured in the catalogue. And they also pose questions related to these topics for their customers, wondering: "What are some of the family traditions that make you feel connected to your past? How is your household different from the one you were brought up in? What makes women have the inner strength to get divorced?" (Littrell and Dickson 2010, 153). Customers' answers to these questions are summarized by a volunteer in the United States and then sent to the women in India. Customers also get the opportunity to ask questions in this exchange, asking: "Does TV play a role in shaping the values of your children?" and "What do you do in your free time?" (153). This second question generated a lively discussion among the women in India about the American notion of "free time." As Littrell and Dickson note: "For women who may walk several hours to collect water or take their children to school, the concept of free time was puzzling" (153). This back-and-forth engagement of women who live across the world from one another is a kind of cosmopolitanism; it is transnational connection through learning about the differences and particularities of one another's lives. I had this experience first-hand during my interviews with the women in the Udan Mandel cooperative. After I had asked them questions about their lives and their work, they asked me: Are you married? Do you have children? My yes and no answers, respectively, confused them. They expressed their sympathy for my lack of children. I explained it was my choice. My answer was unintelligible to them on two levels: first, they wondered, how could it be a choice? And second, why would one ever make such a choice? In the ensuing conversation we talked about birth control, gender expectations, social norms, and the importance and value of family. All of us learned a bit more about ourselves, each other and the gendered norms of our respective cultures and societies. This type of exchange promotes feminist cosmopolitan ideals of the awareness of the ways in which we are positioned differently in the world, as well as an openness to transformation of our own framework and worldview.

SEWA enacts cosmopolitanism in a similar way to Tagore's locally rooted globalism. SEWA's two-pronged strategy of struggle and development keeps the focus on the local needs of each community, but their vision of social justice also connects these local struggles for decent work, freedom from police violence and harassment, and access to natural resources such as water for farming to larger structural issues such as global economic policies and institutions, including the World Bank, IMF, World Trade Organization, and the International Labor Organization (ILO). As previously mentioned in chapter 1, SEWA members have attended international conferences and formed international organizations. They were instrumental in getting the ILO to recognize home-based work as work and in passing ILO policies that provide access to training and collective bargaining for home-based workers. This policy goes far beyond SEWA workers to redefine work in ways that better fit many workers in the global South who work in the informal economy. The policy also leaves less room for exploitation of home-based workers because they are now recognized as workers by the ILO and can be covered and protected by its policies and recommendations. SEWA's active engagement in changing international policy illustrates the feminist cosmopolitan ideal of recognizing systemic power imbalances and encouraging global dialogue about international problems not in spite of differences, but with full awareness of them.

In addition to their participation in formal international organizations, such as the ILO, SEWA also has global connections through its participation in a number of grassroots coalitions: HOMENET, an international network of home-based workers; STREETNET, a worldwide network of street vendors; GRASSNET, an international network of grassroots handicraft workers; and the Global Trading Network of Grassroots Entrepreneurs. Participation in these global coalitions provides an opportunity to learn from the experiences of others, as well as forge bonds of solidarity across borders that increase the collective strength and bargaining power of the organizations both in their home countries and at the international level.

The relationship between the local and the global in these organizations is complex and evolving. But in them I find a model of global justice that respects and values differences among people as sources of learning and creativity. Each organization is committed to challenging structural injustice in all its forms, including gender injustice. Their approach to issues of injustice exemplifies feminist relational cosmopolitanism because of their recognition of interdependence evidenced through their collective work, their recognition of difference as a valuable source of learning and transformation, and their challenges to systemic injustice and colonialism.

In the next chapter, I show how Iris Marion Young's social connection theory provides a framework for global justice that focuses on our connections through our material relationships of production and consumption. Her social connection theory, combined with feminist relational cosmopolitanism, underscores how the practices of SEWA and Marketplace India contribute to building nonexploitive economic relationships through institutions and practices of economic solidarity, both within and across borders.

CHAPTER 5 | Responsibility for Global Justice
and Transnational Feminist
Solidarity Projects

IN CHAPTER 4, I EXPLORED COSMOPOLITANISM as a framework for
addressing issues of global justice. Cosmopolitanism advocates transnational ethical obligations, and it has the potential to recognize the importance of diversity. As we saw, some cosmopolitan approaches veer into
an individualist ethical universalism, while some acknowledge a shared
responsibility for global poverty based on supporting unjust institutions
but ignore the importance of a gendered analysis of poverty (Nussbaum
2002; Pogge 2002). In contrast to these approaches that emphasize human
similarity, I introduced an approach that values particularity and diversity, while still appealing to human unity (Tagore 1918). Often the cosmopolitan model is based upon a rights framework, especially cosmopolitan
models that derive from Kant's Enlightenment philosophy.

As discussed in chapter 2, the rights framework, although extraordinarily important in twentieth-century struggles for justice, has limitations.
Currently, rights claims can only be made within nation-states, and in rare
cases, at the International Criminal Court and the European and Inter-
American Courts of Human Rights. There is as of yet no elaborated set of
international law that can ground claims, for instance, to universal human
rights. Beyond this general practical limitation of relying on rights as a
paradigm for transnational justice, there are also conceptual issues with
rights theory. Significant limitations for feminists include its emphasis on
individualism, its presumed Western bias, the privileging of legal and political rights over social and economic rights, and, finally, a kind of moral
minimalism that pervades rights theory. This moral minimalism—typified
by the idea that fundamental rights primarily involve protection from abuse

of state power and noninterference in pursuing one's goals—leaves aside not only questions of structural injustice but also what responsibilities we have to one another beyond protection and noninterference. Addressing our responsibilities to one another provides an important supplement to thinking about morality primarily in terms of rights. The issue of responsibility applies to multiple contexts—to interpersonal relations, to family, to communities, to the state, and globally.[1] Therefore, approaches to global justice must engage both responsibility and justice.

In her later work, Iris Marion Young develops a conception of political responsibility that focuses on our responsibility for justice. Rather than a rights-based model, her model looks at material and social connections as the basis for responsibility for justice (Young 2003, 2004, 2006, 2011). In what follows I explicate Young's social connection model of responsibility, which she also calls political responsibility. Positioned between statist (nation-based) conceptions of justice, which view our obligations of justice holding between members of the same political community, and what she calls "cosmopolitan-utilitarians," who argue that we have moral obligations to everyone equally, Young's model of political responsibility provides a broad and flexible framework for justice claims because it accounts for justice claims transnationally as well as within nations.[2] The focus on structural processes allows for the fact that some such processes are organized by state policies, such as the multiple structural processes that come into play to produce homelessness. And the social connection model also accounts for transnational structural processes, such as economic relations of production and consumption. The social connection model offers both an account of structural injustice and an articulation of our responsibility for such injustice.

Moreover, unlike the predominant cosmopolitan approaches (individualist and institutional), Young's theory of political responsibility attends to differences and the impact that differences of power and social position make on our everyday lives and opportunities. Young's focus on social connection preserves significant insights from feminist work about intersectionality and privilege that are lost in rights discourse. This marrying of an analysis of structural injustice with our place in it and our responsibility for it allows for a fine-grained, specific, and nuanced analysis. I argue that Young's approach to unjust social systems and her acknowledgment that each of us is placed differently in those systems provides an important resource for engaging with questions of gender oppression globally, while being attentive to intersectionality and power relations. I show how her transnational view of responsibility and justice offers a framework that makes social oppression and economic exploitation central to her analysis, and also accounts for the complex and multiple ways each of us is positioned in social structures. She includes dimensions of power and privilege in her structural analysis, which reflects the ways that structural processes confer benefits and disadvantages on each of us.

In the first two sections of this chapter, I explicate Young's account of political responsibility and address criticisms of it. Specifically, I address Carol Gould's criticisms that, first, Young's concept of political responsibility is too broad; and second, we should focus on promoting rights (Gould 2009). Later I address Ann Ferguson's concerns that Young's theory of political responsibility does not address gender specific injustice such as honor killings; and that her concept of political responsibility requires a prior sense of political solidarity (Ferguson 2009d). These criticisms parallel the approaches to global gender justice that I have discussed earlier; Gould promotes the rights approach and Ferguson addresses the issue of cosmopolitanism, which tries to negotiate between cultural sovereignty and universal moral standards. In response, I show that Young's approach helps to frame violence against women in a different way than a rights-based approach or a cosmopolitan approach because she foregrounds structural injustice and attends to differences in power.

I take up the project of our responsibility to foster alternative nonexploitative, nonoppressive institutions, by extending Young's theory to look at the ways that global cross-border alliances can positively promote not only changes in unjust institutions and structures at the transnational level but also foster new local institutions, organizations, and practices that are fairer and more just. For example, Young discusses activism against sweatshop labor as one collective action aimed at changing working conditions in countries that routinely exploit their (usually female) textile workers through long hours, low wages, and unsafe working conditions. Changing these conditions is obviously an important goal of global justice. Relatedly, I ask: What types of institutions, organizations, and practices can be fostered in distant local contexts through supporting practices and policies that are worker friendly?

I argue for including support of cooperatives and Fair Trade as part of our collective work to promote transnational justice for workers. I counter the position that Fair Trade and cooperatives are merely individualist, and pro-capitalist measures. Fair Trade is part of a larger solidarity economy. And its history as an alternative to standard trade policies, its focus on living wages, and its commitment to transparent and fair social relations situate it within the political context of a cooperative social enterprise against the dominant values of the competitive and profit-driven aims of capitalism. I show that Young's model of political responsibility applies to Fair Trade as well as the anti-sweatshop movement. I depart from Young's concept of political responsibility, which focuses solely on collective action, by emphasizing the connection between our individual actions and collective actions and their impact on local, state, and transnational institutions.

In the second half of this chapter I characterize Young's concept of political responsibility as a feminist approach and apply this approach to cultural and economic issues in transnational feminism. Although Young's account of political responsibility does not focus specifically on gender justice, it offers a powerful framework for analyzing and criticizing what Alison Jaggar has called "gendered cycles of vulnerability" (Jaggar 2014a, 2014c). These gendered cycles of vulnerability are created by gendered and raced structural economic forces, as well as gender-specific vulnerabilities to sex trafficking, and sexual violence. Jaggar's concept of gendered vulnerabilities has both a structural aspect and accounts for cultural variability, as does Young's political responsibility model.

Young's approach shares several features with my social justice approach: both include an analysis of structural injustice; and our analysis of structural injustice includes both economic exploitation and social (gender, race, ethnic, cultural) oppression. Both approaches attend to unequal power relations, privilege, social group membership, and diversity.

The conclusion to this chapter draws on the examples of Marketplace India and the Self-Employed Women's Association (SEWA), and it illustrates that their approaches to empowering women and achieving social justice address a range of issues at multiple levels exemplifying a comprehensive approach to issues of social justice. The feminist social justice approaches of SEWA and Marketplace India include not only an emphasis on providing decent work for women but also a wide range of issues, including environmental issues, land reform, and violence against women. Moreover, as previously discussed, these groups are attentive to diversity and unequal power relations within their organizations while actively fighting economic exploitation and social oppression in society.

Iris Marion Young's Social Connection Model of Responsibility

In several papers and her last book, Iris Marion Young developed a model of responsibility that she called the "social connection model of responsibility," which is a specific type of political responsibility (Young 2003, 2004, 2006, 2011). The main impetus for developing this was to capture a conception of responsibility that accounts for the harms done by structural injustice and to preserve a dual focus on social structures and individual responsibility (Young 2011). Moreover, the social connection model of responsibility can make sense of obligations between distant strangers.[3] Young introduces the social connection model of responsibility as an alternative to the standard liability model of responsibility.

The liability model of responsibility focuses on assigning blame to moral agents and redressing past wrongs, often resulting in punishment for the wrongdoer and compensation for the wronged party. The liability model works within a legal framework and is thus limited to systems in which individuals can make legitimate juridical and political claims. Global justice requires systems and frameworks that go beyond the traditional boundaries of the political as bounded by nation-states; currently, we have limited political and legal recourse for transnational justice claims. Rather than grounding the claims of justice within states, Young argues that obligations of justice arise because we are connected to one another through a variety of complex social structural processes, including economic processes. Our participation in these social processes may not be voluntary and we may not be (indeed, cannot be) aware of the full impact and consequences that our participation in them has on others. Nonetheless, because our actions depend on these social structures and all who are engaged in producing and maintaining them, we bear responsibility for those who are harmed by unjust social structures.

Young distinguishes her model of political responsibility not only from legal liability but also moral responsibility. Moral responsibility, like liability, singles out an individual to blame. Indeed, moral failings are often discussed in terms of fault, blame, guilt, and so on. Whereas this evaluative moral vocabulary might be appropriate for individual or even collective responsibility, Young claims it is not appropriate for political responsibility. Guilt and blame not only single out a particular moral agent and assume that she or he acted voluntarily, with knowledge of the situation, and the intent to harm (all of which are not the case in her political responsibility), but they also detract from possible transformative collective action by focusing on individuals, not the unjust structures and conditions. Young also points out that, as a practical matter, blame and guilt often make people defensive or resentful and this interferes with the possibility of working together for social justice.

Although I see value in leaving aside guilt and blame as we work to transform unjust structures, I question Young's sharp distinction between moral responsibility and political responsibility. Ultimately the personal responsibility that we bear for social injustice is related to what we do or do not do to transform those structures. Like Young, I reject certain features of the liberal view of responsibility that are embodied in the liability model: its individualism and the assumption of voluntariness. But, in contrast to Young, I believe that both moral and political responsibility can be individual or collective, and that they are often related. For example, Young herself seems to connect the two when she discusses the various ways that we can challenge the injustice of sweatshop labor, from social activism, to demanding corporate accountability, to buying Fair Trade.

Young highlights five features of the social connection model of responsibility that distinguish it from the liability model: (1) It does not single out one person or even a specific group to blame while absolving others (everyone is responsible, but to different degrees and in different ways). (2) It questions normal and accepted background conditions (while the liability model is applied only when the normal background conditions are violated). (3) It is more forward looking than backward looking (the social connection model aims to transform institutions to be more just, whereas the liability model seeks compensation for past harms). (4) It is a shared responsibility, meaning that each individual bears personal responsibility (rather than a collective responsibility borne by the group). (5) This responsibility can only be discharged through collective action. Thus, as Young says, "Responsibility derived from social connection, then, is ultimately *political responsibility*" (2006, 123, emphasis in original). According to Young, we have a political responsibility to transform unjust social structures.

We have this political responsibility because each and every one of us bears responsibility for structural injustice, including those subject to it. How best then to fulfill this responsibility? Young specifies that political responsibility based upon social connection can only be fulfilled through collective action. Simply stated, because structural injustice is the result of various complex social processes and the resultant social structures that involve multitudes, the only way to transform these processes and structures is through collective, not individual, action (see Young, 2006, 123 and 2011, 111–113).

I believe Young draws too sharp a line between individual and collective action; the relationships between individual and collective action are complex and contextual. Changing unjust social structures relies on both individual and collective action; as I have argued throughout this book, structural injustice cannot be remedied by individual action, but ultimately it is individuals who come together to engage in collective action leading to structural change. Moreover, this connects moral responsibility and political responsibility; if we are morally complicit in maintaining structural injustice, then it is our political responsibility to engage in the collective work of changing unjust institutions. Young draws a distinction between moral and political responsibility that mirrors her distinction between individual and collective action. But a personal sense of moral responsibility provides motivation for working to change structural injustice, thus connecting it to political responsibility.

Two practical examples that seem to defy a sharp line between individual action and collective action are petitions and boycotts. In the case of a petition, it relies on many individuals signing for its legitimacy as a tool of political and social pressure and change. One could say that the individuals become a collective by their shared interest in, and commitment to, for instance, anti–sex trafficking. Likewise, boycotts rely on individuals not buying a product or shopping at a retailer. In this sense, it is an action by a series of individuals rather than a group. Contrast these activities to a sit-in or demonstration, which is clearly a collective action.

Young's own earlier work on "Gender as Seriality" provides a way of thinking about this connection between individuals and groups.[4] Drawing on Sartre's idea of "seriality," Young discusses the formation of the group "women." She describes the formation of "women" using the example of people waiting for a bus. While they are waiting they are individuals until something happens that binds them together, such as the bus being very late or not showing up. She articulates a concept of women that is not identity based, but situation based, capable of collective action, and nonessentialist. This fluid way of describing group formation as a collection of individuals bound together by a situation mediates viewing collective action as completely separate from individual action.

On my view, boycotts are both collective action and individual action; and I argue that Fair Trade, when seen in its historical and political context as a social movement, is both collective and individual action in this same sense. While boycotts rely on individual action, a group collective action such as a protest or demonstration outside the same store may accomplish similar, related goals of withdrawing financial support from products and retailers that violate human rights or that engage in unfair labor practices. For example, the Coalition of Immokalee Workers has a Fair Food campaign that works to improve the labor conditions of farmworkers. Based on the earlier struggles of the United Farmworkers, who famously urged boycotts of grapes, the groups working with the Fair Food campaign organize and support marches and demonstrations to put public pressure on owners of restaurants and grocery stores who have not yet signed on to the Fair Food agreement.[5]

Both individual and collective actions come from one's specific social position. According to Young, one's social position affects not only the degree and kind of responsibility one has for structural injustice but also what one is best situated to do to work for social justice (2006, 126). Her account of structural injustice applies to both national and transnational contexts. In *Responsibility for Justice*, Young uses the story of Sandy, a young, single mother with two children, to illustrate the structural injustice of homelessness in the national context of the United States. As an example of transnational structural injustice, she uses sweatshops. Moreover, she highlights the anti-sweatshop movement as an example of a social movement that connects consumers in the global North with producers in the global South through relations of production and consumption.

These two different examples reveal that in different contexts and different situations, political responsibility may involve engaging with different social structures. In the case of homelessness in the United States, structural constraints on housing and employment include laws, urban development plans, and availability of jobs, training, and education, as well as the many other factors that Young discusses. In the case of global justice for workers, there is not a set of international laws, but there are international organizations that set guidelines and policy, such as the International Labor Organization. In the first case, the social structures that most immediately impact upon homelessness are within a national context, and political responsibility in this case means transforming those state policies and laws that contribute to homelessness. In the second case, taking political responsibility means directing our collective action to transnational actors, such as transnational corporations, and the laws and economic policies that reinforce their power, as well as engaging with international labor organizations to set fair policies and guidelines. As Young points out, social structural processes act as constraints on our actions. At the same time, these social structures are the result of social processes and therefore are amenable to change through collective action.

Members of both SEWA and MarketPlace India engage in collective action to change laws, policies, and social norms at the local, national, and transnational level. Feminists who support these organizations through buying their products, political advocacy, and their own efforts to change unjust laws, policies, and social norms in their own local, and national context, as well as the shared arena of transnational contexts, engage in a type of multilevel, multifaceted political solidarity that recognizes that women's struggles differ in different social and national contexts, while they are also linked through transnational structural injustice.

Young suggests one can assess proper courses of action by considering the following four parameters: power, privilege, interest, and collective ability (Young 2006, 2011). Although she does not highlight gender in her political responsibility model, nor claim that it is a feminist model, I believe that these parameters are part of what makes Young's model distinctively feminist. Specifically, her parameters of power and privilege draw directly on feminist concepts of social location, power, privilege, and intersectionality. These parameters may also be useful for thinking about our responsibility in relation to gender injustice transnationally. Including power and privilege in a transnational theory of justice distinguishes our roles in both producing and challenging that injustice, and the structural aspect provides a material basis for transnational solidarity.

As Young notes, once we recognize that we are responsible for structural injustice on the basis of our connections with others, even people we have never met and who are far away, we may feel lost as to how to discharge that responsibility or personally overwhelmed at the enormity of it. Although each of us has responsibility for remedying structural injustice, we cannot all do everything. Instead, we need to work from where we are, based on our social position, that is, based on our place in these very social structures that produce injustice. Young discusses power, privilege, interest, and collective ability in the context of the anti-sweatshop movement. Each agent has power based on her or his position in structural processes, and agents "should focus on those [structural injustices] where they have a greater capacity to influence structural processes" (Young 2011, 144).

As an example, the anti-sweatshop movement put pressure on major retailers and multinational corporations because they could, in turn, exert pressure on the overseas factories with whom they contracted. Young urges us to focus on where we have the most power to effect change; as a faculty member, that might mean that I should focus on ensuring that my campus does not buy clothing produced in sweatshops. But we also need to recognize who is best placed to actually change the unjust conditions, and to put pressure on them to do so; this would mean recognizing that multinational corporations that contract with overseas factories have more power to effect change in this situation, perhaps even more power than nonbinding international guidelines and protocols.

Often international human rights organizations focus on the most egregious violations of human rights, so the types of everyday injustice faced by those working long hours for low pay in factories only come to attention when the media reports that a factory burned down. This was the case in Bangladesh in November 2012 when a fire broke out in a garment factory outside Dhaka and over one hundred workers who were locked inside burned to death; at the time, it was one of the worst industrial tragedies ever to occur in Bangladesh (Bajaj 2012).[6]

In this case, questions were raised about who bore the responsibility for the unsafe working conditions. Retailers like Wal-Mart denied a connection to the Bangladesh factory, and the owners of the factory were charged with criminal negligence a year later. For these clear violations of human rights, the liability model works to make those directly responsible for the conditions that caused the deaths of the workers accountable for their negligence. However, this only underscores the retroactive focus of the liability model versus the proactive focus of the social connection model. The social connection model aims to transform working conditions before a major tragedy, not in response to it. Moreover, the liability model treats the exploitation of workers and the unsafe conditions in which they work as an aberration, rather than as a consequence of the structural inequalities produced by global capitalism. It also isolates the responsibility for these unsafe working conditions; the responsibility often falls upon individuals who are themselves severely constrained by the pressures of global structural inequality. The local factory owners should, of course, bear some responsibility for locking the factory doors, but a large share of responsibility also belongs to transnational corporations for their lack of oversight into the conditions of the workers in their subsidiary overseas operations and for profiting from the exploitation of the workers.

Holding different social positions with their respective differences in power and privilege requires each of us to take action in different ways. With this in mind, what can those who are not factory owners and not CEOs of Wal-Mart do to ensure safe and just working conditions? Young suggests that what we can do depends not only on power but also on privilege. In the case of clothing manufacturing, middle-class consumers in the United States enjoy quite a bit of privilege; that is, they benefit from having a wide array of inexpensive clothing from which to choose. Those who are relatively privileged within structural processes have special responsibilities to undermine the structural injustice that benefits them. Young claims that those in the middle class and above have an obligation to buy products, such as Fair Trade clothing, that are not produced under sweatshop conditions. With this example, we can see that consumers stand in a relation of both moral and political responsibility to the workers who make the products they use. As individuals, their everyday choices affect people's working conditions, health, and safety. But buying Fair Trade is not enough; morally conscious consumers must work to change the political and economic conditions that perpetuate economic exploitation.

Later in this chapter, I discuss buying Fair Trade as a positive step toward social and economic justice by promoting alternative institutions in the textile and garment-producing industries, which are primarily in the global South. I argue that although buying Fair Trade does not appear to meet Young's criteria for collective action, Fair Trade is a social movement that is part of the larger solidarity economy movement. Additionally, Fair Trade purchases often support collective political action, as is the case with MarketPlace India and SEWA.

In addition to power and privilege, interest and collective ability round out what Young calls the parameters of reasoning with regard to our political responsibility. Young claims, somewhat controversially, that because victims of structural injustice have unique interests in undermining it, they ought to take responsibility for doing so (Young 2011, 145). To continue with the sweatshop example, workers should take responsibility for challenging and changing the poor conditions that they work under. This may seem to some like "blaming the victim." For instance, Carol Gould says: "The implication that the exploited workers share responsibility for the systems that oppress them seems counterintuitive, at least from a view that takes seriously the fact of their exploitation itself" (2009, 203). Gould believes that Young's political responsibility model holds too many accountable and, in this case, the wrong people. But as I argue in the next section, this aspect of Young's account is valuable. It acknowledges that those who are oppressed by structural injustice have agency, even though they do not stand in the same relationship to processes of structural injustice as consumers in the global North or as the managers and bosses in their factory. Acknowledging that those who are oppressed and exploited have a role in challenging and transforming systemic injustice recognizes that those who are oppressed can also organize collectively for social justice.

The final parameter, collective ability, asks us to draw upon the resources of organized groups that we are already a part of, such as churches, unions, and other associations. Each of these groups has members who act together, thus multiplying the effects of positive action toward social change. Collective ability is especially useful when those in less powerful social positions make claims on those in more powerful social positions.

For instance, when faculty support students to request from the administration that the university not purchase sweatshop clothing. Or when a more experienced SEWA leader or organizer goes along with a newer group of SEWA members to meet with city officials. Taken together, these features—power, privilege, interest, and collective ability—offer some guidelines for political practice. As Young points out, this political practice relies on broad-based social engagement by individuals working as part of a group or collective to transform unjust social structures.

Young bases her model of political responsibility on social activism and civic engagement. And her inclusion of social position, power, and privilege in an account of structural injustice allows for a fine-grained analysis of the variety of injustices and their relationship to one another. It also captures the way that individuals are differently situated within social structures. While the focus of Young's political responsibility is on social structural processes, her recognition of the varying levels of privilege and power within, and as a result of, these social structural processes is particularly important for feminist analyses. Before examining feminist dimensions and applications of Young's political responsibility, I turn to some criticisms of her model.

Criticisms of Young's Political Responsibility

Many social and political theorists view Young's model of political responsibility as an important contribution to conceptualizing a transnational model of social justice; it provides a necessary supplement to the liability model of responsibility. Yet her conception of political responsibility is not without critics. Here I take up what I consider sympathetic criticisms by feminists who engage with Young's work to promote transnational justice and are themselves involved in articulating conceptions of transnational justice. In this section, I address two general concerns about political responsibility: first, it does not adequately locate and individuate who is responsible; and second, it focuses on the harms caused by structural injustice, rather than promoting a positive solution to those harms, such as fostering institutions that advocate for human rights.

Carol Gould questions the broadness of Young's model of responsibility. She claims, "if everyone is responsible, then no one is" (2009, 202). She believes that Young's concept of political responsibility is too capacious and is therefore unable to hold individuals accountable. According to Young, individuals are accountable because of their participation in social and economic processes that produce structural injustice, but they are not equally accountable. Young points out that our responsibility varies depending upon our privilege, power, interest, and ability to take action. Young points out that although everyone is responsible (for participating in, and therefore working against, structural injustice), some are more responsible than others, such as those who have greater power to change the unjust institution. In the case of sweatshops, this would be multinational corporations that contract with the subsidiary factories and the retailers that buy their products.

Gould worries that the social connection model does not sufficiently differentiate between the responsibility of the workers to transform the unjust labor conditions they work in and the responsibility of the multinational corporations that play a major role (and have a compelling interest) in maintaining exploitative working conditions. Young explicitly addresses the issue of varying degrees and types of responsibility. She states, "shared responsibility does not mean equal responsibility" (Young 2004, 381). And she argues that differences in kind and degree of responsibility correlate with an agent's position within social structures (Young 2006, 126). Acknowledging that each of us has a responsibility to transform unjust political and social structures from our own position reinforces the need for transnational coalitions where different groups work on different aspects of an issue, such as labor justice or environmental justice.

Gould believes that Young's concept of political responsibility overemphasizes avoiding harm to others. Gould rightly points out that responsibility has both a negative and a positive sense: causing harm versus helping or caring for. Correspondingly, our negative duty is to avoid harming others, and our positive duty is to establish just institutions that promote human rights. Gould argues that Young's account of responsibility focuses on the negative aspect of responsibility and duty because Young is more concerned with mitigating the harms caused by structural injustice than about the importance of developing transnational institutions that protect and promote human rights.

In what follows I provide three different responses to this criticism. First, Young's concept of political responsibility can be extended to support the responsibility of states to promote, protect, and uphold rights. Second, perhaps Young's lack of focus on rights was intentional; rights have only limited power to address structural injustice. And, third, Young does not neglect this positive aspect of advocating for rights and transforming institutions; she and Gould simply emphasize different sides of responsibility.

Young's model of political responsibility can be used to support institutions that protect and promote human rights. For instance, Serena Parekh argues that Young's idea of political responsibility can be extended to justify states' responsibility for preventing structural injustice and women's human rights violations such as violence against women (2011). Significantly, Parekh draws on Young to talk about states' role in preventing future injustice by changing the political culture and developing institutions that promote human rights. This extension of Young's work addresses Gould's concern about our (and states') obligations to develop and support institutions that promote human rights. Three features of political responsibility support Parekh's argument about states' responsibilities: First, they are in a privileged position to change social structures. Second, because political responsibility is forward-looking, it mandates political action. And, third, states can play a special role in collective or joint action. Parekh convincingly argues that Young's concept of political responsibility can be extended to justify states' responsibility in not only protecting but also promoting human rights. Parekh's extension of Young's theory addresses Gould's criticism. Although Young may not have emphasized human rights in her theory of political responsibility, it can be extended to support the positive development of institutions that promote human rights.

Yet Young's lack of emphasis on human rights may have been intentional. She does not assume that states, or even international organizations, can be most effective in securing transnational justice. And rights are enforced by states and promoted by transnational organizations. Young's model of political responsibility focuses on civic engagement and social activism rather than traditional political and legal institutions. She is skeptical of the role of established institutions to address structural injustice: "the rules and practices of these institutions [states and international institutions] are more aligned with the powers and processes that produce or perpetuate injustice than with those who seek to undermine it" (Young 2011, 151). Young's observation about state and international institutions as perpetuating the status quo, rather than supporting radical struggles for justice, resonates with other feminist criticisms of governmental and non-governmental organizations (NGOs) discussed in chapter 3.

For instance, feminists observe that donor funding constrains NGOs' political activism, and that United Nations conferences and forums are accessible mainly to elite, middle-class women (Romany 1995; Engle 2006; INCITE 2007). Human rights remain the paradigmatic framework for issues of transnational justice, both in international documents and institutions and in philosophical literature. Young's model of political responsibility, though, goes beyond what rights models typically do. A rights model that focuses on legal and political rights can be compatible with economic exploitation, whereas political responsibility allows for a more thoroughgoing criticism of structural injustice. As I have argued, structural injustice includes structural oppression and economic exploitation. Rights focuses on individual instances of injustice, such as a case of discrimination in housing or employment, whereas challenges to structural injustice include challenging the social and economic systems that produce discrimination.

In spite of Young's skepticism about the efficacy of traditional institutions to undermine structural injustice, she recognizes that institutions, if transformed, can play an important role. On this, both Gould and Young agree. Gould says, "there is a need for structural transformation in these institutions themselves . . . institutional problems require institutional solutions" (Gould 2009, 206–207). Similarly, Young calls for collective action "directed at transforming the structures"; furthermore, she claims that the demands of justice call upon us to work jointly "to make better institutions" (Young 2004, 381, 384). Finally, Young claims, "political responsibility in respect to structural injustice . . . often requires transforming institutions and the tasks they assign" (Young 2004, 385). Here, Young and Gould appear to be in agreement about the importance of developing better, more just institutions, both nationally and transnationally. But Young's skepticism about the role of institutions such as the state and international organizations to address injustice at all levels is well founded; as I have argued, the rights discourse utilized by these traditional institutions often leaves aside issues of structural injustice. Young's work on political responsibility provides an important criticism of, and supplement to, rights theory.

Political responsibility differs from rights theory because it does not rely on atomistic individualism but emphasizes social connection; it has a structural analysis, recognizes power differences, and focuses on economic and social injustice. Young's concept of political responsibility relies on a commitment to social justice. As I have argued throughout this book, a social justice framework can better address the myriad injustices than rights theories, including gender injustice. A social justice framework questions and challenges the "normal background conditions" that the rights framework leaves intact. Social justice examines "whether the background conditions of people's actions are fair, whether it is fair that whole categories of persons have vastly wider options and opportunities than others, how among the opportunities that some people have is the ability, through the way institutions operate, to dominate or exploit others, or benefit from their domination and exploitation" (Young 2011, 38). Key to the account of social justice is recognition of the different social positions of those participating in and constrained by social structures. Exploitation, oppression, and domination address aspects of injustice that escape accounts of rights because the individualistic discourse of rights lacks a power analysis.

Moreover, Young's theory of political responsibility not only provides an account of our role in promoting and protecting the rights of "distant others" but also illuminates the ways that we are involved in undermining those rights. As Young points out, oftentimes injustice, including violations of rights, is intentional and willful and attributable to a specific person or persons; those cases can be addressed through a liability model. But the cases of injustice that her political responsibility model is meant to capture are the injustices that result from the myriad actions of multiple individuals behaving according to accepted norms and constrained by structures and institutions. It is the cumulative result of these individual actions that forms and shapes the social institutions that result in basic structures that systematically disadvantage some groups and privilege others.

For example, when I go into a major discount retailer to buy inexpensive clothing produced by sweatshops, my behavior is legal and, in fact, rational. But cheap prices rely in part on cheap labor, and so buying these clothes in the context of an unjust economic system that encourages factories to move to the global South and produce clothing without regard for minimal labor regulations unwittingly supports and contributes to structural injustice. The "Babies in the River" story discussed in the Introduction highlights the dual imperative of social change: we must do what we can at the moment through available means to curtail human rights abuses and positively promote institutions that will protect human rights in the future. At the same time, we must change the social institutions and structures that perpetuate systemic injustice. This is clear in discussions of how to alleviate global poverty—simply recognizing economic and social rights is not enough, nor is advocating individual solutions to global inequality. We must transform the structures that continue to perpetuate these unjust institutions. Keeping this dual focus in mind shows that both individual actions, such as buying Fair Trade, and collective actions, such as changing unfair labor regulations and trade policies, contribute to social and political change.

Looking at a specific example may help to clarify what Young's social connection theory can help us to analyze, articulate, and ultimately mobilize in our projects for social justice. The social connection theory can help to mobilize cross-border solidarity by holding transnational corporations accountable in the countries in which they are based. This cross-border solidarity can be used to prosecute some cases of violence against women. In 2007, Margarita Caal Caal, an indigenous woman from Guatemala, was raped and evicted from her home (Daley 2016, 1). Her rape and eviction were tools of violent sexual intimidation by a multinational corporation eager to claim her land; she and ten other women from her village were gang-raped by employees of a subsidiary of Hudbay Mineral Incorporated. They were unable to pursue justice in Guatemala for a variety of reasons: a corrupt government, an ineffective court and legal system, and social discrimination and marginalization. As indigenous Mayan women, they suffered from linguistic, cultural, and political marginalization in Guatemala; they took their case to Canada because Mayan villagers have had little legal success in Guatemala. In the past, such cases had little chance of being heard in Canadian courts: "Their lawyers have often tried to get cases heard on the basis of violations of human rights or international criminal law. But most were told that Canada had no jurisdiction, and that their claims would be more appropriately heard in the country where the events took place, even if that country's courts were notoriously corrupt or otherwise dysfunctional" (Daley 2016, 11).

The women have now filed a negligence suit against Hudbay Mineral. Unable to get justice through either their own courts or international courts on the basis of human rights claims, their lawyers turned to the strategy of prosecuting parent multinational companies for the behavior of their subsidiaries overseas. This strategy is remarkably similar to that of the anti-sweatshop movement when they challenged Nike and other large transnational corporations about the working conditions in their overseas factories. In fact, it draws on and builds upon this strategy: "The behavior of multinational companies working in poor countries has come under increasing fire in recent years. Social expectations have changed, experts say, with many citizens of rich countries demanding that corporations be more responsible in the countries where they operate" (Daley 2016, 11). In this case, there are multiple injustices and violations of human rights. The mining company denies the local population's land rights. Their mining operations have caused extensive environmental damage, including erosion, sedimentation to groundwater, and river contamination. Security forces employed by the mining company have beaten, shot, and killed protesters. Denying traditional land ownership, they have forcibly evicted families from their homes, and then burned the homes down. And using sexual violence as a tool of intimidation, employees of the mining company have raped the eleven women named in the lawsuit.

As noted, human rights violations are difficult to pursue transnationally, and often impossible to pursue in the country where they occurred, especially if the government is complicit in the violations, or benefits from the presence of the multinational corporation in the country, or the claimants are members of socially marginalized minority groups. Additionally, such issues as environmental damage, land claims, and the marginalization of the Q'eqchi' people do not all fit easily within the human rights framework. The route of pursuing the claim of negligence by the parent corporation in Canada was made possible by the activism of groups like the anti-sweatshop movement, and the consequent social pressure by consumers for large multinational corporations to ensure that suppliers do not violate human rights in the making of a product, or in this case, the extracting of a resource.

One of the ways Young's theory goes beyond individualist cosmopolitanism and rights theory is by locating our responsibility in our participation in social structures that systematically perpetuate injustice, which makes us each personally responsible for contributing to injustice, and therefore also responsible for rectifying it. In this case, the injustices are severe and multiple, and our responsibility as consumers of products that employ rape, murder, and arson as tactics of intimidation is a weighty one. Political responsibility is the responsibility to recognize the ways that these systems of production and consumption implicate us in grievous wrongs, and it should motivate us to transform systems of structural injustice. As Young notes, transforming the institutions and structures that result in injustice is an ongoing, shared task that each of us must take up from our own social position. As consumers, we are implicated in systems of unjust production, and both our individual choices and collective political actions matter.

Sweatshops and Fair Trade

In this section, I argue that Fair Trade production and consumption can be one strategy (among other strategies) for transforming unjust institutions and creating institutions that are more equitable. Contrary to critics who dismiss Fair Trade as an individualist, consumer-based approach that cannot resolve large-scale issues of economic injustice and exploitation, I argue that Fair Trade can play a positive role in transforming unjust institutions across national borders. Young mentions Fair Trade in her later work, but she does not develop it as a way to promote transnational justice (Young 2011, 133). I show how Fair Trade is not only consistent with Young's political responsibility model but also extends it by linking individual action and collective action and showing how both transform social institutions.

First, I discuss the history of Fair Trade as a social movement that focuses on poverty alleviation, noting that as a social movement Fair Trade fits with Young's criteria of collective action. Next using MarketPlace India as an example, I discuss the ways that Fair Trade can foster a type of transnational solidarity among women. This solidarity is not only economic but also political in two senses. First, MarketPlace India members engage in activism to improve the conditions of their lives, so the economic support provided, in turn, supports their social and political activism. Second, consumers in the global North buying MarketPlace products intentionally support a South/North economic solidarity project. Organizations that focus on women's empowerment by combining opportunities for decent work with opportunities for developing leadership go well beyond simply protecting workers' rights; they provide a workplace that is inclusive and democratic. And the leadership skills developed in the cooperative carry over beyond the workplace to the women's communities as they engage in social activism. There is a close connection between cooperatives and Fair Trade; many Fair Trade products are made by cooperatives. As discussed in chapter 3, cooperatives are explicitly committed to economic and social egalitarianism. Cooperatives consider environmental responsibility and sustainability among their goals. Additionally, many cooperatives have a social dividend model where some of the profits are used for a community project or to build infrastructure.

Fair Trade first emerged in the 1950s in Great Britain, the Netherlands, Germany, Canada, and the United States as Alternative Trade Organizations were formed with the explicit goal of resolving inequitable trade relations between producers and consumers, and for providing access to international markets for artisan producers and small businesses (Littrell and Dickson 2010, 8). The term "Fair Trade" replaced "Alternative Trade" in the 1980s, thirty years after the Alternative Trade Movement began. From the beginning, organizations that promoted Alternative/Fair Trade shared a common purpose and vision: "providing new opportunities for small producers who would otherwise not be able to participate in the global economy due to lack of political and economic power" (Littrell and Dickson 2010, 8). Oxfam in the United Kingdom was among the early organizations promoting Fair Trade by selling crafts in their stores and offices.

Fair Trade may seem to provide only a small-scale solution to access to global markets, but the consequences for producers are big; without Fair Trade many of them would lack basic necessities such as enough food, adequate shelter, and basic health care. Moreover, Fair Trade is not only based on relationships between producer, purchaser, and consumer; it creates relationships within local communities and economies both in the global South and the global North. In the global North, Fair Trade is a social movement, like the anti-sweatshop movement. There are Fair Trade–designated cities and schools, and the process of passing the resolution to designate a city or school as Fair Trade is a collective, public, and political process. So, while individual consumption may not meet the criteria of collective action that Young holds as necessary for political responsibility, participating in the Fair Trade movement certainly does. Moreover, when Young mentions Fair Trade as a part of consumer awareness about the conditions of workers in the global South, she mentions it as continuous with the efforts of the anti-sweatshop movement: "more consumers have taken an interest in 'fair trade' consumption, such as buying products through firms that deal directly with workers under fairer-than typical conditions" (Young 2011, 133). Elsewhere, Young cautions anti-sweatshop activists in the global North against calling for boycotts of products produced in sweatshops, reminding us that the workers need their jobs in spite of the exploitative conditions under which they work (Young 2004). The solution is clear: work for fair labor conditions everywhere. Fair Trade producers have already undertaken this project proactively.

Soon after her mention of Fair Trade, Young dismisses it as impractical because of the limited options for Fair Trade clothing and other Fair Trade products. As I discuss later, supporting Fair Trade producers may, in turn, help to increase the number of Fair Trade options. In another place, purchasing Fair Trade is seen as a viable option only for the middle class (Young 2011, 145; see also Jaggar 2014a, 176). But this seems to soften the force of Young's argument. Once we acknowledge our social connection through producer and consumer relationships, and accept our political responsibility to transform the unjust institutions and structures related to those relationships, then we should also support alternatives to free trade and exploitative work conditions such as Fair Trade. Young bases her caution about boycotts on the reasonable assumption that people need to engage in paid labor. Given that the social connection model is based on our material and economic relations to one another, supporting Fair Trade businesses is consistent with Young's view of political responsibility.

Creating fairer, more just institutions and workplaces is the necessary correlate of transforming the exploitative labor and trade relationships through our collective action; recognizing this connection undermines criticism that Fair Trade is simply a reformist, individualist approach to social change. If I frequent retailers who are known to have deplorable conditions for their overseas workers, then I contribute to perpetuating those conditions. Conversely, when I buy Fair Trade, I contribute to promoting and perpetuating fair and safe working conditions, a living wage, and environmental sustainability. When Young says: "we should also ask whether and how we contribute by our actions to structural processes that produce vulnerabilities to deprivation and domination for some people who find themselves in certain positions with limited options compared to others," I take this to mean that we should ask ourselves both how our individual actions and our collective actions contribute to these processes (Young 2011, 73). Arguably, individual actions do not have the same amount of impact as the collective actions of getting a large university campus to ensure that the clothing it sells is not made in sweatshops and is designated as Fair Trade, or as participating in the anti-sweatshop or Fair Trade movements. But these things are not mutually exclusive. There are several parallels between Fair Trade and the anti-sweatshop movement. Both rely on consumer education, acknowledge the connections between producer and consumer, and promote better working conditions for producers. Because of this, I see them as different aspects of the same project working toward transnational labor justice.

Like the anti-sweatshop movement, one of the primary aims of Fair Trade is to educate consumers about the conditions and lack of opportunities that producers face in their daily lives. One hallmark of the movement from the beginning was to educate consumers by sharing the stories of the artisan producers, through informational brochures, tags on items, and educational forums and events in the stores. This served to establish relationships between consumers and producers, even a kind of solidarity, as both producer and consumer acknowledged that they were in a mutual relationship. With the advent of the Internet, these relationships could become more direct, interactive, and sustained.

For example, MarketPlace India has online forums on their website in which producers and consumers can interact and exchange stories. SEWA shares its research and information about the organization on their website. Both organizations welcome visitors who are interested in and supportive of their work. These opportunities to interact and share stories, not only of the impact of the consumer on the producer but to be able to share hopes and dreams, fosters relationships of both economic and political solidarity. For example, as discussed in chapter 1, Marketplace India develops leadership skills and promotes activism among its workers. They also stay in touch with consumers by sending regular email updates. An email sent in March 2016 advertises new products and says "Share Our Vision, Share Our Activism" (MarketPlace India, March 2016). One of the links on their website, "Share Our Activism," shares current activist projects; in one such project Marketplace women were concerned about teacher absenteeism (a widespread problem in India). Teachers in India, like in many other countries, are underpaid and overworked. Because of this, many take second jobs which conflict with their teaching schedule. Most members of MarketPlace India value education; they often stopped formal education in middle school, and now they want their children to finish their formal schooling and graduate from high school. They want them to have the opportunities that education can provide. These members voiced their complaints about teacher absenteeism and met with the board of education. Their meeting with the district education board resulted in more teachers being hired, teachers showing up for work more consistently, and less administrative duties for teachers, affecting two thousand children (MarketPlace India website). The social and political activism and leadership skills of MarketPlace India members are fostered through their involvement in the production cooperatives for which they work. So, although my purchasing a beautiful jacket from Marketplace India is not activism, it supports activism as well as provides a sustainable living for cooperative members.

Moreover, Fair Trade guidelines go far beyond simply protecting workers' rights, or fair pay; they include environmental responsibility, an egalitarian and democratic workplace, inclusive and fair hiring and promotion practices, and often a social dividend (money set aside by the group for a collective project, such as building a school, a clinic, or a road). Fair Trade involves not only producers' cooperatives but also growers' cooperatives; for instance, the well-known nonprofit Equal Exchange, which primarily sells coffee, tea, and chocolate. As discussed in chapter 3, cooperatives promote worker autonomy and collective aims, and they are based on a set of values derived from utopian socialism. Fair Trade provides small businesses, small farmers, and a variety of cooperative enterprises access to international markets. Fair Trade presents itself as an alternative to charity or development aid (Nicholls and Opal 2004, 25). But some may still object that it is a commercial, market-based approach to poverty alleviation, rather than a structural approach. As I have been arguing, we need multiple approaches to promote social change both "from above" and "from below." Of course, human rights violations in workplaces both domestic and overseas need to be stopped. But that still leaves intact the macroeconomic system that relies on the exploitation of labor to maximize profits. When consumers from the global North buy Fair Trade products from the global South, we support alternative institutions and organizations—like worker-managed enterprises and cooperatives—in the global South.

Fair Trade and Neoliberal Capitalism

Both critics and supporters of Fair Trade question its place in the neoliberal capitalist system. As we saw in chapter 3, some feminist critics argued that microcredit furthered the aims of neoliberal capitalism because it focused on individual solutions to poverty alleviation instead of structural solutions. Similar criticisms have been made of Fair Trade; some claim that it is an individualist, consumerist strategy that reinforces rather than challenges the values and aims of neoliberal capitalism. If this is the case, they argue, we should reject Fair Trade as a viable strategy that contributes to poverty alleviation in the global South. In this section I argue that the goals of Fair Trade are contrary to the values and aims of neoliberal capitalism, such as unregulated markets, Free Trade, and the maximization of profit. Specifically, Fair Trade seeks to transform exploitative economic and social institutions and instead promotes justice and dignity for workers.

Fair Trade counters many of assumptions of laissez-faire capitalism; specifically, it undermines three core assumptions: markets are self-regulating, free trade benefits everyone, and profit is the ultimate goal of an economic system. Comparing free trade to Fair Trade, Charlotte Opal and Alex Nicholls summarize the classic free trade theory of Adam Smith and David Ricardo like this: "Under free trade, both parties are better off: international trade is thus a win-win situation in which everyone benefits" (Nicholls and Opal 2004, 17). Feminist philosopher Ann Cudd adopts this formula when discussing the best strategies for alleviating poverty and also for promoting gender equality, claiming that "engaging in commerce that is free, fair and looks to long-run mutual advantage is the best strategy for fighting poverty, both because it has the right aims and because it is a viable strategy from the perspective of the rich" (2014, 218).

Earlier in the essay she uses the term "free and fair trade," combining what she calls the "free and fair trade assumption" with the "surplus value assumption" (Cudd 2014, 210). Taken together, these assumptions claim that each person can produce more material goods than she or he needs to survive, and that trading these surplus goods enhances everyone's well-being. However, "free and fair trade" is an oxymoron. Free trade maximizes owners' profits, is unregulated, and is determined by the market; Fair Trade maximizes workers' earnings, is regulated, and often includes buffers from the abrupt vagaries of the market, especially for commodities like coffee and chocolate. In fact, the explicit objectives of Fair Trade are counter to free trade: "Fair Trade has three interlinked aims: to alleviate extreme poverty through trade; to empower smallholder farmers and farm workers to use trade relationships as a means of enhancing their social capital; and *to support the wider campaign for global trade reform and trade justice*" (Nicholls and Opal 2004, 25, emphasis mine).

The emergence of the Alternative/Fair Trade movement in the 1950s was in part a response to the deregulation of trade that followed the Second World War. This liberalization of trade was followed by structural adjustment conditions on lending by the World Bank and the International Monetary Fund, which stipulated an increased level of trade liberalization. As Joseph Stiglitz and other writers on globalization and Structural Adjustment Programs have pointed out, the imposition of trade liberalization on developing countries in the global South has merely served to increase their poverty and undermine local (national) economies. Moreover, it enhances the bargaining power of already wealthy countries, which as Thomas Pogge points out, is one of the many injustices of the current global economic and political order (2002).

Free trade fails to deliver on its promise to make everyone better off. In fact, it increases wealth inequality; the rich get richer and the poor get poorer. The effects of free trade's failure are both macroeconomic and microeconomic. The free trade policies of neoliberal globalization impoverish entire countries, increasing their debt, forcing devaluation of currency, and hurting economies by importing subsidized products that undermine local businesses and agriculture. While these macroeconomic effects of free trade must be addressed collectively and politically by changing international economic and trade policies, the microeconomic effects can be partially mitigated through Fair Trade networks. The microeconomic effects of neoliberal globalization include increased unemployment and lack of access to basic social services, such as health care, education, and childcare because of privatization. Together, the lack of income and the lack of free access to basic services such as health care, especially in states without entitlement programs like unemployment and social security (which includes most nonwealthy countries), has disastrous consequences for peoples' lives, including death from malnutrition or lack of medical care. Income-generating projects can make the difference between life and death on a microeconomic level; and one common income-generating project for women is the production of items for the Fair Trade market. Fair Trade connects workers in the global South with markets. In some cases, Fair Trade organizations create new jobs and provide skills training, such as Marketplace India. In other cases, Fair Trade organizations support already existing projects, such as the coffee farmers supported by Equal Exchange.

Iris Young and Ann Cudd both use Nike as an example of a positive change in transnational production. Their different treatments of this example provide an illuminating contrast between embracing capitalism as the solution to poverty and criticizing it as one of the sources of poverty and economic inequality. Both see Nike's response to the anti-sweatshop movement to improve working conditions in its overseas factories by raising wages, providing safer working conditions, and limiting hours as a positive step. Young frames this change as the outcome of a social movement that exemplifies social connection through the recognition of our responsibility for unjust labor conditions as consumers of products made under those conditions. For her, collective political action such as the anti-sweatshop movement can lead to positive social transformations that hold corporations accountable. Capitalism is not the solution; it is the problem.

For Cudd, Nike is the model of a successful transnational business because they made these changes and put a system of monitoring their factories into effect, and she downplays the role of public pressure that precipitated these positive changes. Although Cudd acknowledges that Nike made the positive changes under pressure from "critics" of sweatshop conditions, she praises Nike for mandating improved labor conditions in its overseas factories. She even says that in cases where the factories are found not to be complying with these improved labor conditions that Nike has mandated, "the origin of the abuses is often local" (Cudd 2014, 216). One of the reasons for this local abuse is that "it is so profitable to run a factory that contracts with a transnational firm like Nike. But that profitability depends on keeping wages as low and productivity as high as possible" (Cudd 2014, 216). But low wages and high productivity to maximize profit is business as usual for capitalism, not (just) a local abuse by some factory manager in the global South.

One of the most powerful features of Young's social connection model is that it includes questioning background conditions.[7] Questioning background conditions in the case of low-paid factory workers (usually women) in the global South producing for consumers and transnational corporations in the global North will lead us to issues of structural injustice, including trade and economic policies, the flexibility and casualization of labor, the increasingly fluid movement of capital across borders, the feminization of certain types of work, and the legacies of colonialism and the current practices of resource extraction.

As I discuss in chapter 3, cooperatives that sell in Fair Trade markets provide one alternative to transnational factory work. Fair Trade must meet International Labor Organization standards in terms of workers' rights and working conditions, and includes many other positive goals, such as environmental responsibility. These positive guidelines are especially important because social justice issues are often interrelated, and environmental damage has a disproportionately negative effect on poor, rural women in the global South. In this way, Fair Trade goes beyond human rights discourse by including environmental degradation and environmental injustice.[8]

Political Responsibility as a Feminist Model

As we have seen, Young's model of political responsibility draws attention to both systemic injustice and to our place in its production and reproduction. It can help us to analyze both intrastate and interstate social structural processes, as in the case of homelessness in the United States, and sweatshop labor in the global South. It is not limited to, nor focused on, women or gender. It is a normative model that broadens the concept of responsibility, basing it on social connection. Although gender is not explicitly thematized in Young's model of political responsibility, I contend that it is a feminist model, and because of this it can be a useful model for transnational feminist activists and theorists. Like many transnational feminist approaches, Young's political responsibility illuminates transnational economic and social structures while also recognizing national and local social structures, and the complex interplay among them. Young's model of political responsibility also holds that one's place in the social structures plays a significant role in a persons' range of opportunities; she recognizes the role of power in both structural injustice and social norms and categories. Young's parameters for reasoning about the type of actions we should take to remedy structural injustice include power and privilege, both of which are key concepts for feminists. Feminists make explicit this connection among structural oppression, one's place in social structures, power, and privilege. Holding a dominant social position (power) in relation to an axis of oppression confers privilege or unearned advantage.

Feminist analysis, similar to Young's political responsibility, claims that even though the privilege that we have is the result of social processes and structures that we do not control, we are responsible for challenging the social, political, and economic structures that result in our privileged position. Privilege is often invisible to those who have it, so the first task is to recognize that we have privilege. Secondly, using privilege responsibly means using it to undermine the very structures that confer it, by transforming the social structural processes and institutions that give us privilege. As in Young's model of political responsibility, we are implicated in unjust structural systems and processes because they confer an unearned (and unfair) advantage on us, and therefore we have a responsibility to work to change these unjust systems so that they do not produce unjust consequences. Economic, political, legal, and social systems do not operate in isolation, and strategies for transforming them must also be multifaceted.

Power, privilege, and intersectionality play a significant role in feminist analyses; feminist theory has consistently examined and articulated the relations among women that both bring us together and divide us. Young's theory of political responsibility acknowledges our interdependence, our social location, and our embeddedness in unequal relations of power, all of which are important elements in my feminist social justice approach. She employs a nonideal approach to questions of justice, focusing on structural, economic, and social processes to develop her account of political responsibility. And her grounding in empirical examples highlights the connection between theories and practices. Finally, her approach relies on normative notions of social justice, including anti-oppression and anti-exploitation. As I have argued, these norms provide a more comprehensive framework for gender justice.

Political Responsibility and Transnational Feminism

Political responsibility, like transnational feminism, emphasizes not only our connections across borders but also maps out a guide for political action based upon our responsibility for structural injustice. Some feminists think that political responsibility cannot address significant questions for transnational feminism: How does political responsibility connect to issues of women's cross-border solidarity? Can political responsibility address concerns regarding women's rights as human rights, such as honor killings or systematic sexual violence? For instance, Ann Ferguson argues that political responsibility needs to be based on a solidarity paradigm of social justice. And she does not believe Young's concept of political responsibility can address issues of violence against women, especially instances in which the violence is legitimated through social and cultural norms (Ferguson 2009d).

Solidarity forms the political ground from which we act to challenge systems of injustice. Ann Ferguson and Iris Marion Young both agree that global justice requires transnational solidarity. Their positions differ on whether solidarity is prior to, and more fundamental than, political responsibility. Ferguson holds that political responsibility needs to be based on solidarity practices, whereas Young claims that such solidarity practices arise as a way to fulfill political responsibility (Ferguson 2009d, 186). Young's model of political responsibility arises from our connection to others through social structural processes, and to the extent that those processes result in structural injustice, we (everyone involved in the processes) are responsible for it; on Young's model this responsibility requires that we act collectively in order to transform the institutions and processes to be more just. On more than one occasion, Young mentions that transforming these institutions will involve groups of people in different social locations and positions with varying amounts of power and privilege working together, for instance, workers unionizing, activists calling attention to exploitative working conditions, executives in multinational corporations changing policies and practices to treat workers fairly, and states passing laws for fair wages and worker safety or upholding such laws if they are already in place. This resonates with Ferguson's claim that solidarity practices and networks play an essential role in achieving global justice. For Young, once we recognize that we are responsible for systemic injustice, it follows that we should work to change the institutions that perpetuate systemic, structural injustice. Yet she does not fully articulate the connection between the recognition of our responsibility and our commitment to social justice. Significantly, the commitment to social justice required by the solidarity justice model Ferguson proposes grounds our motivation for working against unjust social structures. Thus, Ferguson's articulation of the solidarity justice model makes an important contribution toward a more comprehensive framework for conceptualizing global justice (Ferguson 2009d). The solidarity justice model supplements and extends Young's social connection model, contributing to a more comprehensive framework for understanding transnational social justice activism. Justice solidarity also provides a way to think about solidarity that is not simply identity based.

Young's political responsibility model relies on our connection through structural and institutional processes, making it useful for analyzing transnational feminist solidarity. But critics argue that it does not provide guidance in the case of abuses of women in other countries (Ferguson 2009d). Western feminists have often focused on gender-specific violence, such as female circumcision, domestic abuse, and honor killing, as the locus for transnational feminist theorizing and activism. This is especially true of some proponents of the "women's rights as human rights" position; unfortunately, this position often uses culturalist explanations for gender injustice (Bunch 1993, 1995; Okin 1999; Nussbaum 2000). Defending a view of women's human rights transnationally has been a vexed question, seemingly resulting in a dilemma between imposing a universalist model of human rights that postcolonialist feminists critique as imperialist, or adopting a relativist stance that limits our political and moral responsibility (Ferguson 2009d, 188; Gimenez 2009, 44–45).

As I discuss in chapter 2, some proponents of the "women's rights as human rights" position frame the argument as an opposition between respecting cultural traditions, on the one hand, and achieving gender equality, on the other. As I have argued, the culturalist explanation for women's subordination is misleading because it isolates and individuates cultures; it views cultures as ahistorical and internally homogeneous; and it fails to distinguish between pernicious and benign aspects of social and cultural norms. Perhaps Young intentionally shifted away from issues that assumed an underlying cultural cause or explanation.[9] Critics claim that her model of political responsibility cannot account for cases of gender abuse, such as honor killing, because presumably honor killing results from individuals expressing religious or cultural ideologies, rather than resulting from structural connections. Young's model of political responsibility seems to be silent on these issues. However, we have seen through Parekh's analysis that Young's political responsibility can be extended to offer a justification for states to protect women from violence. And the case of Margarita Caal Caal and the other ten women gang-raped as a violent tool of corporate intimidation stands as a powerful testament to the ways that consumer pressure and social activism can provide a powerful channel for working to hold perpetrators of violence against women accountable through transnational remedies. These examples show ways that Young's political responsibility can address issues of violence against women, both nationally and transnationally.

In cases where Young's model of political responsibility is not sufficient, other models that address more directly issues of violence against women can work in concert with it. Just as Young's model of political responsibility supplements, but does not replace, the liability model, the political responsibility model may need to be supplemented by other models of justice as well, for instance, the feminist relational cosmopolitan model I develop which is attentive to particularity and power differences. Her hesitancy to intervene in issues of gender abuse that have occupied so many Western feminists aligns with her focus on structural injustice. Culturalist explanations of women's subordination shift attention away from a focus on systemic structural processes, such as the disproportionately negative impact of the economic policies of neoliberal globalization on women. Alison Jaggar makes a similar argument in "Saving Amina?," arguing that feminists such as Susan Okin and Martha Nussbaum wrongly attribute gender injustice to cultural explanations rather than structural economic processes (Jaggar 2005).

As I have argued in chapter 3, these structural economic processes have gendered effects further disadvantaging women who are already vulnerable. A framework of gendered vulnerabilities provides a way to think about women's issues in both national and transnational contexts. Alison Jaggar develops such a framework "transnational cycles of gendered vulnerability" as a methodology that can account for significant cross-border phenomena that primarily affects women (Jaggar 2014a, 2014c). This framework provides a structural analysis that prioritizes gender without reducing or oversimplifying the variety of women's different social locations and experiences. For instance, transnational cycles of gendered vulnerability can help to account for sex trafficking, and women's immigration from the global South to the global North to perform care work and domestic work such as housework, childcare, and elder care (Jaggar 2014a, 2014c). These transnational cycles of gendered vulnerability are related to cycles of gendered vulnerability that also occur within national contexts, specifically women's place in the family as caregiver and women's access to paid work outside the home. In both cases, women's opportunities and vulnerabilities are structured by a number of complex structural factors, including economic, political, and sociocultural.

I have suggested that transnational feminist analyses look to grassroots women's organizations to inform transnational feminist activism and theory. When we adopt this model, we see the relationships among local, national, and transnational gendered vulnerabilities, both the similarities and the divergences. Whereas care work and sexual objectification, commodification, and control of women seem to be transnational structures, the opportunities and restrictions on women's labor vary widely from place to place. Of course, opportunities for paid work are structured by national economies, transnational economic policies, and local conditions; additionally, access to paid labor is further conditioned by one's gender, race, and education as well as other factors. Each of us can contribute to transnational solidarity from our different social locations, nations, and material circumstances.

SEWA and MarketPlace India as Models for a Feminist Social Justice Approach

In the rest of this chapter, I look at the ways the model for social justice used by SEWA and MarketPlace India works on a number of levels and how it addresses systemic power differences, social exclusion, and interpersonal and intergroup dynamics at each level. Political responsibility is based on our social connections, that is, our material, economic connections grounded in our roles as workers (producers) and consumers. Because of this, I have argued that this concept implies not only that we need to act collectively to change large-scale institutions that perpetuate economic injustice, but that we also need to develop social and economic institutions that are equitable, fair, and just. SEWA and MarketPlace India both aim toward justice for women workers, realizing that this entails not only economic changes but also social and political changes.

SEWA recognizes that structural injustice must be addressed at the macro-level, and it has worked through international organizations, as well as the Indian government. As an organization and a social movement, it works to address the multiple and reinforcing levels of injustice and inequality simultaneously, rather than at one level or in one sphere in isolation. SEWA begins with an eleven-point set of goals: employment, income, nutritious food, health care, childcare, housing, asset[s], organized strength, leadership, self-reliance, and education. Their primary point of action is at the intersection of gender and labor, which grounds their work "in the material conditions that shape the lives of most women on the planet: their location in the organizations of production and reproduction" (Gimenez 2009, 45). Informal labor is an area of particular importance for women in India and throughout the global South. As previously mentioned, the informal economy makes up the largest sector of the economy for most countries of the global South, and women make up the largest percentage of workers in the informal economy. SEWA's work is guided by the needs of its members rather than professionalized leadership or outside donors. The model that SEWA uses for social change recognizes that systemic change must happen on a variety of levels—local, state, national, and international—and that these systems are interactive and mutually reinforcing. SEWA members, leaders, and researchers also articulate a sense of solidarity while honoring diverse identities and experiences.

For example, when the police in Ahmedabad were harassing vegetable vendors, members of SEWA joined together on the streets to witness and document the harassment. Next, SEWA's founder, Ela Bhatt, met with the police commissioner, but this failed to stop the harassment, so SEWA staged a protest on Independence Day, August 15, 1978. This resulted in spaces for vendors being "chalked" in the market, giving them temporary legitimacy. However, the harassment continued, and because of an unrelated incidence of violence in the area, the market area was closed off; the vendors were not allowed to set up and sell their goods. In response, sixteen SEWA members, along with Ela Bhatt, met with the police commissioner to argue for legalized vending. The police commissioner was unresponsive and blamed the women's poverty on a lack of family planning, asking each woman how many children she had. His question reveals negative gender and cultural stereotypes about lower caste women, and a view of poverty as an individual, rather than a systemic issue. His strategy backfired, however, when a member of the SEWA group asked him how many children his mother had (Bhatt 2006, 85). Although the police commissioner did not change his mind about allowing the women to sell at the market, this question revealed his own biases about caste and gender, and his biases were challenged by the woman who felt empowered to speak up.

After their negotiations failed yet again, the women decided to "occupy the market," setting up their wares in defiance of the continued denial of recognizing their legitimacy as vendors. Police presence was strong with vans ready to transport the women to jail. However, no arrests were made; in addition to the vendors, other SEWA members and organizers showed up to protect the vendors who refused to leave. And the longtime customers of the vendors showed up to buy from them, as before. The police made no arrests and withdrew completely, leaving SEWA members in charge of traffic and public safety in the congested area. But the women vegetable vendors had inspired others: "After the first day, the women's determination and efficiency must have impressed the other traders in the market, for surprisingly, the men volunteered their help and gave their full support to the women they once looked down on. The cooperative spirit of the market was unprecedented" (Bhatt 2006, 86). This illustrates the interdependence of those at the market, and their customers, and the cooperation and solidarity that result from that recognition of interdependence.

But street vending remained illegal even after this action of civil disobedience and solidarity with other vendors. After more meetings, a temporary solution was forged: SEWA members were able to use their SEWA identity cards as vending licenses. However, this agreement between SEWA and city officials ended when the municipal government changed. Additionally, there was social unrest and riots over issues of reserved seats for "scheduled castes and backward tribes" for admission to medical school. During meetings with municipal officials to secure the vending licenses, one judge blamed the women's poverty on their move to the city: "Why did you leave your villages and come to the city? Don't you see that is the root of your problem?" (Bhatt 2006, 86). After unsuccessful attempts at resolving the issue at the municipal and state level, SEWA took the case to India's Supreme Court, arguing, "the vendors' constitutional right to trade was being violated by the municipality"; they ultimately won the case (Bhatt 2006, 88).[10]

After the positive outcome of the Supreme Court case, negotiations were made with the municipal government to find solutions acceptable to the vendors and the city, including special vendor spaces in the new market, a refrigerator for the wholesale market, and buses for transport between the wholesale market and the vending spaces. Due to a change in municipal government (again), these changes were not implemented, and despite the Supreme Court victory, the vegetable vendors of Manekchowk market still experienced harassment, including fines, extortion, and physical abuse. In 2006, there were 41,000 SEWA vendors in Ahmedabad alone. In spite of the persistence of harassment from police and self-imposed neighborhood power-mongers, the vendors continue to work toward making the Supreme Court judgment, which protects and defends their right to sell their goods legally and without harassment, a reality.

But this will only be possible if several things are taken into account. First, city officials must respect and implement national laws. At a broader level, the important role that the vendors play in the economy must be recognized; approximately half of those with low incomes as well as many from the middle class buy their basic necessities from street vendors. And, from an even more general perspective, the dependence of the formal economy on the informal economy should be considered. The vendors, and other workers in the informal economy, allow the formal economy to function because the formal economy outsources some of its labor and functions to the informal sphere (Damodaran 2015). Additionally, urban planning and development must take vendors into account: "street vendors in the cities of India need a comprehensive policy that will integrate their livelihood and their concerns for market space, licenses, and financial and civic services into urban planning" (Bhatt 2006, 93).

Many other factors play a role in the precarious lives and livelihoods of the SEWA vendors in Ahmedabad; many of them are the sole support for their families, and many did migrate from rural areas to the city. These issues are, in turn, linked to other issues—some of the rural to urban migration results from the inability of small farmers to make a living from their land; this in turn is linked to the incursion of Monsanto in farming practices, selling and regulating GMO seeds and the expensive fertilizer needed for the seeds.

Also, the textile industry and the cotton mills have long been a mainstay of the local economy in Ahmedabad; the mills primarily employed men. But massive mill closings between 1980 and 1990 left 100,000 men unemployed; not all were able to find other work. The mill closings were related to the flood of cheap imports fueled by the liberalization of trade, specifically the lowering of tariffs on imports demanded by structural adjustment programs. When the mills closed, many women sought work in the informal sector to support their families; one third of the women vendors in Ahmedabad are the sole earners in their families.

This one local case shows how multiple systems interact and affect the daily lives of women vendors in Ahmedabad, and this can provide insight into how an intersectional, multisystems analysis might work in other cases. On the transnational level, trade policies, structural adjustment policies imposed by the World Bank and the International Monetary Fund, intellectual property laws, and international law regarding the scope and power of transnational corporations like Monsanto all affect the situation and daily lives of the women vendors. At the national level, this is the case for laws regulating vending and workers' rights, as well as government subsidies for unemployment, and policies for economic growth. At the local level, this is true for urban planning and design, as well as support and cooperation from municipal officials and police. SEWA's grassroots approach begins with a specific issue or problem—in this case, police harassment of women vegetable vendors—and aims to address the problem at all levels: local (meetings with local officials, political activism, demonstrations, and civil disobedience), national (Supreme Court case), and transnational (ILO policies and international solidarity). Addressing the issue in all its complexity involves taking a feminist social justice approach, which recognizes systemic and structural injustice, the importance of relationships, the acknowledgment that we stand in unequal relationships of power, the significance of social location, and the many facets of even a single issue when struggling for social justice.

Moreover, in seeking a solution to the issue of police harassment, SEWA vendors developed leadership skills and engaged in political activism that had real effects on their daily lives. These earlier successes paved the way for further success. When I visited Manekchowk in November 2006, the vegetable vendors had formed a cooperative; they had secured their own stall and had joined together to rent a van to transport their goods to the market, rather than carry them on their heads. In this case, the vendors' cooperative benefits the women by sharing the cost of transportation, the cost of renting the stall, and having the political clout of a collective group (in Ahmedabad in 2004, there were 80,000 vendors total) to organize for their right to sell their goods without fear of arrest, extortion, or harassment. These changes also affected the women's level of confidence and self-respect. While the perception of the women's power and social position by others is more difficult to measure than the tangible results of sharing a van and a market stall, we can see its practical implications by the fact that the male vendors acted in solidarity with them when they occupied the market. In chapter 3, I have articulated these interconnections among changes in social, economic, and cultural position within the women's local contexts.

These complex connections among the social, economic, and cultural positions of women can also be illustrated by the complicated relationship between gender and culture within the practices of MarketPlace. MarketPlace artisans explicitly draw on traditional methods of textile production, such as batik and block printing. They also include embroidery on every item, a signature of their production, based on traditional cultural designs and aesthetics. My initial interest in MarketPlace India was that it seemed like a concrete, real-life counterexample to the prevalent view that culture and women's rights were at odds; in MarketPlace I saw women drawing upon traditional cultural practices to achieve their economic rights, and, in turn, I saw women who had developed confidence and skills as workers mobilize that power into social recognition

and cultural capital.[11] This left me wondering about the relationship between culture and women's equality; in this instance, they were clearly
not at odds.

Upon further investigation, the complex and multifaceted relationship
between cultural traditions, social norms, and gender roles and expectations became clearer. Drawing on traditional Indian textile methods of
fabric dyeing and clothing design is an intentional strategy; it keeps an
aesthetic tradition alive, and there is a niche for handmade ethnic products
in the United States consumer market. Artisans producing clothing sold
by MarketPlace work in a flexible and supportive environment. Artisans'
hours are flexible; they may work at home or at the cooperatives' shared
space. Each artisan learns different aspects of producing an item (cutting,
sewing, embroidery, quality control, etc.) so that she may change jobs
within the cooperative, and not get bored. Creative work with dignity is
the hallmark of the organization.

Clearly, some cultural traditions such as traditional textile production and design are benign in terms of gender equality. However, many
feminists see gender segregation (purdah) as a violation of women's rights
and an impediment to gender equality. All-women's cooperatives and
workplaces allow women to work without violating the community gender
norms of purdah; yet working outside the home may at the same time
push against those community norms. These trade-offs can be thought of
as "bargaining with patriarchy" at the systemic level, negotiating among
the multiple social systems that constrain our actions (Kandiyoti 1988). At
the level of individual agency, it can be thought of as a trade-off between
welfare agency and feminist agency (Khader 2014).

These trade-offs are not unique to a specific group of women but result
from the ways that each of us is positioned in social structural systems in
multiple and complex ways. Social norms, such as gender roles and religious and cultural expectations, both constrain and enable. MarketPlace
reinforces gender norms not only by allowing for a women-only work-
space but also by the type of work engaged in: clothing production.
Chosen because many women already know how to sew and embroider,
clothing and textile production are typically women's work. But in this
case, the conditions of labor are fair and just, rather than exploitative. The
benefit to gender traditional labor is that it draws upon skills many women
already have; the drawback is that it serves to reinforce gender norms
and stereotypes about "women's work." Of course, this issue of gender-
segregated occupations is not unique to MarketPlace or to India but can be
considered in the larger global context.

Conclusion

In this chapter, I have argued that Iris Marion Young's theory of political responsibility provides a framework for transnational justice that is useful for feminists. Because her theory focuses on structural injustice, it can be applied to both national and transnational social and economic structures. Political responsibility arises out of her idea that we are connected to others through relationships of production and consumption. Given this, I have argued that one aspect of feminist transnational solidarity relies on supporting just economic institutions such as Fair Trade cooperatives. Cooperatives and Fair Trade are part of a larger economic solidarity network (Ferguson 2009a, 2009b). Ann Ferguson characterizes economic solidarity as "a set of economic and political networks that include worker and consumer-owned cooperatives, rural farmers' unions, fair trade networks, local social money and bartering networks, and the global food sovereignty movement advocating locally grown food and ecologically-sustainable development" (Ferguson 2009b, 242).

Economic solidarity has a long and varied history. The International Solidarity Economy Group held a meeting in Lima, Peru, that brought together for the first time representatives from economic solidarity projects around the world (Miller 2009, 27). Then, at the World Social Forum in 2001, a global solidarity network was proposed, and in 2007, at the US Social Forum, a US Solidarity Network was formed (Ferguson 2009a; Kawano 2009). The projects and institutions that are part of solidarity economics share the commitment of people before profit, as well as commitments to environmental sustainability and egalitarian social relationships. Actively supporting projects, institutions, and organizations structured around economic solidarity contributes to strengthening both the global economic solidarity network and the individual economic solidarity projects on the ground whether they are local, like CSA (community-supported agriculture), or far away, like Fair Trade items produced in India and marketed in the United States. Supporting women's cooperatives contributes to workers' economic empowerment and has a positive impact on their quality of life. Moreover, these solidarity economies provide an alternative to neoliberal corporate capitalism (Ferguson 2009a, 2009b).

Resistance to corporate capitalism takes place at multiple levels from building solidarity among alternative economic institutions, including cooperatives and Fair Trade, to workers' rights, and collective organizing and action. Young's social connection theory of political responsibility offers a material base upon which to understand our obligations to one another based upon our relationships in systems of production and consumption.

However, Young does not highlight the gendered aspect of production and consumption: both are highly gendered. SEWA and MarketPlace India locate their work for gender equity in the context of economic relationships through their focus on women workers. Their strategies for resisting economic exploitation reveal a position that is grounded in feminist social justice norms of anti-oppression and anti-exploitation. Their local, collective activism addresses gender and caste oppression, as well economic exploitation; they begin from their concrete, material situation and work for social justice at the structural level. Their strategy for organizing recognizes that the economic system is structured through racial, ethnic, caste, and gender divisions.

Many occupations are gender segregated throughout the world, including the textile and garment industries. And the work of social reproduction (care and domestic work) still falls primarily on women. Some feminists argue that this common location in the relations of production and reproduction could provide a base for political organization and mobilization as working women, resulting in a "working women's feminism" (Gimenez 2009). Martha Gimenez develops the idea of working women's feminism from a theoretical Marxist standpoint. She claims that it will result from the contradictions of global capitalism, and the deepening of class, socioeconomic, race, and ethnic inequalities among women; working women's feminism involves acknowledging divisions and antagonisms among women with the aim of collectively transforming social relations of exploitation and domination.

From a different angle, SEWA and MarketPlace address this same intersection—women as workers, not theoretically, but practically, because material conditions and access to basic goods shape the range of opportunities and life chances for everyone. In both cases, the intersection of gender and class (women and work) is a starting point for analysis and action, rather than a totalizing framework. Beginning from real-life situations reinforces the need for a multilevel, multisystems analysis; systemic injustice operates differently in different situations and contexts. The feminist social justice approach does not reduce this complexity but includes issues of relationality, power differences, intersectionality, and multiple social locations as important considerations for questions of justice. Recognizing how we are (differently) positioned in and by social structures and working against their unjust consequences can be a common starting point for feminist social justice projects. Looking at the ways that social structures have gendered effects, such as the feminization of poverty, can provide guidance for specific projects and collective actions that feminists might take up to change those social structures.

| Conclusion

IN THE HYPOTHETICAL STORY of "Babies in the River," we were asked to make a choice between pulling the babies out as they went by us before they drowned or going upstream to stop the person(s) responsible for throwing them in. This choice, like so many hypothetical choices, is a stark lose/lose situation. Of course, we must somehow do both. In our daily lives, and in the situations discussed in this book, we see that working simultaneously at the local and the global level (even if not always at the same time or by the same people) and ensuring that basic needs in daily life are met, while still fighting for structural change, are all necessary for real progress toward social justice. Even more important is understanding when we are throwing the babies in the river ourselves. Social institutions and norms, cultural traditions and practices, and political and economic systems do not somehow exist outside of us. Each of them is created and sustained by human energy, activity, and labor.

Because our actions create and sustain institutions, policies, and practices, we can also change them through our actions. In this book I have drawn out the connections among individual actions and collective action, and social and political transformation both theoretically and practically. Collective social movements require an ongoing and sustained commitment to social justice by many individuals. Social change occurs at many levels, including political and legislative, but informal systems and practices are outside the realm of policy and law and must be addressed by other means.

To illustrate this connection among different avenues to promote the same goal, let me return to the issues of the anti-sweatshop movement, Fair Trade, and cooperatives. In chapter 5, I explicated Iris Marion Young's account of political responsibility, which claims that we each have a personal and shared responsibility for working to change unjust social, institutional systems from which we benefit. For Young this means that we have an obligation to engage in collective action aimed at transforming the institutions and social structures that result in unjust consequences. Unlike institutional cosmopolitans, who advocate a general responsibility to change the global economic institutions that support the unjust world order, she narrows down this huge responsibility by claiming that our own responsibility to change those systems is based on our causal relationship to them. In order to move forward with this large task, Young suggests we start with the issues we are best situated to address effectively. For transnational justice, this involves specifically the relationships of consumers in the global North to producers in the global South. While Young focuses on what consumers can do to put pressure on transnational corporations that violate workers' rights by requiring long hours with inadequate pay and no benefits in unsafe conditions, I take up what we might also do to promote more alternatives on the ground for producers to ensure better working conditions. I advocate supporting Fair Trade and workers' cooperatives by purchasing their products.

Radical political thinkers have often dismissed these alternatives as individualist or pro-capitalist, or as part of a neoliberal consumer strategy that ultimately benefits transnational corporations. Yet this obscures the connection between collective political actions aimed at changing unjust structures and intentional, politically informed ethical choices. Through legislation and activism we can work to make transnational corporations have decent pay, benefits, and safe working conditions; this addresses structural injustice at the level of a specific institution. But we must also advocate the radical restructuring of work or working relationships and address the asymmetries built into current trade access and policies. One viable method of restructuring work relationships is through workers' cooperatives. As discussed in chapter 3, cooperatives emerged out of the historical context of utopian socialism. They have an explicit commitment to social cooperation, democratic participation, and egalitarian relationships. Moreover, cooperatives subsume economic goals to social aims; in this system, people are not human resources serving the goal of the company and its profit. Instead, they are creative partners and co-owners shaping the direction and policies of their workplace and their role within it. Like cooperatives, Fair Trade is a part of the solidarity economy.

As discussed in chapter 5, Fair Trade provides access for small producers to the import/export market. It also promotes an alternative for consumers who care about the conditions for workers to ensure that the products they use are made under fair and safe conditions. The case of collective political action to participate in the anti-sweatshop movement falls under Young's definition of political responsibility, whereas buying Fair Trade does not. This is because she does not view Fair Trade as a collective action, and only collective actions can transform the institutions that contribute to structural injustice. But our individual ethical choices can support alternatives to unjust institutions. I have argued that Fair Trade and the anti-sweatshop movement are both part of the same larger project of promoting and supporting fair working conditions; when we support Fair Trade and cooperatives, we contribute to a larger movement for a solidarity economy.

This leads me to think that the lines drawn between ethics (seen as focusing on individual actions) and politics (viewed as involving promoting structural change) are too sharp. How we act and what we do on an individual level often have political consequences and ramifications. Conversely, large-scale structural change must be accompanied by changes in other areas: informal institutions, policies, social norms, and individual behavior and practices. In the context of discussing inadequate analyses of global gender disparities, Alison Jaggar claims that when Western philosophers focus on the "bad decisions made by poor women out of ignorance or false consciousness," they misperceive the proper focus of gender justice, which is institutions and structures (2014a, 178). She distinguishes such an ethical approach from a political one: "Although ethics does assess individual choices, the primary tasks for political philosophers is to consider the social institutions that make various menus of options socially available and assign costs and benefits to various decisions" (Jaggar 2014a, 178).

In the same volume, whose theme is poverty, agency, and human rights, Serene Khader explores the question of women's empowerment and agency in relation to microcredit projects. She notes that some feminists have criticized the role of microcredit for perpetuating global inequality because its focus on individual women and their choices draws attention away from the unjust global economic order that creates and sustains poverty. Khader says, "I am sympathetic to these critiques of the structural discursive effects of microcredit, but they are out of the scope of Kabeer's analysis—and mine" (2014, 235). What I have been suggesting in this book is that social justice includes attention both to issues traditionally labeled as ethical, especially those regarding individuals' range of choices, opportunities, and interpersonal relationships, and to what is traditionally labeled as questions for political philosophers, specifically whether or not institutions are just. In real life, ethics and politics are not so easily separated; our actions always take place within a social and political context. Yet that social and political context is not fixed or permanent, but is itself the result of our actions and social processes. A comprehensive feminist social justice approach recognizes that there is an interactive and dialectical relationship between the various aspects of our lives and the ways in which our options are molded and constrained by unjust institutions. As discussed in chapter 3, in order to exercise agency, we must have meaningful choice and having meaningful choice relies upon our material, economic, social, and political context, which is shaped by economic, political, and cultural institutions.

An understanding of the connections among individual actions, social norms, contexts, and institutions reveals a more complicated relationship between one's individual actions and structural change. For example, recall the women in MarketPlace India who were able to work outside the home because it was an all-female workplace. This allowed them to both conform to gendered cultural and religious norms of gender segregation and to challenge those same norms by working for pay outside the home. Likewise, the Self-Employed Women's Association (SEWA)'s initial project was to help home-based workers, who were primarily Muslim and observing purdah by working at home, to get higher wages for their work. Not only were they successful at raising the wages for that particular group of women, but also later SEWA introduced the convention to recognize home-based work at the International Labor Organization. The Home Work Convention is hailed as a significant milestone in strengthening "the human rights claims of women as workers in the global economy and reflect[s] the growing importance of social and economic rights" (Reilly 2009, 126).

SEWA and MarketPlace India recognize that gendered norms vary from community to community and that challenging gender discrimination and women's subordination cannot be separated out from other forms of oppression and exploitation which may be more severe and more detrimental, such as poverty, violence against women, religious violence, and caste discrimination. Although neither SEWA nor MarketPlace was formed explicitly to combat domestic violence, recall the examples of Asmita who was being abused by her in-laws, and of the MarketPlace worker whose coworkers took her in and then confronted her husband about his abuse. In both cases the combined economic and social support provided a base from which to challenge and stop domestic violence.

As I have been arguing, social change requires changes at multiple levels: micro, meso, and macro. On the micro-level, changes in behavior, practices, and interpersonal relationships; on the meso-level, changes in family relationships, education, media, and municipal and state-level policies; and on the macro-level, changes in national laws, and international policies and the unjust global economic order. Each of these levels plays a role in challenging and changing structural oppression, including gender oppression. As noted in chapter 5, social structural processes act as constraints on our actions, yet at the same time these social structures are the result of social processes and can be changed through collective action. I propose this multilevel systems approach to social justice as a methodology that is in keeping with feminist calls for an intersectional approach to dismantling structural injustice. In practice, remedying one form of injustice may take priority over another, or be at odds, at least temporarily. On-the-ground solutions are not always clear or easy, but commitment to values of diversity and social justice can move us forward.

Every theory and strategy has assumptions and normative commitments. In the course of this book, I have tried to make visible some of the normative commitments of dominant approaches to global gender equality, approaches such as universal human rights, neoliberal economic projects, and ethical individualist cosmopolitanism; all three approaches share a normative commitment to a strongly individualist self. This emphasis on individualism rather than on our mutual dependence influences other aspects of ethical and political projects, such as notions of freedom, and social goals. In the context of neoliberal economics, individual freedom relies on maximizing choice. Neoliberal economic policies ostensibly increase "freedom" through privatization, deregulation, and free trade policies (which are designed to favor wealthy industrialized countries and wealthy elites within countries). Because these policies create wealth for some and poverty for others, we can see that a systemic view of our mutual economic dependence structured through unequal power relationships yields a different picture of freedom, not individual choice but the eradication of poverty.

In contrast to the individualistic view of freedom as a type of laissez-faire license to do what one wants, Ela Bhatt sees economic freedom as freedom from poverty: "the problem of poverty and loss of freedom are not separate" (Bhatt 2000, 1). Calling economic power the "Second Freedom" after the political power of India's independence (the "First Freedom"), Bhatt notes that this Second Freedom involves increasing the competencies of economically and socially marginalized women to find their voices and to gain visibility through the process of working together to challenge their oppression, exploitation, and marginalization. Traditional philosophical approaches of rights theory and cosmopolitanism often privilege a notion of the self as atomistic, rather than as interconnected. But this exaggerated ideal of independence carries over to undermine collective projects and public goods. In order to acknowledge our vulnerabilities, dependence, and connections to others, we need to begin from a methodological commitment to interdependence, rather than independence.

A second related methodological assumption is that one aspect of our identities can be singled out or privileged in analyses. This move relies on both the abstraction of individuals from social systems characteristic of the abstract universalistic frameworks of liberalism and neoliberalism, and from its staunch individualism. The assumed neutrality of these frameworks makes it crucial that those with nondominant identities challenge this neutrality by asserting themselves as a group to claim rights, recognition, or restitution under a system that purports to support equality through its neutrality, but in fact undermines it. Color-blindness in the law can simply serve to protect social biases of racial discrimination and relegate social and economic issues to the private sector. But as we have seen, substantive economic and social equality are necessary preconditions in order to realize the civil and political rights afforded and protected by formal equality.

Focusing on social structures as processes and structural injustice as a particular type of moral harm provides a method of analysis that recognizes connections on the basis of material, structural relationships rather than a shared identity. I will not revisit here the question of a shared identity among women epitomized by the essentialist-difference debate among feminists (Spelman 1988; Fuss 1989; Butler 1990; Weir 2013). Moving away from woman as an identity category, feminists have proposed several ways to understand gender as relational, contextual, and produced through one's position in social structures, for instance as seriality, social location, standpoint, and postionality (Rich 1984; Alcoff 1988; Young 1994; Hartsock 1998). Each of these understandings views "woman" not as a pregiven social identity and "women" not as a pregiven social group, but as produced through social and structural processes; significantly, these social and structural processes are multidimensional, shaping us not only as women but also as raced, ethnic, poor or middle class or rich, religious or secular, "First World" or "Third World." Just as earlier discussions among academic feminists highlighted the tensions between assuming "women" was a necessary category for a feminist politics and acknowledging that categories inevitably erased difference and ignored complexity, a central issue for transnational feminism centers on a similar tension: given the variety and diversity of woman's experiences across the globe, on what and how can a transnational feminist politics be grounded? Chandra Mohanty has called for an inclusive feminist politics that would be decolonizing, anti-capitalist, and allow for solidarity (Mohanty 2003).

I suggest a shift from identity to intersectionality in two ways: first, a shift from an identity-based model of feminist politics to an intersectional model of feminist social justice; and second, that this intersectional model can be thought of as a type of methodology or tool of analysis. Feminist solidarity on this model would not be based on identity but on a shared commitment to social justice, and a feminist methodology that can analyze and challenge injustice without reinscribing identity categories. Intersectionality is oriented toward undoing structural injustice in ways that identity is not. For this reason, feminists should take up intersectionality rather than identity to ground our emancipatory feminist struggles.

The third methodological assumption that underlies much traditional political theory is an interest-based model of politics. Often political endeavors are seen in terms of interest; usually groups pursue their interests in opposition to other groups. Sometimes these interests are in terms of resources; sometimes they are claims to rights. In the United States, conflicts in interest emerged between African American males and white women over voting rights in the late nineteenth century. And interest groups often lobby for more resources for their particular cause, such as for national funding for medical research. In interest politics, the relationship between different groups is often agonistic and competitive. Unfortunately this paradigm characterizes politics at both the domestic and international level, as various interest groups and countries jockey for power and position. This competitive political paradigm is closely tied to the methodological assumptions of individualism and identity. But interdependence and intersectionality require a new political paradigm, one that recognizes the multifaceted character of injustice and the ways in which all of us are affected by and implicated in systems of injustice. Working against systemic injustices is a collective project. This collective project requires a shared commitment to social justice that is open ended. Working and thinking together in this way will require sociopolitical imagination. Therefore, I call for a shift in our political praxis from interest to imagination.

From Individualism to Interdependence

As we have seen, liberal political approaches begin from a strong view of abstract individualism. Proponents of these approaches claim that this is necessary to override abuses of individuals within groups, particularly by those with more power such as male elders. Yet feminists have pointed out that this "Robinson Crusoe" approach denies human dependence as necessary for our survival and socialization. If we truly were independent, no one would live to adulthood. Not only do we need the care of parents when we are babies and children, we often need the care of others in our lives when we are ill, go through surgery, or become elderly. In addition to this practical material and emotional care, we are also dependent on others for nearly every aspect of meeting our day-to-day basic needs, from eating to the clothes we wear. Institutional cosmopolitanism gestures toward this economic interdependence, and social connection theory makes it even more explicit. Interdependence is an inescapable condition of human life.

In a different way, Tagore expresses well the idea that we are connected as humans. Tagore emphasizes that humans are part of societies, and that valuing sociality and community is an aspect of our humanness. Adopting this view as the starting point for an ethics and politics would set us on a different path. Rather than beginning from the hypothetical assumption of radical independence and then having the task of justifying our ethical obligations to one another, we should begin from the reality of interdependence, knowing that we have ethical obligations to one another and working together to ensure that those obligations are fulfilled to the best of our ability.

The feminist social justice approach that I am advocating not only acknowledges our interdependence but also values it. Beginning from the reality of interdependence makes our normative ethical and political commitments clearer, as we saw in institutional cosmopolitanism and in social connection theory; we are complexly related in systems of production and consumption as well as through the global political and economic order. On the positive side, valuing our interdependence also means that we engage in collective projects, support public goods, and value relationships and communities.

From Identity to Intersectionality

As noted in the Introduction, feminists who try to organize women's emancipatory struggles around their identity as women arrive at an impasse, because sex is not separable from other aspects of social group identity, and aspects of identity are interrelated. Additionally, focusing on identities as the main site for emancipatory movements runs the risk of individualizing and psychologizing what is a collective, political struggle. Recently, several feminist theorists have explored the activist roots and political potential of theories of intersectionality (May 2015; Hancock 2016; Hill Collins and Bilge 2016). I cannot do justice to their individual and complex arguments here, but one shared theme is that intersectionality is not an apolitical focus on identities. The power and radical political potential of intersectionality comes from its articulation of social norms and oppressive structures and institutions, and from the analyses of the ways that these shape and constrain us. Furthermore, an intersectional approach calls upon us to transform these unjust structures and institutions in multiple ways. As Vivian May puts it: "intersectional concepts of liberation approach the world's possibilities pragmatically, in the here and now, and idealistically, with an eye toward more utopian goals of eradicating inequality, exploitation and supremacy, both at the micropolitical level of everyday life, and the macropolitical level of social structures, material practices and cultural norms" (2015, 5).

In this book we have seen how the women in SEWA and MarketPlace India work to challenge and change structural constraints and oppressive systems at both the micro- and macro-levels. From coming together to intervene when a coworker is experiencing domestic violence to forming unions and winning Supreme Court cases, the women in MarketPlace India and SEWA, many of whom lack formal education and come from the lower caste, continue to fight against economic exploitation and social oppression based on gender and caste; they challenge cultural norms around prescribed behaviors and practices. Their activism is a model of women coming together to work for social transformation; beginning from their own experiences as poor, uneducated, lower caste women, they challenge the social structures that oppress and exploit them. Their work together as members of cooperatives and unions provides a livelihood for each woman, and also a place to grow their collective strength to take on these larger challenges to social, economic, and political institutions together.

From Interest to Imagination

Some philosophers suggest that moral imagination can be a resource for individuals to better understand the situations and lives of those very different from themselves. But moral imagination is primarily discussed as an individual capacity, a "thinking about" rather than a "thinking with." When we engage in the collective project of working for social justice, sociopolitical imagination can be a valuable resource as we think with others to envision a better world.

This type of sociopolitical imagination may begin from specific local struggles and emerge out of specific historical and political contexts. SEWA was inspired by Mohandas K. Gandhi and continued his commitment to social justice by working with poor women. According to Ela Bhatt, "Gandhiji's thinking has shown us the way, a clear direction, leading us to commitment, sustained efforts, a gentle but firm belief in women's leadership in social change, and *willingness to see beyond what was around.* What has been inspiring about this search is realizing how much we did and can do much much more, how significantly we transformed the place and time we have been through, and what is more inspiring is that it did not occur to us not to" (Bhatt 2000, 2, emphasis mine). This "willingness to see beyond what was around" and the commitment to "think with" rather than merely think about those who are disadvantaged exemplify a political paradigm of sociopolitical imagination.

Sociopolitical imagination requires openness and a willingness to be transformed through the processes of collaboration. For instance, collaboration between those with formal education and those without is valued in SEWA: "A woman who has studied land tenure rights in the university has a lot to learn from women who actually cultivate the land and who understand village land politics. They are essential to each other in developing new models of women's collective access to land" (Rose 1992, 89). Sociopolitical imagination helps us to envision radically different social, economic, and political relationships based on acknowledging and valuing our interdependence.

In a fitting image of transformation, Emily Kawano uses the example of a caterpillar changing into a butterfly. This metamorphosis involves imaginal cells:

> These cells have a different vision of what the caterpillar could be and in fact they are so different from the original cells that they are attacked and killed by the immune system. Still, more and more imaginal cells continue to develop. They begin to find each other and, recognizing each other as part of the same project of metamorphosis, they begin to form clusters. Eventually, these clusters of imaginal cells begin to work together, taking on different functions, and building a whole new creature . . . they build a new organism which emerges from the chrysalis as the butterfly. (Kawano 2009, 15)

The imaginal cells are aptly named, as they have a different vision of what could be and they can only achieve this vision through their collective strength.

While writing this book, the limitations of theory and language were often apparent to me as I tried to figure out the ways that traditional philosophical theory could analyze and illuminate complex situations of actual injustice in all its dimensions. This task is made difficult by the disciplinary nature of philosophy, which is to abstract and generalize. Yet simply describing particular situations errs on the other side; it may capture the complexity of real life, but it lacks a normative framework. In exploring issues of global justice for women, I took my cue from women's organizations that were concerned both with women's basic needs and with combatting structural injustice. Often white academic feminists from the global North privilege gender in their analyses of oppression, creating what can be called a "gender-first" feminism. But gender-first feminism often de-emphasizes other aspects of identity, as we have seen in the debate about culture and gender equality.

The limitations of language became apparent during the course of writing this book: Should I follow the convention in philosophy by talking about global gender justice? Should I adopt the language of transnational feminism and discuss transnational feminist solidarity? How is the social justice framework I describe and advocate feminist if it does not privilege gender? Is the primary aim of feminism to challenge sexism and gender domination or to improve women's welfare? And what happens when these conflict? And there were more questions: how do I write about women, knowing that there is no such category, without adjectival overload?

One thing that happened in the course of writing is that my thinking and language began to change: from global gender justice to feminist global justice or feminist social justice, and from transnational feminist solidarity to feminist transnational solidarity projects. Both of these changes reflect moving from trying to articulate feminism as singular and unified to an understanding of feminism as diverse and plural. The shift in language also corresponds with a change in focus from an account of justice focused on gender and women to an intersectional feminist method of thinking about the ways that projects of justice must attend to various aspects of exploitation, oppression, and domination.

Moving from individualism to interdependence, from identity to intersectionality, and from interest to imagination reorients our methodology to a collective, collaborative and open enterprise working together in full awareness of our diversity toward a shared vision of a just world.

We cannot know in advance exactly the form and shape that this will take. But we can begin from a multilevel systemic approach to recognizing and working against injustice in all its forms: economic exploitation, social oppression, and the psychological domination of internalized oppression. We can also be confident that these forms of injustice arise in different ways in different contexts, and that collaboration requires deep listening and a commitment to collective action. Feminists contribute significant methodological tools to the pursuit of social justice. A feminist social justice methodology can inform theories of global justice that continue to either leave women out or assume that women constitute a coherent category. A grounded, pragmatic feminist social justice approach offers an integrated method for analysis and action that opens up new concepts, new strategies, and new visions for a just world.

NOTES

Introduction

1. The three book-length studies are Ela Bhatt, *We Are Poor, But So Many: The Story of Self-Employed Women in India*; Kalima Rose, *Where Women Are Leaders: The SEWA Movement in India*; and Mary A. Littrell and Marsha A. Dickson, *Artisans and Fair Trade: Crafting Development* (MarketPlace India). For names and authors of the reports and booklets from SEWA, see Bibliography.

2. I develop my feminist social justice approach from various approaches to social justice, which are usually employed separately. A notable exception is "The Red, the Green, the Black and the Purple: Reclaiming Development, Resisting Globalization," where Kum-Kum Bhavani, John Forna, and Molly Talcott bring together the frameworks of socialism, environmentalism, critical race theory, feminism, and sexuality. Their approach, like mine, is inspired by and informed by practices of resistance of people in the global South. I contrast my feminist social justice approach to "rights-justice" approaches. Rights-justice approaches focus on political and legal equality, and often ignore structural injustice. While making an important contribution to working for justice and equality, rights-justice approaches generally are individualist and state-centric. Furthermore, economic institutions often fall outside the purview of this approach.

3. See Meyers and Kittay, eds. (1987), Held (2006), Nedelsky (2011), and Weir (2013).

4. Kimberle Crenshaw is credited with coining the term "intersectionality" in her article, "Mapping the Margins: Intersectionality, Identity Politics and Violence Against Women of Color" (1991). In their recent book, *Intersectionality* (2016), Patricia Hill Collins and Silma Bilge suggest that the roots of the concept begin earlier. They note the importance of the Combahee River Collective Statement, and also Deborah King's article, "Double Jeopardy," in laying the groundwork for the idea of intersectionality.

5. Some feminists have criticized the liberal feminist position that endorses primarily legal and political sanctions to remedy what they see as broader-based societal problems. They term the liberal feminist reliance on the state "carceral feminism" because it endorses state power, including punitive measures, against marginalized populations.

Janet Halley has also criticized the international feminist movement for including violence against women as a violation of human rights. Halley calls this type of feminism "governance feminism." These criticisms view liberal feminism with its reliance on laws, the justice system, and established institutions as increasing state power over the already disenfranchised.

6. Economic Policy Institute, "What is the gender pay gap and is it real?, https://www.epi.org/publication/what-is-the-gender-pay-gap-and-is-it-real/#epi-toc-13. Accessed August 12, 2018.

7. Iris Marion Young, *Justice and the Politics of Difference* (Princeton, NJ: Princeton University Press, 1990), 57. Although Young is discussing the powerless specifically with reference to the working class, much of what she says can be generalized to those who are socially marginalized on the basis of other types of social group membership.

8. Here I am following Mohanty in her usage of "Third World women" as a political term that includes women from the global South, as well women of color in the global North.

9. Young makes a sharp distinction between moral and political responsibility, but I argue that the distinction she draws is too clean, and that these types of responsibilities overlap, especially in accounts like hers that recognize our social connection as the source of responsibilities.

10. This insight is not specific to feminism. Martin Luther King Jr. famously said, "Injustice anywhere is a threat to justice everywhere" (West 2015, 244).

11. I have heard this story in various community organizing situations. It is an adapted version of an oft-told parable—popularized in the 1930s by social reformer and community organizer Saul Alinksy. I have also drawn from Aaron Schutz's version of this story.

12. I have adapted this version from versions I have heard and from "The Parable of the River and What Organizing Is Not" posted by Aaron Schutzwww.educationaction.org/uploads.

13. Paraphrased from "The Parable of the River and What Organizing Is Not" by Aaron Schutz.

14. United Nations Development Programme, The 2016 Human Development Report—India country profile (http://hdr.undp.org/en/countries/profiles/IND).

15. In both these cases I use "Third World" because it is in Spivak's quote, and because it is consistent with the language Mohanty uses in her discussion of SEWA.

Chapter 1

1. Information about these organizations was obtained through my research visits to MarketPlace India in 2004, 2005, and 2017 and to SEWA in 2005, 2006, and 2017 as well as through several research publications by SEWA purchased while there. In addition to my firsthand experience of these organizations, I have drawn on three book-length studies (Kalima Rose, *Where Women Are Leaders: The SEWA Movement in India*; Ela Bhatt, *We Are Poor but So Many: The Story of Self-Employed Women in India*; and Mary A. Littrell and Marsha A. Dickson, *Artisans and Fair Trade: Crafting Development*) as well as a number of articles. Quotations from MarketPlace members in italics without a citation are drawn from the interviews I conducted during my research.

2. Mission statement for MarketPlace: Handwork of India website; accessed February 3, 2018. https://www.marketplaceindia.com/

3. Here I depart from my usage of "global South" and follow Mohanty, Narayan, and others' use of "Third World" to refer to both women in the global South and women of color in the diaspora. In this sense "Third World" has a political meaning of resistance and solidarity, and it is not merely a descriptor.

4. One example of a singular approach to justice issues is the focus on human rights; I discuss the limitations of such a singular focus in chapter 2. The human rights framework has been tremendously important in international and transnational struggles for justice. At the same time, it has also been criticized as imperialist and insensitive to cultural context. In the 1980s and 1990s, feminists concerned with international women's rights and global gender justice adopted the strategy of working for women's rights as human rights. While the framework of universal human rights has certainly been useful for securing some gains for women, it often minimizes the importance of historical and cultural contexts, and historically has emphasized political and legal rights at the expense of economic and social rights. Through examples, I show the importance of attention to cultural context and historical specificity, and that economic and social rights and political and legal rights cannot be pried apart.

5. I address empowerment further in chapter 3.

6. Much has been written about both the benefits and the limitations of poverty alleviation projects that focus on women and income generation. I take up this issue in chapter 3, arguing that the approach taken by MarketPlace India and SEWA differs from the approach taken by microfinance institutions (hereafter MFIs) and is therefore not subject to the same criticisms.

7. See, for instance, Charlotte Bunch (1993, 1995) and Susan Moller Okin (1999, 2000).

8. I have attended the Non-Governmental Organizational Forums of the United Nations Conferences on Women in Nairobi, Kenya, in 1985, and in Beijing, China, in 1995. Participating in these forums broadened my perspective on "women's issues." In 1985 I vividly remember seeing a fuel-efficient stove made from a coffee can and wondering how that was a "women's issue." The explanation—that women were primarily responsible for gathering firewood, a difficult and time-consuming task, and for cooking meals—combined aspects of concern for the environment and the disproportionately negative impact of environmental destruction on women, as well as an analysis of gender and labor. Participating in these conferences where I met and learned from women involved in social change and women's issues from all over the world impacted my perspective on women's issues and feminism. In addition, I have met with women's organizations working for gender equity and social change in a number of places, including many countries in the global South, and these experiences have continually challenged my settled perceptions and much of the dominant discourse in academic feminism.

9. See chapter 3 for a fuller discussion of cooperative principles and history.

10. These were the numbers when I conducted my fieldwork and did interviews in February and March 2004. Current numbers are available on the MarketPlace India website; in February 2018, MarketPlace India was working with over four hundred members in eleven cooperatives.

11. This was the most recent report available at the time of writing.

12. I discuss resistance and hostility to the change in gender roles, and women's empowerment further in chapter 3.

1. We can see the evolution of human rights discourse as striving to overcome this initial insensitivity to cultural, religious, ability, and even class-based differences through its successive iterations in the United Nations Declarations on the Rights of Indigenous Peoples, the Rights of the Disabled, and Peasants Rights.

2. I adopted this term, "transnational feminist advocacy," from Niamh Reilly (2009).

3. See, for example, the essays in Rebecca Cook, *Human Rights of Women: National and International Perspectives* (Philadelphia: University of Pennsylvania Press, 1994), especially Singh, and the essays in Julie Peters and Andrea Wolper, *Women's Rights, Human Rights: International Feminist Perspectives* (New York: Routledge, 1995), especially Friedman, Saurez Toro, and Stamatopoulou.

4. This division between the public and private spheres is a well-known characteristic of political liberalism. The public sphere includes politics and work, whereas the private sphere is comprised of home, family, and domestic life. Typically, contemporary justice theorists have held that justice operated only in the public sphere. John Rawls's influential *Theory of Justice* articulates this position. For an excellent feminist critique of political liberalism's division between public and private spheres, see Susan Moller Okin's *Justice, Gender and the Family* (New York: Basic Books, 1989).

5. The film *The Vienna Tribunal: Women's Rights Are Human Rights* (directed by Gerry Rogers, Augusta Productions, 1994) vividly captures testimony from a number of women.

6. As Nivedita Menon discusses in "Abortion and the Law" (*Canadian Journal of Women and the Law* 6, no. 1 [1993]), characterizing sex-selective abortion as sexual violence may play into the push to restrict abortions, thus pitting two important issues for women and feminists against one another—the issue of access to abortion versus the sex discrimination of sex-selective abortion.

7. For an excellent overview of the issue of women's rights as human rights, see Peters and Wolper (1995).

8. I characterize this perspective as both "Western" and from the global North, although I recognize that these are not identical. The discourses and policies of the West and those of the global North are both dominant discourses of privileged groups, but they do not divide up the world in precisely the same way. For example, Asian countries such as Japan and China get Orientalized by discourses of westernization. Yet as a wealthy, postindustrial nation, Japan may share with Northern European countries and the United States an economically privileged position similar to that of the global North. In contrast, while Greece shares Western heritage and discourse with the wealthy, postindustrialized nations of Europe and the United States, it is arguably part of the global South because of its economic situation. There isn't one (singular) "dominant" position. My thanks to Shelley Park for this point.

9. See also Dorothy Roberts, *Killing the Black Body: Race, Reproduction, and the Meaning of Liberty* (New York: Pantheon, 1997); and her "Race and the New Reproduction," in *The Reproductive Rights Reader: Law, Medicine, and the Construction of Motherhood*, edited by Nancy Ehrenreich, 308–319 (New York: New York University Press, 2008).

10. Although feminist critiques of rights come from several different directions, there are some overlapping concerns: the concepts of self and identity presupposed by

universal rights. The self is assumed to be individualistic, atomistic, rational, and devoid of particular features or identity. These assumptions are criticized by care ethicists and communitarian feminists. Identity is assumed to be individual and abstract, and devoid of any constitutive commitments to cultural or religious beliefs. (These assumptions are criticized by postcolonial feminists and communitarian feminists, and feminist anthropologists.) Socialist feminists are concerned with the lack of focus on economic and social rights in a world in which there is deep and growing social and economic inequality, and in which current economic institutions seem geared to exacerbate this inequality, or at best attempt to ameliorate it through redistribution rather than widespread radical reform of institutions; this concern is also shared by socialist feminists and some postcolonial feminists.

11. See Carol Gilligan, *In a Different Voice: Psychological Theory and Women's Development* (Cambridge, MA: Harvard University Press, 1982).

12. There are a number of anthologies with essays by feminist moral and political theorists which come directly out of Gilligan's work; see, for instance, Kittay and Meyers (1987); Cole and Coultrap-McQuin (1992); and Larrabee (1993).

13. Barbara Ehrenreich and Arlie Hochschild (eds.), *Global Woman: Nannies, Sex Workers, and Maids* (New York: Metropolitan Books, 2002) vividly demonstrates the global chains of care and dependency when care work for children, elders, the ill, and the house is provided by immigrant women who leave their own children behind to care for others. For an excellent discussion of Filipina women who leave their own children behind to raise other people's children as their nannies, see Rhacel Salzar Parennas (2001, 2002).

14. For an excellent argument that this self-in-relation implies new theories of identity and freedom, see Allison Weir, *Identities and Freedom* (Oxford, UK: Oxford University Press, 2013).

15. I use the terms "postcolonial feminists," "feminists of color," and "white Western feminists" with some reservations recognizing (along with Mohanty [1991] and many others) that these categories are problematic and may best be thought of as identifying an analytic perspective rather than a social location. Moreover, the categories themselves are not mutually exclusive.

16. For an excellent and extended discussion of these issues, see Uma Narayan, *Dislocating Cultures*, especially chaps. 1, 2, and 3. My discussion here is deeply indebted to her work.

17. See Anne Phillips, *Multiculturalism Without Culture* (Princeton, NJ: Princeton University Press, 2007) for a nuanced argument about the debate between multiculturalists and liberal theorists on the role of culture and cultural groups in politics, policy, and societies.

18. See Saba Mahmood, *The Politics of Piety* (Princeton, NJ: Princeton University Press, 2005) for a study of the way that religious identity can be constitutive of, and inseparable from, women's sense of self and identity. See Allison Weir, *Identities and Freedom* (Oxford, UK: Oxford University Press, 2013) for the philosophical implications for identities and freedoms when particular identities are acknowledged as constitutive of the self.

19. See Mahmood, *The Politics of Piety*; and Naila Kabeer, "Empowerment, Citizenship and Gender Justice: A Contribution to Locally Grounded Theories of Change

in Women's Lives," in *Ethics and Social Welfare* 6, no. 3 (2012): 216–232. I owe the formulation of this point to Shelley Park.

20. Anne Phillips also claims that culture plays an important role in peoples' lives, but that the notion of culture has been simplified and reified in the liberal-multicultural debate. See her *Multiculturalism Without Culture* (2007), especially chaps. 1 and 2.

21. This point, the conflict between a universal human rights and a respect for cultures that presumably leads to a cultural and ethical relativism that undermines the claim of universality for human rights, has been the source of much debate for philosophers and anthropologists. See the *Anthropology Newsletter* (2000) for an overview of this debate among anthropologists. Two philosophers who address this question head-on in recent work on human rights are Robert Paul Churchill and Carol Gould. Robert Paul Churchill claims that an acceptance of universal human rights is compatible with value pluralism. Further, he argues that the criticism of Western cultural imperialism about the universality of human rights can be mitigated by recognizing that they are defeasible (i.e., not absolute) and by acknowledging that although human rights norms apply cross-culturally, their application is open to discussion and interpretation. See his *Human Rights and Global Diversity* (2006, chaps. 2 and 3) for a full discussion of this issue. Carol Gould makes a distinction between two types of universality: an abstract universality that often results in imposing "Western liberal conceptions of norms of development and rights under the guise of the universally human" (Gould 2004, 51) and what she calls "concrete universality," wherein norms develop out of conversation and consensus. See her *Globalizing Democracy and Human Rights* (2009, ch. 2) for a fuller discussion.

22. See Uma Narayan, *Dislocating Cultures* (2010, ch. 2) for an excellent discussion of the politics and historical context of sati and the feminist literature around the topic.

23. For a more detailed analysis of sati, and of the Roop Kanwar case, see Narayan (1997, ch. 2); Lata Mani, "Contentious Traditions: The Debate on SATI in Colonial India," *Cultural Critique* (Fall 1987); and Veena Talwar Oldenburg, "The Roop Kanwar Case: Feminist Responses," in *Sati, The Blessing and the Curse: The Burning of Wives in India*, edited by John Stratton Hawley (Oxford, UK: Oxford University Press, 1994).

Chapter 3

1. Anibal Quijano, in "The Coloniality of Power," discusses the connections among colonialism, capitalism, and racial domination; he makes clear connections to the racialized exploitation of labor. Maria Lugones extends his analysis to incorporate a gendered as well as the racialized colonial labor system; see her "The Coloniality of Gender."

2. The report defines the "brink of poverty" as making $47,000 a year for a family of four.

3. Sylvia Chant expands the notion of the feminization of poverty, arguing that it does not capture women's unpaid labor within the home; she argues instead for a more expansive notion of "feminization of responsibility or obligation." See her "Exploring the 'Feminisation of Poverty' in Relation to Women's Work and Home-Based Enterprise in Slums of the Global South" (Chant 2014).

4. Some argue that globalization is not a new phenomenon, but has been going on as long as commerce, trade, travel, and immigration. However, there are undeniably new aspects of globalization in the contemporary world. Inda and Rosaldo point out five important flows typical of contemporary globalization: images, ideologies, capital, people,

and commodities (Inda and Rosaldo 2003, 4). Arjun Appadurai offers a similar five-fold framework for thinking about the cultural dimensions of global flows: ethnoscapes (people); mediascapes (media/images); technoscapes (technologies); financescapes (monetary flows); and ideoscapes (ideologies usually connected to the state) (Appadurai 1996). Technology, specifically the Internet, social media, and cell phones, make transnational communication easier than ever.

5. For general discussions of globalization see Joseph Stiglitz, *Globalization and Its Discontents*, and *Making Globalization Work*; Arjun Appadurai, *Modernity at Large: Cultural Dimensions of Globalization*; Patrick O'Meara, Howard D. Mehlinger, and Matthew Krain (eds.), *Globalization and the Challenges of a New Century*; and Jan Pieterse (ed.), *Global Futures: Shaping Globalization*. For critiques of globalization, see Tony Smith, *Globalisation: A Systematic Marxist Account*; Kevin Danaher (ed.), *Democratizing the Global Economy*; Jeremy Brecher, Tim Costello, and Brendan Smith (eds.), *Globalization from Below: The Power of Solidarity*; and David Solnit (ed.), *Globalize Liberation: How to Uproot the System and Build a Better World*. For analyses of the differential gendered aspect of globalization and how it impacts women, see *Global Woman: Nannies, Maids and Sex Workers in the New Economy*, Barbara Ehrenreich and Arlie Hochschild (eds.); *Women and Globalization*, Delia D. Aguilar and Anne E. Lacsamana (eds.); *Gender and Globalization: Patterns of Women's Resistance*, Erica G. Polakoff and Ligaya Lindo-McGovern (eds.); *Globalization and Third World Women: Exploitation, Coping, Resistance*, Ligaya Lindo-McGovern and Isidor Walliman (eds.); *The Gender of Globalization: Women Navigating Cultural and Economic Marginalization*, Nandini Gunewardena and Ann Kingsolver (eds.); and *Women's Activism and Globalization: Linking Local Struggles and Transnational Politics*, Nancy A. Naples and Manisha Desai (eds.).

6. To be fair, globalization has positive as well as negative effects. Some argue that one of the positive effects of globalization is that it fosters transnational ideas and concepts such as human rights and gender equality. Specifically, they claim that globalization helps to promote the discourse of human rights and gender equality through a wider circulation of international treaties, documents, and so on; through increased access to political, cultural, and social situations and circumstances outside one's own via media, social media, and the Internet; and through the increased possibility of transnational activism. Given my argument in chapter 2 about the limitations of rights discourse, even this "positive" aspect of globalization is ambiguous.

7. In part, this was initiated by a "conscientisation" approach developed by Paulo Freire in his popular education approach in Latin America.

8. *Microfinance* covers a variety of institutions and is often used synonymously with *microcredit* and sometimes *microenterprise*; here I will use *microfinance* and *microcredit* interchangeably following the practice in the literature on women and development. See Beatriz Armendariz and Jonathan Morduch, *The Economics of Microfinance* (2nd ed., 1–27), for a clear concise explanation of the history and differences. In short, microcredit is the practice of simply offering small, collateral-free loans to the poor, while microfinance covers a broader range of financial services, including savings and insurance as well as loans.

9. These objectives are listed in Lamia Karim (2008, 9) and are originally from the Grameen website.

10. Anapurna Pariwar, an NGO in India, also uses this joint liability group model. A recent study of Annapurna Pariwar found both benefits and drawbacks to this model of group lending. On the one hand, it strengthened relationships among group members who had to rely on one another's responsible and timely repayment for future loans; on the other hand, making future loans contingent on all group members' ability to repay loans on time often strained relationships within the group (Krenz et al., "Exploring Women's Empowerment Through 'Credit-Plus' Microfinance in India," *Affilia: Journal of Women and Social Work* 29, no. 3 [2014]: 310–325).

11. There are a number of issues here that I cannot fully address. Apparently, these MFIs do not challenge the idea of women being the traditional custodians of family honor. Moreover, NGOs focused on improving women's lives should avoid penalizing them with jail time, especially as it may result in divorce, which will only exacerbate a woman's social exclusion and economic deprivation in the context of rural Bangladesh.

12. See Karim (2008, 21). She states that 100 out of 230 NGO beneficiary households were engaged in moneylending in Krishnonagar.

13. Elizabeth Bowman and Bob Stone, "Cooperatives: A Brief Introduction to Their Types, History and Social Change Prospect," in the Center for Global Justice Newsletter (December 2007): 1–5, p. 1. See also International Cooperative Association website, http://ica.coop/en/whats-co-op/co-operative-identity-values-principles/. Accessed April 29, 2014.

14. See also *Worker Cooperatives in Theory and Practice* by Mary Mellor, Janet Hannah, and John Stirling, p. 37. They refer to Six Rochdale Principles originating in Rochdale and adopted by the International Cooperative Alliance in 1934; these principles are still recognized as fundamental to cooperatives worldwide.

15. There are several other well-known historical examples. For instance, the cooperatives that flourished under the Paris Commune in 1871. And more recently, Mondragon in Spain (founded in the mid-twentieth century) exemplifies a successful multifaceted group of cooperatives. And in 1968 in the wake of liberation struggles and a call for new nonhierarchical institutions, the idea of "self-management" and cooperatives was reintroduced the world over. In the past three decades, cooperativism has emerged most prominently in Latin America: cooperatives in Cuba, Zapatista "communities of struggle," the occupation of unused land (Brazil), and the cooperativization of factories (in Argentina and Uruguay) all provide new hope for future economic democracies.

16. Note that the names here are fictional because these quotes are unattributed in Littrell and Dickson (2010).

Chapter 4

1. Cosmopolitan approaches include political, economic, cultural, and moral approaches. For a brief overview of the distinctions among different types of cosmopolitanism, see Eduardo Mendieta (2009) and Miller (2011, especially p. 393). Moral cosmopolitanism usually employs a universalism that abstracts from all particular features and identities; following Carol Gould I call this "abstract universalism." My criticism of universalism is directed toward this type of abstract universalism that overemphasizes rationality as the main criteria for inclusion in moral considerations, and employs a type of methodological individualism. Along with Gould, I argue for a concrete universalism that emerges from dialogue and consensus.

2. I use the term "relational cosmopolitanism" to highlight the features of Tagore's view that provide a distinct contrast to mainstream views of moral cosmopolitanism. Tagore recognizes human interdependence, values human and cultural diversity, and acknowledges that we can and should be transformed by our relationships with one another. Emphasizing relationality also follows recent developments in contemporary feminist theory that recognize that major concepts such as autonomy and freedom are relational, rather than strictly individualist.

3. I raise several of these criticisms in McLaren (2001, 2007). See also Sarah Clark Miller (2010, 2011).

4. Other philosophers offer a modified version of Nussbaum's individualist cosmopolitanism. For instance, Kwame Anthony Appiah's rooted cosmopolitanism gives more credence to local attachments and affiliations than Nussbaum's cosmopolitanism does. Appiah in "Patriotism and Cosmopolitanism," his response to Nussbaum's essay, counters her lack of acknowledging the importance of place and particular identities, communities, and traditions with the idea of a "rooted cosmopolitanism." Rather than arguing that one's identity is contingent and accidental as Nussbaum does, he notes that each of us comes from a specific home, with specific traditions, and that these may influence the ways that we make meaning of our lives. Appiah's rooted cosmopolitanism values particularity and one's specific identities. However, in his book-length treatment of cosmopolitanism, *Cosmopolitanism: Ethics in a World of Strangers*, he favors commonality over difference. Here Appiah characterizes cosmopolitanism as conflicting strands. On the one hand, cosmopolitanism enjoins us to have a universal concern for others on the basis of their shared humanity. And on the other hand, cosmopolitanism urges us to value and respect difference and human diversity. However, he ultimately argues that our shared human history and identity ought to hold more weight than our particular stories and homes. Like Nussbaum, he valorizes rationality and values our shared, common, human identity.

5. Feminists who advocate care cosmopolitanism, for instance Sarah Clark Miller and Fiona Robinson, also point out the limitations of the justice framework used by moral cosmopolitans such as Pogge and Nussbaum.

6. Here I am in agreement with Sarah Clark Miller, who notes that shifting the framework away from the justice model allows us to ask different questions (see Miller 2011). One of the primary limitations of the moral cosmopolitan framework is its neglect of the role of culture and identity in moral life. See Anne Phillips, *Multiculturalism Without Culture*, for an extended argument on the role that culture plays in our moral and social lives.

7. See, for example, Martha Nussbaum et al., *For Love of Country?*; Kwame Anthony Appiah, *Cosmopolitanism: Ethics in A World of Strangers*; Seyla Benhabib, *Another Cosmopolitanism*; Pheng Cheah and Bruce Robbins (eds.), *Cosmopolitics: Thinking Beyond and Feeling Beyond the Nation*; and Carol Breckenridge et al. (eds.), *Cosmopolitanism*.

8. This list is far from exhaustive. But it gives some sense of the historical persistence of the interest in cosmopolitanism and the range of traditions, approaches, and positions addressing cosmopolitanism.

9. I do not discuss cosmopolitanism and immigration. For discussions of cosmopolitanism and immigration see, for example, Seyla Behabib, *Another Cosmopolitanism*;

Joseph Carens, "Cosmopolitanism, Nationalism and Immigration: False Dichotomies and Shifting Presuppositions"; Peter Higgins, "Open Borders and the Right to Immigration"; and Jose Jorge Mendoza, "Does Cosmopolitan Justice Ever Require Restrictions on Migration?."

10. Care cosmopolitanism is a notable exception to this.

11. See also Fiona Robinson, *Globalizing Care: Ethics, Feminist Theory and International Relations*.

12. See Walter Mignolo, "The Many Faces of Cosmo-polis: Border Thinking and Critical Cosmopolitanism," in *Cosmopolitanism*, edited by Breckenridge et al., 157–187 (Durham, NC: Duke University Press, 2002).

13. Other feminist cosmopolitans include those adopting a framework of care (Sarah Clark Miller, Fiona Robinson); those coming from a critical theory framework (Seyla Benhabib), and those engaging with the framework of multiculturalism (Anne Phillips). My approach here is closest to those coming out of a care ethics framework, as there is much overlap between our criticisms of justice-oriented moral cosmopolitanism.

14. Although the essay was originally published in 1994 in the *Boston Review*, it was reprinted as the book *For Love of Country?* along with responses in 2002. I focus on this essay rather than her subsequent books, *Frontiers of Justice: Disability, Nationality, Species Membership* and *Political Emotions: Why Love Matters for Justice*, in order to draw a sharper contrast among the types of cosmopolitanism I am describing.

15. In the preface to *For Love of Country?*, Nussbaum addresses an American audience in the aftermath of the terrorist attacks on the World Trade Center on September 11, 2001. In the immediate wake of this attack, many Americans reacted by adopting an aggressive and uncritical patriotism that drew sharp distinctions between "us" (American citizens) and "them" (everyone else, especially those in the Middle East). Cosmopolitanism offers a position that rejects this sharp distinction between "us" and "them" by claiming that national boundaries are arbitrary, and by asserting that our overriding moral obligation is to all humans, not only fellow citizens.

16. Sarah Clark Miller identifies similar shortcomings in moral cosmopolitanism: hyperindividualism, abstraction, idealization, and acontextuality; I adopt these features to evaluate Nussbaum's position. See Sarah Clark Miller "Cosmopolitan Care" (2010) and "A Feminist Account of Global Responsibility" (2011).

17. It should be noted, however, that much of her work is dedicated to an exploration of the emotions and their importance for moral life. She develops a view of the importance of emotions for political justice in her *Political Emotions: Why Love Matters for Justice.*

18. In her later work on cosmopolitanism, she draws more extensively on Tagore than she does in this earlier essay, but she continues to view him within the Western liberal tradition.

19. Nussbaum makes the connection between Kant's cosmopolitanism and the Stoics' cosmopolitanism even more explicit in her article "Kant and Stoic Cosmopolitanism," upon which I also draw.

20. But if capacity for moral reason is the basis for respect for persons, this excludes young children, those with severe cognitive disabilities, and those with certain types of dementia. Much has been written about the problems with defining personhood primarily on the capacity to reason, and I cannot fully discuss this literature here.

21. For her full argument, see *Frontiers of Justice* (2006).

22. In Nussbaum's *Political Emotions*, she draws on other works of Tagore, notably his lectures on nationalism upon which I also draw.

23. Thanks to Grant Cornwell for drawing my attention to this distinction.

24. Nussbaum does not specify who these critics of the Enlightenment are.

25. Other philosophers make similar distinctions; for instance, Judith Butler talks about "contingent universals." Charles Taylor discusses the role of dialogue and the importance of moral pluralism. Jurgen Habermas develops a dialogic approach based on the ideal speech situation. And Alison Jaggar has developed a feminist dialogue approach to global issues.

26. See, for instance, Vandana Shiva et al., *The Mirage of Market Access: How Globalization Is Destroying Farmers' Lives and Livelihoods* (New Delhi: Navdanya Research Foundation for Science, Technology, and Ecology, 2003)..

27. Interactional cosmopolitans postulate fundamental principles of ethics, while institutional cosmopolitans postulate fundamental principles of justice. Both are concerned with individual humans as the object of moral concern, and both view the scope of justice as global. I use the term "individualist cosmopolitan" to refer to Nussbaum's view because it calls attention to the conception of self embedded in her cosmopolitan theory. Institutional cosmopolitans include Thomas Pogge and Charles Beitz; interactional cosmopolitans include Henry Shue, David Luben, and Robert Nozick. There are many further distinctions among cosmopolitan views, such as cosmopolitans who believe that global justice requires a full equality of opportunity (equalitarianism) and those that believe that a certain minimal standard is required (sufficientarians). For my purposes, I focus on the difference between cosmopolitan views that are individualist versus those that are institutional, and those that advocate for a strong universality based on similarities among humans versus those that find connection across difference to be enough to ground moral concerns.

28. Walter Mignolo also emphasizes diversity as central to cosmopolitanism.

29. Like others who discuss cosmopolitanism, notably Kant and Derrida, Tagore discusses hospitality. I will not go into this topic here, but I plan to develop it in a separate essay.

30. Tagore paints the values of "the East" in very broad strokes; he could even be accused of Orientalism because of the generalizations he makes about "the East" and his romanticism of the values and lifestyle of "the East." However, I think it is instructive to see his valorization of "the East" (Asia and Asian values) as a form of resistance to imperialism.

31. Interestingly, his view on history appears contradictory. He states: "There is only one history—the history of man (sic)" (1918, 36). And yet he also claims that each people has its own history and borrowing other's history only serves "to crush your life" (38). This may be explained by his belief that "All national histories are merely chapters in the larger one" (36).

Chapter 5

1. There is a large body of Anglo-American feminist work on care and responsibility; oftentimes the language of care and responsibility is contrasted with the language of rights and justice. Moreover, care and responsibility have sometimes been criticized as

limited to the interpersonal realm, whereas rights and justice hold sway in public arenas and in politics. However, one hallmark of feminist work is questioning the line between the private and the public; we need justice in the family as well as caring in public life (e.g., see Okin, Kittay, Tronto, and Held). Blurring the line between public and private likewise exposes the overlapping intersections of ethics and politics, which I take up later.

2. Young mentions John Rawls and David Miller as representatives of the position that obligations of justice arise from a shared political community, and Peter Singer and Peter Unger as representatives of the cosmopolitan-utilitarian position.

3. This is, of course, the classic problem for cosmopolitanism: how to justify our global moral obligations to those "distant strangers" who are not in our nation or community. For Young, these moral obligations turn into political obligations or political responsibility.

4. Iris Marion Young, "Gender as Seriality: Thinking about Women as a Social Collective." *Signs* 19, no. 3 (Spring 1994): 713–738.

5. In addition to the Coalition of Immokalee Workers, the National Farmworker Ministry, the Young Adult and Youth Alliance (YAYA), and the Student Farmworker Alliance are directly involved in the Fair Food Alliance.

6. Just one year later, 1,129 workers were killed and 2,500 were injured when a fire broke out in Rana Plaza in Dhaka Bangladesh and the building collapsed. To date, this has been the deadliest incident in the garment industry worldwide. Patricia Hill-Collins and Sirma Bilge note: "Using intersectionality as an analytic tool sheds light on how some of the key features of the Rana Plaza collapse led to global social protest. [B]ecause the Rana Plaza collapse highlights how capitalism and nation–state policies converge to shape the inequalities in the global garment industry, intersectionality suggests new avenues of investigation for social protest" (2016, 144).

7. Elizabeth Ashford notes in "Responsibility for Violations of the Human Right to Subsistence" that the intrapersonal trade-off between not being able to feed your child or accepting a job at a sweatshop takes place against the background condition of severe poverty; "This indicates that moral responsibility for sweatshop labor is shared in large part by those responsible for the background persistence of severe poverty" (Ashford 2014, 115). This loses some of the specificity of Young's model (and is more in line with a cosmopolitan model like Pogge's), but it is consistent with Young's desire to question background conditions.

8. Environmental justice (formerly termed *environmental racism*) examines the differential impact on poor communities and communities of color of the effects of decisions such as where to locate garbage dumps, nuclear plants, large factories, and toxic waste sites. Access to clean and safe drinking water is a major issue in the global South, particularly in rural areas. For urban slum dwellers, access to drinking water means gathering the water from a common tap, often waiting hours in line. For rural women, it means getting water from a well or river, often walking miles there and back. Therefore, access to clean and safe water is simultaneously a women's issue, a health issue, and an environmental issue. Issues of environmental justice, such as access to safe water, often have a differentially negative impact on poor women of color.

For the most part, this has not been an issue in wealthy, industrialized nations of the global North. A notable exception is the contamination of the drinking water in Flint, Michigan, in the United States in 2014–2016. In the case of Flint, political decisions were made to cut costs by routing water through old pipes containing lead. Although the city and the mayor were notified that lead contamination exceeded what was deemed safe, no attempt was made to change the water delivery system or to notify the households receiving the lead contaminated water. Children, both boys and girls, under the age of six whose brains are still rapidly developing stand the most to lose from this horrible violation. It places an ongoing burden on their mothers, who are likely the primary caretakers, to be vigilant about cognitive impairment, provide conditions to offset possible cognitive impairment, and to provide care for those children permanently affected by the contaminated water.

In the global South, too, women are primarily responsible for children, and primarily responsible for providing the water for drinking, cooking, bathing, and cleaning. Solutions to issues such as how to secure access to water, whether to safe drinking water or water for irrigation, are complex and multifaceted. In India, for instance, a series of dams was planned in the Narmada River valley to provide access to water for irrigation and drinking water. However, the dams flooded tribal lands and displaced entire villages. Affected villagers staged public protests, risking arrest and violence (Roy 2001). The dam project was a project of the Indian government, so at first glance it seems as though Indian nationals are best situated to object to the project. However, national infrastructure projects take place within the constraints of international policies and practices of large corporations. In her account of the reasons for the need for the massive project of multiple dams along the sacred Narmada River, Arundhati Roy makes connections between the government decision, the industries stealing power without paying, and the privatization of power and electricity prompted by privatization and reforms required by structural adjustment.

9. During a 2003 interview with a Turkish journalist about women's issues, Young was asked about her views on veiling. She replied that she thought too much attention was given to these identity issues and not enough attention to issues such as domestic violence, violence against women, and economic issues. I was present at the interview, and I was also interviewed.

10. Uma Narayan cites this example of one measure of SEWA's success at protecting the rights of informal workers. (See "Workers in the Informal Sector: Special Challenges for Economic Human Rights," *Feminist Economics* 13, no. 1 [January 2007]: 101–116.)

11. As discussed in chapter 3, economic empowerment does not necessarily or directly lead to feminist empowerment and gender equality. Only in conjunction with other social changes (e.g., leadership development, political activism) will economic and feminist empowerment coincide.

BIBLIOGRAPHY

Abu-Lughod, Lila. "Dialects of Women's Empowerment: The International Circuitry of the Arab Human Development Report 2005." *International Journal of Middle East Studies* 41, no. 1 (2009): 83–103.

Abu-Lughod, Lila. *Do Muslim Women Need Saving?* Cambridge, MA: Harvard University Press, 2013.

Abu-Lughod, Lila. "Do Muslim Women Really Need Saving? Anthropological Reflections on Cultural Relativism and Its Others." *American Anthropologist* 104, no. 3 (September 2002): 783–790.

Aguilar, Delia, and Anne Lacsamana, eds. *Women and Globalization.* Amherst, NY: Humanity Books, 2004.

Alcoff, Linda. "Cultural Feminism versus Post-structuralism: The Identity Crisis in Feminist Theory." *Signs* 13, no. 1 (1988): 405–436.

Alexander, M. Jacqui, and Chandra Talpade Mohanty, eds. *Feminist Genealogies, Colonial Legacies, Democratic Futures.* New York: Routledge, 1997.

Allen, Amy. *The Power of Feminist Theory: Domination, Resistance, Solidarity.* Boulder, CO: Westview Press, 1999.

Anderson-Gold, Sharon. *Cosmopolitanism and Human Rights.* Cardiff, Wales: University of Wales, 2001.

An-Na'im, A. "Promises We Should All Keep in Common Cause." In *Is Multiculturalism Bad for Women?*, edited by J. Cohen, M. Howard, and M. Nussbaum, 59–64. Princeton, NJ: Princeton University Press, 1999.

Appadurai, Arjun. *Modernity at Large: Cultural Dimensions of Globalization.* Minneapolis: University of Minnesota Press, 1996.

Appiah, Kwame Anthony. "Cosmopolitan Patriots." In *For Love of Country: Debating the Limits of Patriotism*, edited by Joshua Cohen, 21–29 Boston: Beacon Books, 2002.

Appiah, Kwame Anthony. *Cosmopolitanism: Ethics in A World of Strangers.* New York: Norton, 2006.

Armendariz, Beatriz, and Jonathan Morduch. *The Economics of Microfinance* (2nd ed.). Cambridge, MA: MIT Press, 2010.

Ashford, Elizabeth. "Responsibility for Violations of the Human Right to Subsistence." In *Poverty, Agency, and Human Rights*, edited by Diana T. Meyers, 95–118. New York: Oxford University Press, 2014.

Asian Communities for Reproductive Justice. "Reproductive Justice: Vision, Analysis and Action for a Stronger Movement." In *Women's Lives: Multicultural Perspectives*, edited by G. Kirk and M. Okazawa-Rey, 242–246. Boston: McGraw-Hill, 2010.

Aziz, Nikhil. "The Human Rights Debate in an Era of Globalization: Hegemony of the Discourse." In *Debating Human Rights: Critical Essays from the United States and Asia*, edited by Peter Ness, 32–55. London: Routledge, 1999.

Bajaj, Vikas. "Fatal Fire in Bangladesh Highlights the Dangers Facing Garment Workers." *New York Times*, November 26, 2012, A4. Accessed November 24, 2016. http://www. nytimes.com/2012/11/26/world/asia/bangladesh-fire-kills-more-than-100-and-injures-many.html?_r=0

Bales, Kevin. "Because She Looks Like a Child." In *Global Woman: Nannies, Maids and Sex Workers in the New Economy*, edited by Barbara Ehrenreich, 207–229. New York: Metropolitan Books, 2003.

Banerjee, Sharmistha, and Tina Mukherjee. "Empowerment Enabling Empowerment." In *The Lightning of Empowerment: Gender Equality Development and Women Empowerment*, edited by D. Bhowmik, J. K. Pandey, A. K. Chintu, and R. Ranjan, 223–237. Delhi, India: Globus Press, 2015.

Bar On, Ami, and Ann Ferguson, eds. *Daring to be Good: Essays in Feminist Ethico-Politics*. New York: Routledge, 1998.

Bartky, Sandra Lee. *Femininity and Domination: Studies in the Phenomenology of Oppression*. New York: Routledge, 1990.

Basu, Amrita. "Globalization of the Local/Localization of the Global: Mapping Transnational Women's Movements." In *Feminist Theory Reader: Local and Global Perspectives* (3rd ed.), edited by Carole R. McCann and Seung-Kyung Kim, 63–71. New York: Routledge, 2013.

Batliwala, Srilatha. "Taking the Power Out of Empowerment: An Experiential Account." *Development in Practice* 17, no. 4 (August 2007): 557–565.

Beck, Ulrich. *The Cosmopolitan Vision*. Translated by Ciaran Cronin. Cambridge, UK: Polity Press, 2006.

Benhabib, Seyla. *Another Cosmopolitanism*. Oxford, UK: Oxford University Press, 2006.

Benhabib, Seyla. *Claims of Culture: Equality and Diversity in the Global Era*. Princeton, NJ: Princeton University Press, 2002.

Benhabib, Seyla. "The Generalized and The Concrete Other: The Kohlberg-Gilligan Controversy and Moral Theory." In *Women and Moral Theory*, edited by E. F. Kittay and D. T. Meyers, 154–177. Totowa, NJ: Rowman and Littlefield, 1987.

Benhabib, Seyla. *Situating the Self: Gender, Community and Postmodernism in Contemporary Ethics*. New York: Routledge, 1992.

Bhatt, Ela. *Beyond Microcredit: Structures that Increase the Economic Power of the Poor.* Gujarat, India: SEWA Academy, Mahila SEWA Trust, 1995a.

Bhatt, Ela. *Cooperatives and Empowerment of Women*. Gujarat, India: SEWA Academy, Mahila SEWA Trust, 1995b.

Bhatt, Ela. *Towards Second Freedom*. Gujarat, India: Mahila SEWA Trust, 2000.

Bhatt, Ela. *We Are Poor, But So Many: The Story of Self-Employed Women in India*. New Delhi: Oxford University Press, 2006.

Bhatt, Ela, and Bishwaroop Das. *Mainstreaming the Informal Sector Women.* Gujarat, India: SEWA Academy, Mahila SEWA Trust, 1995.

Bhavani, Kum-Kum, John Forna, and Molly Talcott. "The Red, the Green, the Black and the Purple: Reclaiming Development, Resisting Globalization." In *Critical Globalization Studies*, edited by Richard P. Appelbaum and William I. Robinson, 323–332. New York: Routledge, 2005.

Bhowmik, Sharit K., and Kanchan Sarker. "Worker Cooperatives as Alternative Production Systems: A Study in Kolkata, India." *Work and Occupations* 29, no. 4 (2002): 460–482.

Biswas, Soutik. "India's Microfinance Suicide Epidemic." *BBC News*, 2010. Accessed December 21, 2017. https://www.bbc.com/news/world-south-asia-11997571

Boserup, Esther. *Women's Role in Economic Development.* London: Allen and Unwin, 1970.

Bowman, Betsy, and Bob Stone. "Can Grameen Bank-style Microcredit Eliminate Poverty?" *The Center for Global Justice Newsletter* (March 2007): 1–4.

Bowman, Betsy, and Bob Stone. "Cooperatives: A Brief Introduction to Their Types, History and Social Change Prospect." *The Center for Global Justice Newsletter* (December 2007): 1–5.

Brecher, Jeremy, Tim Costello, and Brendan Smith, eds. *Globalization from Below: The Power of Solidarity.* Cambridge, MA: South End Press, 2000.

Breckenridge, Carol, Sheldon Pollock, Homi K. Bhabha, and Dipesh Chakrabarty. *Cosmopolitanism.* Durham, NC: Duke University Press, 2002.

Brett, John A. "'We Sacrifice and Eat Less': The Structural Complexities of Microfinance Participation." *Human Organization* 65, no. 1 (Spring 2006): 8–19.

Brown, Carolyn Henning. "The Forced Sterilization Program Under the Indian Emergency: Results in One Settlement." *Human Organization: Journal of the Society for Applied Anthropology* 43, no. 1 (Spring 1984).

Buckingham, Jane. "Patient Welfare Versus the Health of the Nation: Governmentality and Sterilization of Leprosy Sufferers in Post-Colonial India." *Social History of Medicine* 19, no. 3. (2006): 483–499.

Bulbeck, Chilla. *Re-Orienting Western Feminisms: Women's Diversity in a Postcolonial World.* Cambridge, UK: Cambridge University Press, 1998.

Bunch, Charlotte, and Susan Fried. "Beijing 95: Moving Women's Human Rights from Margin to Center." *Signs* 22, no. 1 (1993): 200–204.

Bunch, Charlotte. "Prospects for A Global Feminism." In *Feminist Frameworks: Alternative Accounts of the Theoretical Relations Between Women and Men*, edited by Alison M. Jaggar and Paula S. Rothenberg, 249–252. New York: McGraw-Hill, 1993.

Bunch, Charlotte. "Transforming Human Rights from a Feminist Perspective." In *Women's Rights, Human Rights: International Feminist Perspectives*, edited by Julie Peters and Andrea Wolper, 11–17. New York: Routledge, 1995.

Bunch, Charlotte, and Susan Fried. "Beijing 95: Moving Women's Human Rights from Margin to Center." *Signs* 22, no. 1 (1996): 200–204.

Butler, Judith. *Gender Trouble: Feminism and the Subversion of Identity.* New York: Routledge, 1990.

Carens, Joseph. "Cosmopolitanism, Nationalism and Immigration: False Dichotomies and Shifting Presuppositions." In *Canadian Political Philosophy: Contemporary Reflections*, edited by R. Beiner and W. J. Norman, 17–35. Oxford, UK: Oxford University Press, 2001.

Carr, Marilyn, Martha Chen, and Renana Jhabvala, eds. *Speaking Out: Women's Economic Empowerment in South Asia*. London, UK: IT Publications on behalf of Aga Khan Foundation Canada and UNIFEM, 1996.

Chant, Sylvia. "Exploring the 'Feminisation of Poverty' in Relation to Women's Work and Home-based Enterprise in Slums of the Global South." *International Journal of Gender and Entrepreneurship* 6, no. 3 (2014): 296–310.

Chant, Sylvia. "Women, Girls, and World Poverty: Empowerment, Equality, or Essentialism?" *International Development Planning Review* 38, no. 1 (2016): 1–24.

Cheah, Pheng, and Bruce Robbins, eds. *Cosmopolitics: Thinking and Feeling Beyond the Nation*. Minneapolis: University of Minnesota Press, 1998.

Chong, Daniel P. L. *Freedom from Poverty: NGOs and Human Rights Praxis*. Philadelphia: University of Pennsylvania Press, 2010.

Chow, Esther N. "Making Waves, Moving Mountains." *Signs* 22, no. 1 (1996): 185–192.

Churchill, Nancy. "Maquiladoras, Migration, and Daily Life: Women and Work in the Contemporary Mexican Political Economy." In *Women and Globalization*, edited by Delia Aguilar and Anne Lacsamana, 120–153. Amherst, NY: Humanity Books, 2004.

Churchill, Robert P. *Human Rights and Global Diversity*. Upper Saddle River, NJ: Pearson Prentice-Hall, 2006.

Coicaud, Jean-Marc, Michael W. Doyle, and Anne-Marie Gardner, eds. *The Globalization of Human Rights*. Paris: United Nations University Press, 2003.

Cole, Eve B., and Susan Coultrap-McQuin, eds. *Explorations in Feminist Ethics: Theory and Practice*. Bloomington: University of Indiana Press, 1992.

Collins, Patricia Hill. *Black Feminist Thought: Knowledge, Consciousness, and the Politics of Empowerment*. New York: Routledge Press, 1990.

Collins, Patricia Hill, and Sirma Bilge. *Intersectionality*. Cambridge, UK: Polity Press, 2016.

Cook, Rebecca J. *Human Rights of Women: National and International Perspectives*. Philadelphia: University of Pennsylvania Press, 1994.

Crenshaw, Kimberlé Williams. "Mapping the Margins: Intersectionality, Identity Politics and Violence Against Women of Color." *Stanford Law Review* 43, no. 1 (1991): 1241–99.

Cudd, Ann E. "Agency and Invention: How (Not) to Fight Global Poverty." In *Poverty, Agency, and Human Rights*, edited by Diana T. Meyers, 197–222. New York: Oxford University Press, 2014.

Daley, Suzanne. "Outcry Echoes Up to Canada: Guatemalans Citing Rapes and Other Abuses Put Focus on Companies Conduct Abroad." *New York Times*, April 3, 2016, p. A1+.

Damodaran, Sumangala. "The Chimera of Inclusive Growth: Informality, Poverty and Inequality in India in the Post-Reform Period." *Development and Change* 46, no. 5 (2015): 1213–1224.

Danaher, Kevin, ed. *Democratizing the Global Economy*. Monore, Maine: Common Courage Press, 2001.

Datta, Punita Bhatt, and Robert Gailey. "Empowering Women Through Social Entrepreneurship: Case Study of a Women's Cooperative in India." *Entrepreneurship Theory and Practice* (May 2012): 569–587.

Drydyk, Jay. "Empowerment, Agency, and Power." *Journal of Global Ethics* 9, no. 3 (2013): 249–262.

Ehrenreich, Barbara, and Arlie Hochschild, eds. *Global Woman: Nannies, Maids and Sex Workers in the New Economy*. New York: Metropolitan Books, 2002.

El Saadawi, Nawal. "Women and The Poor: The Challenge of Global Justice." In *Beyond Borders: Thinking Critically About Global Issues*, edited by Paula S. Rothenberg, 400–408. New York: Worth Publishers, 2006.

Engle, Sally M. *Human Rights & Gender Violence: Translating International Law into Local Justice*. Chicago: University of Chicago Press, 2006.

Escobar, Arturo. *Encountering Development: The Making and Unmaking of the Third World*. Princeton, NJ: Princeton University Press, 1995.

Fallstrom, Jerry. "Senate Oks $2.1 Million For Rosewood Reparations." *Sun Sentinel Tallahassee*, April 9, 1994.

Fanon, Franz. *Black Skin, White Masks*. New York: Grove Press, 1967.

Farmer, Paul. *Pathologies of Power: Health, Human Rights and the New War on the Poor*. Berkeley: University of California Press, 2003.

Ferguson, Ann. "Alternative Economies: Mexican Women Left Behind: Organizing Solidarity Economy in Response." In *Globalization and Third World Women: Exploitation, Coping and Resistance*, edited by Ligaya Lindio-McGovern and Isidor Walliman, 107–119. Surrey, UK: Ashgate, 2009a.

Ferguson, Ann. "CEDESA, Women, and the Food Sovereignty Movement in Mexico." In *Solidarity Economy I: Building Alternatives for People and Planet: Papers and Reports from the 2009 U.S. Forum on the Solidarity Economy*, edited by Emily Kawano, Thomas Neal Masterson, and Jonathan Teller-Elsberg, 241–248. Amherst, MA: Center for Popular Economics, 2009b.

Ferguson, Ann. "Empowerment, Development and Women's Liberation." In *The Political Interests of Gender Revisited: Redoing Theory and Research with a Feminist Face*, edited by Anna Jonasdottir and Kathleen B. Jones. Manchester, UK: Manchester University Press, 2009c.

Ferguson, Ann. "Iris Young, Global Responsibility and Solidarity." In Dancing with Iris: The Philosophy of Iris Marion Young, edited by Ann Ferguson and Mechthild Nagel, 185–197. Oxford, UK: Oxford University Press, 2009d.

Ferguson, Ann. "Motherhood and Sexuality: Some Feminist Questions." Edited by Ann Ferguson. *Hypatia Special Issue: Motherhood and Sexuality* 1, no. 2 (1986): 3–22.

Ferguson, Ann. "Resisting the Veil of Privilege: Building Bridge Identities as an Ethico-Politics of Global Feminisms." *Hypatia* 13, no. 3 (1998): 95–113.

Ferguson, Ann, and Nagel Mechthild, eds. *Dancing with Iris: The Philosophy of Iris Marion Young*. Oxford, UK: Oxford University Press, 2009.

Fraser, Nancy. "From Redistribution to Recognition? Dilemmas of Justice in a 'Postsocialist' Age." *New Left Review* 212 (July/August 1995): 68–93.

Friedman, Elisabeth. "Women's Human Rights: The Emergence of a Movement Perspective." In *Women's Rights, Human Rights: International Feminist Perspectives*, edited by Julie Peters and Andrea Wolper, 18–35. New York: Routledge, 1995.

Friedman, Marilyn. *Autonomy, Gender, Politics*. New York: Oxford Univeristy Press, 2003.

Friedman, Marilyn. "Care and Context in Moral Reasoning." In *Women and Moral Theory*, edited by E. F. Kittay and D. T. Meyers, 190–204. Totowa, NJ: Rowman and Littlefield, 1987.

Friedman, Marilyn. *What Are Friends For? Feminist Perspectives on Personal Relationships and Moral Theory*. Ithaca, NY: Cornell University Press, 1993.

Frye, Marilyn. "Oppression." In *Politics of Reality: Essays in Feminist Theory*, 1–16. New York: Crossing Press, 1983.

Fuss, Diana. *Essentially Speaking: Feminism, Nature and Difference*. New York: Routledge, 1989.

Gavison, Ruth. "On the Relationship Between Civil and Political Rights, and Social and Economic Rights." In *The Globalization of Human Rights*, edited Coicaud, Jean-Marc, Michael W. Doyle, and Anne-Marie Gardner, 23–55. Paris: United Nations University Press, 2003.

Gilligan, Carol. *In A Different Voice: Psychological Theory and Women's Development*. Cambridge, MA: Harvard University Press, 1982.

Gilmore, Ruth Wilson. "In the Shadow of the Shadow State." In *the Revolution Will Not Be Funded: Beyond the Non-Profit Industrial Complex, INCITE*. Boston: South End Press, 2007.

Gimenez, Martha. "Global Capitalism and Women: From Feminist Politics to Working Class Women's Politics." In *Globalization and Third World Women: Exploitation, Coping and Resistance*, edited by Ligaya Lindio-McGovern and Isidor Walliman. Surrey, UK: Ashgate, 2009.

Goetz, A. M., and R. Sen Gupta. "Who Takes the Credit? Gender, Power, and Control over Loan Use in Rural Credit Programs in Bangladesh." *World Development* 24, no. 1 (1996): 45–63.

Goodale, M., ed. "In Focus: Anthropology and Human Rights in A New Key." *American Anthropologist* 108, no. 1 (2006): 1–83.

Gould, Carol. *Globalizing Democracy and Human Rights*. Cambridge, UK: Cambridge University Press, 2004.

Gould, Carol. "Varieties of Global Responsibility, Social Connection, Human Rights and Transnational Solidarity." In *Dancing with Iris: The Philosophy of Iris Marion Young*, edited by Ann Ferguson and Mechthild Nagel, 198–211. Oxford, UK: Oxford University Press, 2009.

Gulli, Hege. *Microfinance and Poverty: Questioning the Conventional Wisdom*. Washington, DC: Microenterprise Unit, Sustainable Development Department, Inter-American Development Bank, 1998.

Gunewardena, Nandini, and Ann Kingsolver, eds. *The Gender of Globalization: Women Navigating Cultural and Economic Marginalization*. Santa Fe, NM: School for Advanced Research Press, 2007.

Gutmann, Amy, ed. *Multiculturalism*. Princeton, NJ: Princeton University Press, 1994.

Hancock, Ange-Marie. *Intersectionality: An Intellectual History*. New York: Oxford University Press, 2016.

Hartsock, Nancy. *The Feminist Standpoint Revisited and Other Essays*. Boulder, CO: Westview Press, 1998.

Hashemi, S. M., S. R. Schuler, and A. P. Riley. "Rural Credit Programs and Women's Empowerment in Bangladesh." *World Development* 24, no. 4 (1996): 635–653.

Hausmann, Ricardo, Laura D. Tyson, and Saadia Zahidi. *The Global Gender Gap Report 2009*. Geneva: World Economic Forum, 2010.

Held, Virginia. *The Ethics of Care: Personal, Political and Global*. Oxford, UK: Oxford University Press, 2006.

Held, Virginia. "Feminism and Moral Theory." In *Women and Moral Theory*, edited by E. F. Kittay and D. T. Meyers, 111–128. Totowa, NJ: Rowman and Littlefield, 1987.

Held, Virginia. *Feminist Morality: Transforming Culture, Society, and Politics.* Chicago: University of Chicago, 1993.

Held, Virginia. *Rights and Goods: Justifying Social Action.* Chicago: University of Chicago, 1984.

Henrich, Joseph, Steven Heine, and Ara Norenzayan. "The Weirdest People in the World," *Behavioral and Brain Sciences* 33, no. 1 (2010): 61–83.

Higgins, Peter. "Open Borders and the Right to Immigration." *Human Rights Review* 9, no. 1 (2008): 525–535.

Hill-Collins, Patricia. *Black Feminist Thought: Knowledge, Consciousness, and the Politics of Empowerment.* New York: Routledge, 1990.

Hill-Collins, Patricia, and Sirma Bilge. *Intersectionality (Key Concepts)* (1st ed.). Cambridge, UK: Polity, 2016.

Himmelfarb, Gertrude. "The Illusions of Cosmopolitanism." In *For Love of Country: Debating the Limits of Patriotism*, edited by Joshua Cohen, 3–17. Boston, MA: Beacon Books, 2002.

Hochschild, Arlie. "Love and Gold." In *Global Woman: Nannies, Maids and Sex Workers in the New Economy*, edited by Barbara Ehrenreich and Arlie Hochschild. New York: Metropolitan Books, 2002.

Hogberg, Ulf, and Ian Dowbiggin. "The Sterilization Movement and Global Fertility in the Twentieth Century." *European Journal of Public Health* 19, no. 1 (November 2008): 262.

Holmstrom, Nancy. *The Socialist Feminist Project: A Contemporary Reader in Theory and Politics.* New York: Monthly Review Press, 2002.

Hossain, Ismail, al-Amin, and Jahangir Alam. "NGO Interventions and Women Development in Bangladesh: Do Feminist Theories Work?" *The Hong Kong Journal of Social Work* 46, no.1–2 (2012): 13–29.

Human Rights Watch. *The Human Rights Watch Global Report on Women's Human Rights.* New York: Human Rights Watch, 1995.

Illich, Ivan. "Development as Planned Poverty." In *The Post-Development Reader*, edited by Majid Rahnema and Victoria Bawtree, 94–101. New York: Zed Press, 1997.

INCITE! Women of Color Against Violence. *The Revolution Will Not Be Funded: Beyond the Non-Profit Industrial Complex.* Cambridge, MA: South End Press, 2007.

Inda, J. X., and R. Rosaldo, eds. *The Anthropology of Globalization: A Reader* (2nd ed.). Oxford, UK: Blackwell, 2003.

Inoue, Tatsuo. "Human Rights and Asian Values." In *The Globalization of Human Rights*, edited by Coicaud, Jean-Marc, Michael W. Doyle, and Anne-Marie Gardner, 116–133. Paris: United Nations University Press, 2003.

International Cooperative Alliance. "About the International Cooperative Alliance." Accessed April 29, 2014. http://ica.coop/

International Labor Organization. "ILO's Global Employment Trends 2013 Report." Accessed June 18, 2015. http://www.ilo.org/global/

Isserles, Robin. "Microcredit: The Rhetoric of Empowerment, the Reality of 'Development as Usual.'" *Women's Studies Quarterly* 31, no. 3–4 (2003): 38–57.

Jaggar, Alison, M. "Are My Hands Clean? Responsibility for Global Gender Disparities." In *Poverty, Agency, and Human Rights*, edited by Diana T. Meyers, 170–194. New York: Oxford University Press, 2014a.

Jaggar, Alison M., ed. *Gender and Global Justice.* Cambridge, UK: Polity Press, 2014b.

Jaggar, Alison M. "L'Imagination au pouvoir: Comparing John Rawls's Method of Ideal Theory with Iris Marion Young's Method of Critical Theory." In *Dancing with Iris: The Philosophy of Iris Marion Young*, edited by Ann Ferguson and Mechthild Nagel, 95–102. Oxford, UK: Oxford University Press, 2009.

Jaggar, Alison, M. "'Saving Amina?': Global Justice for Women and Intercultural Dialogue." *Ethics and International Affairs* 19, no. 3 (2005): 55–75.

Jaggar, Alison M. "Transnational Cycles of Gendered Vulnerability: A Prologue to a Theory of Global Gender Justice." In *Global Gender Justice*, edited by Alison Jaggar. Cambridge, UK: Polity Press, 2014c.

Jaising, Indira. "Violence Against Women: The Indian Perspective." In *Women's Rights, Human Rights: International Feminist Perspectives*, edited by Julie Peters and Andrea Wolper, 51–56. New York: Routledge, 1995.

Jhabvala, Renana. *Structural Adjustment Programme: Issues and Strategies for Action for "Peoples" Sector Women Workers in India.* Gujarat, India: Mahila SEWA Trust, 1995.

Johnson, Susan, and Ben Rogaly. *Microfinance and Poverty Reduction.* UK and Ireland: Action Aid and Oxfam, 1997.

Kabeer, Naila. "Between Affiliation and Autonomy: Navigating Pathways of Women's Empowerment and Gender Justice in Rural Bangladesh." *Development and Change* 42, no. 2 (2011): 499–528.

Kabeer, Naila. "Conflicts over Credit: Re-evaluating the Empowerment Potential of Loans to Women in Rural Bangladesh." *World Development* 29, no.1 (2001): 63–84.

Kabeer, Naila. "Empowerment, Citizenship and Gender Justice: A Contribution to Locally Grounded Theories of Change in Women's Lives." *Ethics and Social Welfare* 6, no. 3 (2012): 216–232.

Kabeer, Naila. "Gender Equality and Women's Empowerment: A Critical Analysis of the Third Millennium Development Goal." *Gender and Development* 13, no. 1 (2005a): 13–24.

Kabeer, Naila. "Is Microfinance a 'Magic Bullet' for Women's Empowerment? Analysis of Findings from South Asia." *Economic and Political Weekly* 40, no. 44–45 (2005b): 4709–4718.

Kabeer, Naila. "'Money Can't Buy Me Love'? Re-evaluating Gender, Credit and empowerment in Rural Bangladesh." *IDS Discussion Paper 363*. Brighton: Institute of Development Studies, University of Sussex, 1998.

Kabeer, Naila. "Resources, Agency, Achievements: Reflections on the Measurement of Women's Empowerment." *Development and Change* 30, no. 1 (1999): 435–464.

Kabeer, Naila. *The Power to Choose.* London: Verso, 2000.

Kandiyoti, Deniz. "Bargaining with Patriarchy." *Gender & Society* 2, no. 3 (September 1988): 274–290.

Kang, Hye-Ryoung. "Transnational Collectivities and Global Justice." In *Gender and Global Justice*, edited by Alison Jaggar, 40–61. Cambridge, UK: Polity Press, 2014.

Kant, Immanuel. "Grounding for the Metaphysics of Morals." In *Immanuel Kant: Ethical Philosophy*, edited by J. W. Ellington and W. A. Wick, 1–62. Indianapolis, IN: Hackett, 1994.

Kapur, Ratna. "Dark Times for Liberal Intellectual Thought." *Profession,* Modern Language Association (2006): 22–32.

Kapur, Ratna. "Precarious Desires and Ungrievable Lives: Human Rights and Postcolonial Critiques of Justice." *London Review of International Law* 3 (2015): 267–294.

Kapur, Ratna. "Sexual Subalterns, Human Rights and the Limits of the Liberal Imaginary." Open Democracy. Accessed August 20, 2014. https://www.opendemocracy.net/ratna-kapur/sexual-subalterns-human-rights-and-limits-of-liberal-imaginary

Karim, Lamia. "Demystifying Microcredit." *Cultural Dynamics* 20, no. 1 (March 2008): 5–29.

Karim, Lamia. *Microfinance and Its Discontents: Women in Debt in Bangladesh.* Minneapolis: University of Minnesota Press, 2011.

Kawano, Emily. "Crisis and Opportunity: The Emerging Solidarity Economy Movement." In *Solidarity Economy I: Building Alternatives for People and Planet: Papers and Reports from the 2009 U.S. Forum on the Solidarity Economy*, edited by Emily Kawano, Thomas Neal Masterson, and Jonathan Teller-Elsberg, 11–23. Amherst, MA: Center for Popular Economics, 2009.

Keating, Christine, Claire Rasmussen, and Pooja Rishi. "The Rationality of Empowerment: Microcredit, Accumulation by Dispossession, and the Gendered Economy." *Signs* 36, no. 1 (2010): 424–440.

Khader, Serene. *Adaptive Preferences and Women's Empowerment.* New York: Oxford University Press, 2011.

Khader, Serene. "Development Ethics, Gender Complementarianism, and Intrahousehold Inequality." *Hypatia* 30, no. 2 (Spring 2015): 352–369.

Khader, Serene. "Empowerment Through Self-Subordination? Microcredit and Women's Agency." In *Poverty, Agency, and Human Rights*, edited by Diana T. Meyers, 223–248. New York: Oxford University Press, 2014.

Kilby, Patrick. *NGOs in India: The Challenges of Women's Empowerment and Accountability.* London: Routledge, 2011.

King, Deborah K. "Multiple Jeopardy, Multiple Consciousness: The Context of a Black Feminist Ideology." *Signs* 14 no. 1 (1988): 42–72.

Kittay, Eva Feder. *Love's Labor: Essays on Women, Equality and Dependency.* New York: Routledge, 1999.

Kittay, Eva Feder. "The Moral Harm of Migrant Carework: Realizing a Global Right to Care." In *Gender and Global Justice*, edited by Alison Jaggar, 62–84. Cambridge, UK: Polity Press, 2014.

Kittay, Eva Feder, and Diana T. Meyers, eds. *Women and Moral Theory.* Totowa: Rowman and Littlefield, 1987.

Kobila, James Mouangue. "Comparative Practice on Human Rights: North-South." In *The Globalization of Human Rights*, edited by Coicaud, Jean-Marc, Michael W. Doyle, and Anne-Marie Gardner, 89–115. Paris: United Nations University Press, 2003.

Koggel, Christine M. 2010. "The Ethics of Empowerment." *Development* 53, no. 2 (2010): 175–178.

Koggel, Christine M. "A Critical Analysis of Recent Work on Empowerment: Implications for Gender." *Journal of Global Ethics* 9, no. 3 (2013): 263–275.

Krenz, Kristen, Dorie J. Gilbert, and Gokul Mandayam. "Exploring Women's Empowerment Through 'Credit-Plus' Microfinance in India." *Affilia: Journal of Women and Social Work* 29, no. 3 (2014): 310–325.

Krishnaswami, Lalita. *Adding Beauty to Lives . . . Work.* Gujarat, India: Gujurat State Women's SEWA Co-operative Federation, 2003.

Krishnaswami, Lalita. *Co-operatives Our Strength.* Gujarat, India: Gujurat State Women's SEWA Co-operative Federation, 2002.

Larrabee, Mary Jeanne, ed. *An Ethic of Care: Feminist and Interdisciplinary Perspectives.* New York: Routledge, 1993.

Lettinga, Doutje, and Lars van Troost, eds. *Can Human Rights Bring Social Justice? Twelve Essays.* Amsterdam, Netherlands: Amnesty International, 2015.

Lindio-McGovern, Ligaya, and Isidor Walliman. *Globalization and Third World Women.* Burlington, VT: Ashgate, 2009.

Littrell, Mary A., and Marsha A. Dickson. *Artisans and Fair Trade: Crafting Development.* Sterling, VA: Kumarian Press, 2010.

Locke, John. "The Second Treatise of Government." In *John Locke Two Treatises of Government,* edited by P. Laslett, 304–477. Cambridge: Cambridge University Press, 1960.

Lorde, Audrey. *Sister Outsider.* Freedom, CA: Crossing Press, 1984.

Lugones, Maria. "The Coloniality of Gender." *Worlds & Knowledges Otherwise* (Spring 2008): 2–17.

Lugones, Maria. *Pilgrimages/Peregrinajes: Theorizing Coalition Against Multiple Oppressions.* New York: Rowman and Littlefield, 2003.

Lugones, Maria. "Playfulness, 'World'-Travelling, and Loving Perception." *Hypatia* 2, no. 2 (1987): 3–19.

MacFarquhar, Neil. "Banks Making Big Profits from Tiny Loans." *New York Times,* April 13, 2010.

Mahmood, Saba. *The Politics of Piety: The Islamic Revival and the Feminist Subject.* Princeton, NJ: Princeton University Press, 2005.

Mani, Lata. "Contentious Traditions: The Debate on SATI in Colonial India." *Cultural Critique* (Fall 1987).

Marketplace India. "Our History." Accessed December 4, 2016. https://www.marketplaceindia.com/category/MarketPlace-History

May, Vivian M. *Pursuing Intersectionality, Unsettling Dominant Imaginaries.* New York: Routledge, 2015.

Mayoux, Linda. "Questioning Virtuous Spirals: Microfinance and Women's Empowerment in Africa." *Journal of International Development* 11, no. 1 (1999): 957–984.

McIntosh, Peggy. "White Privilege and Male Privilege: A Personal Account of Coming to See Correspondences through Work in Women's Studies." Working Paper No. 189. Wellesley, MA: Center for Research on Women, Wellesley College, 1988.

McLaren, Margaret. "Feminist Ethics: Care as a Virtue." In *Feminist Doing Ethics,* edited by Joanne Waugh and Peggy DesAutels, 101–117. New York: Rowman and Littlefield, 2001.

McLaren, Margaret. "Gender Equality and the Economic Empowerment of Women." *Forum on Public Policy* (Spring 2008). Accessed November 18, 2016. http://forumonpublicpolicy.com/archivesspring08/mclaren.pdf

McLaren, Margaret. "Women's Rights and Collective Resistance: The Success Story of Marketplace India." In *Gender and Globalization: Patterns of Women's Resistance,* edited by Erica G. Polakoff and Ligaya Lindio-McGovern, 191–210. Whitby, ON: de Sitter Publications, 2011.

McLaren, Margaret. "Women's Rights and Economic Empowerment: The Story of the Self-Employed Women's Association of India." In *Florida Without Borders: Women at the Intersection of the Local and the Global*, edited by S. K. Masters, J. A. Hayden, and K. Vaz, 99–107. Newcastle, UK: Cambridge Scholars Publishing, 2008.

McLaren, Margaret. "Women's Rights in a Global Context." *Journal of Developing Societies* 23, no. 1–2 (2007): 159–173.

McMichael, Philip. "Globalization and Development Studies." In *Critical Globalization Studies*, edited by Richard P. Appelbaum and William I. Robinson, 111–120. New York: Routledge, 2005.

Mellor, Mary, Janet Hannah, and John Stirling. *Worker Cooperatives in Theory and Practice*. Philadelphia: Open University Press, 1988.

Mendieta, Eduardo. "From Imperial to Dialogical Cosmopolitanism." *Ethics & Global Politics* 2, no. 2 (2009): 241–258.

Mendoza, Jose Jorge. "Does Cosmopolitan Justice Ever Require Restrictions on Migration?" *Public Affairs Quarterly* 29, no. 2 (2015): 175–186.

Menon, Nivedita. "Abortion and the Law: Questions for Feminism." *Canadian Journal of Women and the Law* 6, no. 1 (1993): 103–118.

Menon, Nivedita. "Fighting Patriarchy and Capitalism." *Journal of Contemporary African Studies*, 33 no. 1 (2015): 3–11.

Menon, Nivedita. "Rights. What Are They Good For?" Open Democracy. Accessed August 15, 2014. https://www.opendemocracy.net/nivedita-menon/rights-what-are-they-good-for-0

Menon, Nivedita. "Universalism Without Foundations?" *Economy and Society* 31, no.1 (2002): 152–169.

Meyers, Diana T., ed. *Feminists Rethink the Self*. Boulder, CO: Westview Press, 1997.

Meyers, Diana T. *Gender in the Mirror: Cultural Imagery & Women's Agency*. Oxford, UK: Oxford University Press, 2002.

Meyers, Diana T., ed. *Poverty, Agency, and Human Rights*. New York: Oxford University Press, 2014.

Meyers, Diana T. *Subjection & Subjectivity: Psychoanalytic Feminism & Moral Philosophy*. New York: Routledge, 1994.

Meyers, Diana T. "The Socialized Individual and Individual Autonomy: An Intersection between Philosophy and Psychology." In *Women and Moral Theory*, edited by E. F. Kittay and D. T. Meyers, 139–153. Totowa, NJ: Rowman and Littlefield, 1987.

Mies, Maria. "The Myth of Catching-up Development." In *Ecofeminism*, edited by Maria Mies and Vandana Shiva, 55–69. New York: Palgrave, 1993.

Mignolo, Walter. *The Darker Side of Western Modernity: Global Futures, Decolonial Options*. Durham, NC: Duke University Press, 2011.

Mignolo, Walter. "The Many Faces of Cosmo-polis: Border Thinking and Critical Cosmopolitanism." *Public Culture* 12, no. 3 (Fall 2000): 721–748.

Mill, John Stuart. *On Liberty*, edited by G. Himmelfarb. London: Penguin Books, 1985.

Miller, Ethan. "Solidarity Economy: Key Concepts and Issues." In *Solidarity Economy I: Building Alternatives for People and Planet: Papers and Reports from the 2009 U.S. Forum on the Solidarity Economy*, edited by Emily Kawano, Thomas Neal Masterson, and Jonathan Teller-Elsberg, 25–41. Amherst, MA: Center for Popular Economics, 2009.

Miller, Sarah Clark. "Cosmopolitan Care." *Ethics and Social Welfare* 4, no. 2 (2010): 145–157. doi:10.1080/17496535.2010.484258.

Miller, Sarah Clark. "A Feminist Account of Global Responsibility." *Social Theory and Practice* 37, no. 3 (2011): 391–412.

Mills, Charles. *The Racial Contract.* Ithaca, NY: Cornell University Press, 1997.

Mohanty, Chandra Talpade. "Cartographies of Struggle: Third World Women and the Politics of Feminism." In *Third World Women and the Politics of Feminism*, edited by C. T. Mohanty, A. Russo, and L. Torres, 1–47. Bloomington: Indiana University Press, 1991a.

Mohanty, Chandra Talpade. *Feminism Without Borders: Decolonizing Theory, Practicing Solidarity.* Durham, NC: Duke University Press, 2003.

Mohanty, Chandra Talpade. "Under Western Eyes: Feminist Scholarship and Colonial Discourses." In *Third World Women and the Politics of Feminism*, edited by C.T. Mohanty, A. Russo, and L. Torres, 51–80. Bloomington: Indiana University Press, 1991b.

Mohanty, Chandra Talpade, Ann Russo, and Lourdes Torres, eds. *Third World Women and the Politics of Feminism.* Bloomington: Indiana University Press, 1991.

Moodie, Megan. "Enter Microcredit: A New Culture of Women's Empowerment in Rajasthan?" *American Ethnologist* 35, no. 3 (2008): 454–465.

Nanavaty, Reema. *Does Empowerment Matter for Economic Development?* Gujarat, India: Gujarat State Women's SEWA Co-op, 2000.

Narayan, Uma. *Dislocating Cultures: Identities, Traditions and Third World Feminism.* New York: Routledge, 1997.

Naples, Nancy A., and Manisha Desai, eds. *Women's Activism and Globalization: Linking Local Struggles and Transnational Politics.* New York: Routledge, 2002.

Narayan, Uma. "Global Gender Inequality and the Empowerment of Women." *Perspectives on Politics* 8, no. 1 (2010): 282–284.

Narayan, Uma. "Informal Sector Work, Microcredit and Third World Women's 'Empowerment': A Critical Perspective." Presented by Uma Narayan. *XXII World Congress of Philosophy of Law and Social Philosophy*, 2005.

Narayan, Uma. "Workers in the Informal Sector: Special Challenges for Economic Human Rights." *Feminist Economics* 13, no. 1 (January 2007): 101–116.

Narayan, Uma, and Sandra Harding, eds. *Decentering the Center: Philosophy for a Multicultural, Postcolonial, and Feminist World.* Bloomington: Indiana University Press, 2000.

Nedelsky, Jennifer. *Law's Relations: A Relational Theory of Self, Autonomy and Law.* Oxford, UK: Oxford University Press, 2011.

Ness, Peter, ed. *Debating Human Rights: Critical Essays from the United States and Asia.* London: Routledge, 1999.

Nicholls, Alex, and Charlotte Opal. *Fair Trade: Market-Driven Ethical Consumption.* London: Sage, 2004.

Njoki Njoroge Njehu. "Lila Watson, Globalization: A Path to Global Understanding or Global Plunder?" In *Critical Globalization Studies*, edited by Richard P. Appelbaum and William I. Robinson, 397–402. New York: Routledge, 2005.

Nussbaum, Martha. *For Love of Country: Debating the Limits of Patriotism*, edited by Joshua Cohen. Boston: Beacon Press, 2002.

Nussbaum, Martha. *Frontiers of Justice: Disability, Nationality, Species Membership.* Cambridge, MA: Harvard University Press, 2006.

Nussbaum, Martha. "Kant and Stoic Cosmopolitanism." *The Journal of Political Philosophy* 5, no. 1 (1997): 1–25.

Nussbaum, Martha. "Patriotism and Cosmopolitanism." In *For Love of Country: Debating the Limits of Patriotism*, edited by Joshua Cohen, 3–17. Boston: Beacon Books, 2002.

Nussbaum, Martha. *Sex and Social Justice.* New York: Oxford University Press, 1999.

Nussbaum, Martha. *Women and Human Development: The Capabilities Approach.* Cambridge, UK: Cambridge University Press, 2000.

Okin, Susan Moller. "Feminism, Women's Human Rights, and Cultural Differences." In *Decentering the Center: Philosophy for a Multicultural, Postcolonial, and Feminist World*, edited by Uma Narayan and Sandra Harding, 26–46. Bloomington: Indiana University Press, 2000.

Okin, Susan Moller, ed. *Is Multiculturalism Bad for Women?* Princeton, NJ: Princeton University Press, 1999.

Okin, Susan Moller. *Justice, Gender and the Family.* New York: Basic Books, 1989.

Oldenburg, Veena Talwar. "The Roop Kanwar Case: Feminist Responses." In *Sati, The Blessing and the Curse: The Burning of Wives in India*, edited by John Stratton Hawley, 101–130. Oxford, UK: Oxford University Press, 2007.

O'Meara, Patrick, Howard D. Mehlinger, and Matthew Krain, eds. *Globalization and the Challenges of a New Century.* Bloomington: Indiana University Press, 2000.

O'Neill, Onora. "Justice, Capabilities, and Vulnerabilities." In *Women, Culture and Development*, edited by Martha Nussbaum and Jonathan Glover, 140–152. New York: Oxford University Press, 1995.

Oyeronke, Oyewumi. "Visualizing the Body: Western Theories and African Subjects." In *The Feminist Philosophy Reader*, edited by Alison Bailey and Chris Cuomo, 163–176. New York: McGraw-Hill, 2008.

Parekh, Serena. "Getting to the Root of Gender Inequality: Structural Injustice and Political Responsibility." *Hypatia* 6, no. 4 (2011): 672–89.

Parrenas, Rhacel Salazar. "The Care Crisis in the Philippines: Children and Transnational Families in the New Global Economy." In *Global Woman: Nannies, Maids and Sex Workers in the New Economy*, edited by Barbara Ehrenreich and Arlie Hochschild, 39–54. New York: Metropolitan Books, 2002.

Parrenas, Rhacel Salazar. *Servants of Globalization: Women, Migration and Domestic Work.* Stanford, CA: Stanford University Press, 2001.

Pateman, Carol. *The Sexual Contract.* Stanford, CA: Stanford University Press, 1988.

Pateman, Carol, and Charles Mills. *Contract and Domination.* Cambridge, UK: Polity, 2007.

Pateman, Carol, and Elizabeth Grosz, eds. *Feminist Challenges: Social and Political Theory.* Boston: Northeastern University Press, 1986.

PCI. "Population and Development in the 21st Century." *Report from Population Communications International (PCI).* New York: Population Communications International, 2004.

Petchesky, Rosalind, F. "Human Rights, Reproductive Health, and Economic Justice: Why They Are Indivisible." In *The Socialist Feminist Project: A Contemporary Reader in Theory and Politics*, edited by Nancy Holmstrom, 74–82. New York: Monthly Review Press, 2002.

Peters, Julie, and Andrea Wolper. *Women's Rights, Human Rights: International Feminist Perspectives.* New York: Routledge, 1995.

Pettman, Jan Jindy. "On the Backs of Women and Children." In *Beyond Borders: Thinking Critically About Global Issues*, edited by Paula S. Rothenberg, 437–440. New York: Worth Publishers, 2006.

Phillips, Anne. *Multiculturalism Without Culture.* Princeton, NJ: Princeton University Press, 2007.

Pieterse, Jan Nederveen, ed. *Global Futures: Shaping Globalization.* New York: Zed Books, 2000.

Pogge, Thomas. "Cosmopolitanism and Sovereignty." *Ethics* 103, no. 1 (1992): 48–75.

Pogge, Thomas. *World Poverty and Human Rights Cosmopolitan Responsibilities and Reforms.* Cambridge, UK: Polity Press, 2002.

Polakoff, Erica G., and Ligaya Lindo-McGovern, eds. *Gender & Globalization: Patterns of Women's Resistance.* Whitby, ON: De Sitter Publications, 2011.

Poster, Winifred, and Zakia Salime. "The Limits of Microcredit: Transnational Feminism and USAID Activities in the United States and Morocco." In *Women's Activism and Globalization: Linking Local Struggles and Transnational Politics*, edited by Nancy A. Naples and Manisha Desai, 189–219. New York: Routledge, 2002.

Quijano, Anibal. "Coloniality of Power, Eurocentrism, and Latin America." *Nepantla: Views from South* 1, no. 3 (2000): 533–580.

Rao, Aruna, ed. *Women's Studies International: Nairobi and Beyond.* New York: The Feminist Press, 1991.

Raval, Bijal, with SEWA Research Team. *Multiple Work Status of Women in the Informal Economy.* Gujarat, India: Mahila SEWA Trust, 2001.

Reilly, Niamh. *Women's Human Rights: Seeking Gender Justice in a Globalizing Age.* Cambridge, UK: Polity Press, 2009.

Rendell, Margherita. *Whose Human Rights?* Staffordshire, UK: Trentham Books, 1997.

Rich, Adrienne. "Notes Towards a Politics of Location." In *Blood, Bread and Poetry: Selected Prose, 1979–1985*, edited by A. Rich, 210–231. London: Little Brown & Co, 1984.

Roberts, Dorothy. *Killing the Black Body: Race, Reproduction, and the Meaning of Liberty.* New York: Pantheon, 1997.

Roberts, Dorothy. "Race and the New Reproduction." In *The Reproductive Rights Reader: Law, Medicine, and the Construction of Motherhood*, edited by Nancy Ehrenreich, 308–319. New York: New York University Press, 2008.

Robinson, Fiona. *Globalizing Care: Ethics, Feminist Theory, and International Relations.* Boulder, CO: Westview Press, 1999.

Romany, Celina. "On Surrendering Privilege: Diversity in Feminist Redefinition of Human Rights Law." In *From Basic Needs to Basic Rights: Women's Claims to Human Rights*, edited by Margaret Schuler, 543–554. Washington, DC: Women, Law and Development International, 1995.

Rose, Kalima. *Where Women Are Leaders: The SEWA Movement in India.* New Delhi: Vistaar Publications, 1992.

Rothenberg, Paula S., ed. *Beyond Borders: Thinking Critically About Global Issues.* New York: Worth Publishers, 2006.

Roy, Arundhati. *Power Politics.* Cambridge, MA: South End Press, 2001.

Ruddick, Sara. *Maternal thinking: Toward a Politics of Peace*. New York: Ballatine Books, 1989.

Saha, Poulomi. "Singing Bengal into a Nation: Tagore the Colonial Cosmopolitan?" *Journal of Modern Literature* 36, no. 2 (2013): 1–24.

Sama-Resource Group for Women and Health. *Arts and Women: Assistance in Reproduction or Subjugation?* New Delhi, India: Impulsive Creations, 2006.

Sama-Resource Group for Women and Health. *Unveiled Realities: A Study on Women's Experiences with Depo-Provera, and Injectable Contraception*. New Delhi, India: Impulsive Creations, 2003.

Saurez Toro, M. "Popularizing Women's Human Rights at the Local Level: A Grassroots Methodology for Setting the International Agenda." In *Women's Rights, Human Rights: International Feminist Perspectives*, edited by J. Peters and A. Wolper, 189–194. New York: Routledge, 1995.

Schuler, S. R., M. Hashemi, A. Riley, and A. Akhter. (1996). "Credit Programs, Patriarchy and Men's Violence Against Women in Rural Bangladesh." *Social Science and Medicine* 43, no. 12 (1996): 1729–1742.

Self-Employed Women's Association. Accessed March 2015. http://www.sewa.org/

Self-Employed Women's Association. Annual Report 2015. Published by the Self-Employed Women's Association, Ahmedabad, India, 2015. http://www.sewa.org/Archives.asp

Sen, Amartya. *Development as Freedom*. New York: Knopf, 1999.

Sen, Amartya. "Foreword." In *Pathologies of Power: Health, Human Rights and the New War on the Poor*, edited by Paul Farmer, xi–xvii. Berkeley: University of California Press, 2003: xi–xvii.

Sen, Amartya. "More Than 100 Million Women Are Missing." *New York Review of Books*, December 20, 1990.

Sen, Gita, and Caren Grown. *Development, Crises, and Alternative Visions*. New York: Monthly Review Press, 1987.

SEWA Academy. *Organizing for Change: Unions and Cooperatives*. Gujarat, India: Mahila SEWA Trust, 2000.

Shanley, M. L., and C. Pateman, eds. *Feminist Interpretations and Political Theory*. University Park: The Pennsylvania State University Press, 1991.

Shiva, Vandana. *Globalization's New Wars: Seed, Water & Life Forms*. New Delhi, India: Women Unlimited, 2005.

Shiva, Vandana, Afsar H. Jafri, and Kunwar Jalees. *The Mirage of Market Access: How Globalization Is Destroying Farmers' Lives and Livelihoods*. New Delhi: Navdanya Research Foundation for Science, Technology, and Ecology, 2003.

Shriver Report. "Eleven Surprising Facts about Women and Poverty." Accessed July 29, 2015. http://time.com/2026/11-surprising-facts-about-women-and-poverty-from-the-shriver-report/

Singh, Abhishek, Reuben Oggollah, Faujdar Ram, and Saseendran Pallikadavath. "Sterilization Regret Among Married Women in India: Implications for the Indian National Family Planning Program." *International Perspectives on Sexual and Reproductive Health* 38, no. 4 (December 2012).

Singh, Kirti. "Obstacles to Women's Rights in India." In *Human Rights of Women: National and International Perspectives*, edited by Rebecca Cook, 375–396. Philadelphia: University of Pennsylvania Press, 1994.

Smith, Toni. *Globalisation: A Systematic Marxist Account.* Leiden, The Netherlands: Brill Academic Publishers, 2005.

Solnit, David, ed. *Globalize Liberation: How to Uproot the System and Build a Better World.* San Francisco: City Lights Books, 2004.

Spelman, Elizabeth. *Inessential Woman: Problems of Exclusion in Feminist Thought.* Boston: Beacon Press, 1988.

Spivak, Gayatri Chakravorty. "Can the Subaltern Speak?" In *Marxism and the Interpretation of Culture,* edited by Cary Nelson and Lawrence Grossberg, 296. Chicago: University of Illinois Press, 1988.

Spivak, Gayatri Chakravorty. "Righting Wrongs." In *Human Rights, Human Wrongs,* edited by N. Owen, 168–227. Oxford: Oxford University Press, 2003.

Stacy, Helen M. *Human Rights for the 21st Century: Sovereignty, Civil Society, Culture.* Stanford, CA: Stanford University Press, 2009.

Stamatopoulou, E. "Women's Rights and the United Nations." In *Women's Rights, Human Rights: International Feminist Perspectives,* edited by J. Peters and A. Wolper, 36–48. New York: Routledge, 1995.

Stiglitz, Joseph. *Globalization and Its Discontents.* New York: W. W. Norton and Company, 2003.

Strangio, Sebastian. "Is Microfinance Pushing the World's Poorest Even Deeper into Poverty?" *The New Republic,* December 14, 2011.

Stuart, Sara. "Training and Organizing for Change in India: Video as a Tool of the Self-Employed Women's Association." In *Women's Studies International: Nairobi and Beyond,* edited by Aruna Rao, 75–81. New York: The Feminist Press, 1991.

Tagore, Rabindranath. *The Essential Tagore.* Edited by Fakrul Alam and Radha Chakravarty. Kolkata: Visva-Bharati Publishing Department, 2011.

Tagore, Rabindranath. *Nationalism.* London: MacMillan and Co., 1918.

Tagore, Saranindranath. "Tagore's Conception of Cosmopolitanism: A Reconstruction." *University of Toronto Quarterly* 77, no. 4 (2008): 1070–1084.

Taylor, Charles. "The Politics of Recognition." In *Multiculturalism,* edited by Amy Gutmann, 25–73. Princeton, NJ: Princeton University Press, 1994.

Tripp, A. M. "Challenges in Transnational Feminist Mobilization." In *Global Feminism: Transnational Women's Activism, Organizing and Human Rights,* edited by M. M. Ferree and A. M. Tripp, 296–312. New York: New York University, 2006.

Tronto, Joan C. *Moral Boundaries: A Political Argument for an Ethic of Care.* New York: Routledge, 1993.

Truth and Reconciliation Commission. "About the Truth and Reconciliation Commission." Accessed November 18, 2018. http://www.justice.gov.za/trc/

UNICEF. "India-Statistics, 2015." Accessed July 31, 2015. http://www.unicef.org/infobycountry/india_statistics.html

UNICEF. "The 2014 Human Development Report—Sustaining Human Progress: Reducing Vulnerabilities and Building Resilience." Accessed July 31, 2015. http://hdr.undp.org/en/2014-report

United Nations. "Universal Declaration of Human Rights." Accessed November 18, 2017. http://www.un.org/en/universal-declaration-human-rights/

UNDP Report. *Global Partnership for Development, United Nations Development Programme Annual Report.* New York: UNDP, 2006.

United Nations Development Programme. "The 2016 Human Development Report— India Country Profile." Accessed November 18, 2018. http://hdr.undp.org/en/countries/profiles/IND

United States Census Bureau. "Income and Poverty in the United States, 2016." Accessed December 31, 2017. https://www.census.gov/library/publications/2016/demo/p60-256.html

Visva-Bharati. "Mission and Vision." Accessed November 28, 2015. http://www.visvabharati.ac.in/Mission__Vision.html

Weir, Allison. "Global Care Chains: Freedom, Responsibility, and Solidarity." *Southern Journal of Philosophy* 46, no. 1 (2008): 166–175.

Weir, Allison. *Identities and Freedom: Feminist Theory Between Power and Connection.* Oxford, UK: Oxford University Press, 2013.

West, Cornell, ed. *The Radical King: Martin Luther King, Jr.* Boston: Beacon Press, 2015.

"What Is the Gender Pay Gap and Is It Real?" *Economic Policy Institute.* Accessed August 12, 2018. https://www.epi.org/publication/what-is-the-gender-pay-gap-and-is-it-real#epi-toc-13.

Whelan, Daniel, J. *Indivisible Human Rights: A History.* Philadelphia: University of Pennsylvania Press, 2010.

Wichterich, Christa. "The Other Financial Crisis: Growth and Crash of the Microfinance Sector in India." *Development* 55, no. 3 (2012): 406–412.

Wiser, Scott. "Gender Injustice and the Resource Curse: Feminist Assessment and Reform." In *Gender and Global Justice*, edited by Alison Jaggar, 168–192. Cambridge, UK: Polity Press, 2014.

World Health Organization. "International Covenant on Economic, Social and Cultural Rights." Accessed November 18, 2018. http://www.who.int/hhr/Economic_social_cultural.pdf

Young, Iris Marion. "From Guilt to Solidarity: Sweatshops and Political Responsibility." *Dissent* (Spring 2003): 39–44.

Young, Iris Marion. "Gender as Seriality: Thinking about Women as a Social Collective." *Signs* 19, no. 3 (Spring 1994): 713–738.

Young, Iris Marion. *Justice and the Politics of Difference.* Princeton, NJ: Princeton University Press, 1990.

Young, Iris Marion. "Responsibility and Global Labor Justice." *Journal of Political Philosophy* 12, no. 4 (2004): 365–388.

Young, Iris Marion. "Responsibility and Global Justice: A Social Connection Model." *Social Philosophy and Policy* 23, no. 1 (Winter 2006): 102–130.

Young, Iris Marion. *Responsibility for Justice.* New York: Oxford University Press, 2011.

Zaman, Hasan. *Assessing the Impact of Microcredit on Poverty and Vulnerability in Bangladesh: Policy Research Working Paper 2145.* Washington, DC: World Bank, 1999.

INDEX

Abu-Lughod, Lila, 86–88, 155
Africa, 7–8, 69–70
  Nairobi, Kenya, 2, 239n8
  South Africa, 45–46, 54, 157
  Sudan, 84–85
agency, 8–9, 11, 37, 38, 50–51, 78–79,
  83–84, 95, 101–2, 109–12,
  119–21, 132, 196, 221, 227–28
  welfare agency, 111–12, 120–21, 221
Alinksy, Saul, 238n11
Americas, the
  Canada, 202–3, 204–5
  Guatemala, 202
  Latin America, 7–8, 69–70
  Peru, 222
  United States, 10, 11–12, 15, 26–27,
    32–33, 40, 73, 79, 85, 89–90, 91–92,
    102–3, 124, 156–57, 165–66,
    172–73, 177–78, 193, 195–96,
    204–5, 221, 222, 231
  See also global North
Anthropology, 125, 126, 170
  See also colonialism; ethnocentrism
Appadurai, Arjun, 242–43n4
Appiah, Kwame Anthony, 144–45, 153,
  171, 245n4
Armendariz, Beatriz, 243n8
arranged marriage, 75, 91–92
Ashford, Elizabeth, 248n7
Asia, 7–8, 69–70, 103–4, 113–14, 170
  Afghanistan, 39, 54, 182–83

Bangladesh, 54, 122, 126, 127,
  133–34, 195
Beijing, China, 2, 64, 70
Bhutan, 54
Japan, 170, 174–75
Myanmar, 54
Nepal, 54
Pakistan, 54
Philippines, 79
Sri Lanka, 54
See also India

babies in the river analogy, 20–21,
  201, 225
Basu, Amrita, 69, 70–71
Batliwala, Srilatha, 1, 95
Benhabib, Seyla, 7, 144–45, 149,
  245–46n9, 246n13
Bhatt, Ela, 25, 28, 42–43, 44–45, 46–48,
  50, 51, 53–54, 106–7, 116–17, 120,
  130, 136, 217–18, 229–30, 234
Bhavani, Kum-Kum, 237n2
Bietz, Charles, 163–64, 247n27
Bilge, Silma, 237n4, 248n6
Boserup, Esther, 114
Bowman, Betsy, 129–30
Breckenridge, Carol, 180–81
Bunch, Charlotte, 15–16, 70–71, 82–83
Butler, Judith, 247n25
butterfly analogy, 234
  See also Emily Kawano

McLaren, Margaret, 245n3
Mellor, Mary, 244n14
Mendieta, Eduardo, 144–45, 244n1
Mendoza, Jose Jorge, 245–46n9
Menon, Nivedita, 93–94, 98,
  155–56, 240n6
microfinance, 16–17, 101–2, 108–9,
  111–12, 114, 116, 121–23, 124,
  125–27, 128–30, 132, 133–35, 136–38
  Grameen Bank, 122–23, 124, 126, 133
  microcredit, 122–23, 124, 126–27, 208,
  227–28, 243n8
  microenterprise, 31–32, 129–30, 243n8
  Morduch, Jonathan, 243n8
Mignolo, Walter, 146, 153, 247n28
  See also diversity
Miller, David, 248n2
Miller, Sarah Clark, 146, 149, 151,
  245n3, 246n13
Mills, Charles, 160
Mohanty, Chandra Talpade, 1, 13–14,
  23–24, 27–28, 29, 44, 86–87, 148,
  160, 230–31
  See also transnational feminism
morality and ethics, 7–8, 78–79, 140,
  143, 144–45, 147, 152–53, 154, 156,
  161–63, 166, 172, 179–80, 190–92,
  195–96, 214
  care ethics, 77–78, 79, 80–81 (see also
  Carol Gilligan)
  ethical universalism, concept of, 146
  moral cosmopolitanism, 144–46, 147,
  148–49, 150, 168–69
  moral development, theory of, 77, 148
  moral minimalism, 186–87
  moral pluralism, 247n25

Narayan, Uma, 16, 74–75, 81–82, 83,
  85–86, 91–92, 94
neoliberalism, 3, 27, 58–59, 70, 96–97,
  99, 101–2, 103–5, 113, 115–16,
  125–26, 127–28, 132, 135, 159,
  166, 167–68, 208–11, 215, 222,
  226, 229–30
  multinational corporations, 107
  Nike Corporation, 202–3, 210–11

Smith, Adam, 208–9 (see also
  economics; western philosophy)
  Wal-Mart corporation, 195–96
  World Trade Organization, 66–67,
  99, 104–5
  See also non-governmental organizations
Nicholls, Alex, 208–9
Non-Governmental Organizations
  (NGOs), 2, 28, 38, 64–65, 66–67, 69,
  94–95, 101, 108, 109, 114, 115–17,
  118–19, 120, 122, 125, 126–27, 133,
  135–36, 199–200
  Amnesty International, 15, 63–64
  Anapurna Pariwar, 244n10
  Human Rights Watch, 63–64
  International Labor Organization
  (ILO), 15, 17, 23, 54, 184–85, 193,
  211, 219–20, 228
  International Monetary Fund (IMF),
  99, 104–5, 115–16, 163–64, 184,
  209, 219–20
  Millennium Development Goals
  (MDGs), 95
  UNICEF, 22
  UNIFEM, 106–7 (see also United
  Nations)
  World Bank, 99, 103–5, 115–16,
  163–64, 184, 209, 219–20
  World Economic Forum, 22–23
  World Trade Organization, 66–67,
  99, 104–5
  See also neoliberalism
normative framework, 9–10
Nussbaum, Martha, 17–18, 44, 142–43,
  144–45, 146, 147–48, 149, 150–51,
  152–56, 157–58, 159–61, 162–63,
  168, 169, 170, 171, 172, 173, 174, 215
  See also cosmopolitanism

Okin, Susan Moller, 15–16, 81–84, 215
O'Neill, Onora, 140–41
Opal, Charlotte, 208–9
oppression, 8–9, 11–12, 13, 60, 90, 91,
  97–98, 110–11, 181–82, 189, 235–36
  See also structural violence
Oyewumi, Oyeronke, 81–82

Parekh, Serena, 199, 214–15
Parennas, Rhacel Salzar, 241n13
Park, Shelley, 240n8, 241–42n19
Pateman, Carol, 160
Petchetsky, Rosalind, 15, 72–73, 76–77
Peters, Julie, 15, 77
Phillips, Anne, 242n20, 245n6, 246n13
Pogge, Thomas, 17–18, 142–43, 144–45,
    146, 161–64, 165–68, 209
    See also cosmopolitanism
politics
    political empowerment, 29, 52
    political injustice, 6–7, 9–10, 11–12, 55
    political responsibility, 3–4, 18–19, 63,
        79–80, 159–60, 165, 187–92, 193,
        194, 195–201, 203–4, 205–6,
        211–14, 215, 216, 222–23, 226–27
    See also Iris Marion Young
poverty, 5, 22–23, 44–45, 47–48, 67, 70,
    92–93, 99, 103–4, 110, 114, 120,
    122–23, 128–29, 138–39, 142,
    144–45, 161–64, 179–80, 201,
    209–10, 217, 218, 227–28
    brink of poverty, concept of, 242n2
    feminization of poverty, 102–4,
        148–49, 223–24
    See also economics
power relations, 7, 8, 11–12, 13, 14, 15,
    17–18, 19, 36–37, 60, 84, 89, 110,
    111–13, 115, 116, 117, 126–27, 134,
    141–42, 146–47, 149, 150, 151, 153,
    154, 157–58, 160, 169–70, 172–73,
    178–79, 184, 189, 196–97, 204–5,
    212, 219–20, 229
privilege, concept of, 211–12, 213–14

Quijano, Anibal, 242n1

race and ethnicity, 5, 9–10, 11–12, 14,
    27–28, 45, 65, 80, 81, 84, 86–87,
    113, 117, 131, 148–49, 153–54, 158,
    160, 167, 170–71, 178, 179–81, 182,
    223, 230, 231
    African Americans, 103, 153–54,
        176–77, 231
    Native Americans, 176–77

See also structural injustice
Rasmussen, Claire, 122–23
Reilly, Niamh, 240n2
relationality, 3, 7–8, 14, 16, 18,
    169–70, 223–24
    See also cosmopolitanism
religion, 5, 14, 23, 27–28, 35–36, 38–39,
    45, 46–47, 52–53, 58, 62, 65, 80, 81,
    83–84, 86–87, 89–90, 95, 97–98,
    143–44, 230–31
    Taliban, 39, 182–83
    See also veiling
Renana Jhabwala, 100, 105
Reproduction and culture
    reproductive issues, 62–63, 65,
        72–73, 217
    reproductive justice, 73–75, 119
    See also health and healthcare
responsibility
    standard liability model of
        responsibility, 189–90
    See also political responsibility
Ricardo, David, 208–9
rights, 5, 9–11, 15, 18–19, 30–31, 53–54,
    58–59, 61, 62–69, 70–74, 76–78,
    79, 81–84, 86–89, 90–92, 94, 95,
    96–99, 100, 103, 110, 120, 122–23,
    135, 136, 156, 161–63, 164–65, 172,
    186–88, 192–93, 198, 199–201, 204,
    207–8, 211, 212–13, 219–21,
    222–23, 225–26, 228, 230, 231
    Addams, Jane, 144–45
    economic rights, 15, 18–19, 30–31,
        58–59, 60, 67–70, 72–74, 76–77, 98,
        110, 120, 140–41, 166, 186–87,
        201, 204, 211, 219–21, 228,
        229–30, 239n4
    educational rights, 22, 26, 31–32, 33–
        34, 40–41, 45–46, 50, 58, 63–64, 67,
        68–69, 71, 72–73, 75–76, 88, 101,
        102–3, 105–6, 115–16, 119–21, 131,
        132–33, 136–37, 147, 159, 170, 193,
        206–7, 209–10, 215–17, 228–29, 234
    European and Inter-American Courts
        of Human Rights, 186–87 (*see also*
        human rights)

xenophobia and cultural bias
nationalism, 18, 86
orientalism, 247n30
See also colonialism; ethnocentrism

Young, Marion Iris, ix, 3–4, 10, 12, 18–19, 79–80, 159–60, 165–66, 185, 187–89, 190–92, 193, 194, 195–201, 202, 203–4, 205–6, 210, 211–15, 222–23, 225–27

Social connection model of responsibility, 189–90, 191, 195, 202
See also political responsibility

Yunus, Mohammad, 122

Lightning Source UK Ltd.
Milton Keynes UK
UKHW020017300822
408023UK00006B/1676